BREAD FOR ALL SEASONS

DELICIOUS AND DISTINCTIVE RECIPES FOR YEAR-ROUND BAKING

BY **BETH HENSPERGER**

PHOTOGRAPHY BY **VICTORIA PEARSON**

STYLING BY **JANET MILLER**

CHRONICLE BOOKS

SAN FRANCISCO

Victoria Pearson wishes to extend her special thanks to Janet Miller and her assistant Mary Lou Celona, for their beautiful baking and commitment to the book; Hannah Milman and Darcy Miller for their exquisite styling; Kim Golding, Laura Brooks, and Amy Neusinger for their loyalty and support; AIM Color Lab in Los Angeles for the beautiful color processing; Samy's Camera in Los Angeles for the superb technical support; and Gretchen Scoble for her patience.

Library of Congress Cataloging-in-Publication Data available.

Printed in Hong Kong.

Book and Cover Design: Gretchen Scoble
Composition: On Line Typography
Food Styling: Janet Miller
Prop Styling: Hannah Milman and Darcy Miller

ISBN 0-8118-0582-4 pbk
ISBN 0-8118-0598-0 hc

Distributed in Canada by
Raincoast Books
8680 Cambie St.
Vancouver, B.C. V6P 6M9

10 9 8 7 6 5 4 3 2 1

Chronicle Books
275 Fifth Street
San Francisco, CA 94103

Contents

Baking by the Seasons   On the wall above my work space I have a panoramic photograph by Gus Foster called *Cut Wheat*. It shows a stark sea of gold below a layer of blue prairie sky marbled with cirrus clouds, the two elements cut perfectly in half by the horizon. When I look at the photo, I am reminded that for centuries much of the populated earth was covered by grain fields—a sign of harmony, health, and abundance. Sumerian tablets from 260 B.C. list the flood-bed cultivation of five sacred crops: rice, soy, wheat, barley, and millet. Over the past millennia, similar references to the importance of these crops have been found from Israel to China. Such seasonal fields are the cornerstones of the religions, cultures, and sustenance of all past civilizations based on agriculture. The bread produced from these grains has been part of a world intricately entwined with the cyclical celebrations of life and death.

The evolution of human history perfectly parallels the changes in the planting of grain, baking practices, and milling procedures. The birth of grano culture, the planting of a single strain of edible grass that could be harvested at one time, marks the beginning of true civilization. European maps from past centuries show that geographical boundaries and cultural traits are based on political communities, marriage alliances, land and navigation trade routes, military invasions, and migratory upheavals. The constant movement has changed borders and cross-pollinated cultures so many times that no country in present-day Europe has been untouched by the others, or by influences as distant as India and Africa.

The dynastic map of Europe has constantly redrawn itself. The indigenous peoples of Old Europe such as the Basques still practice baking skills that sustained their ancestors for millennia. The Celts traveled west from the Balkans, settling all across western Europe and the British Isles. The empires and kingdoms of the Egyptians, Greeks, Romans, Franconians, Moors, Ottomans, Austro-Hungarians, French, and British have all left their unique cultural stamp on the families of breads enjoyed in the West today. Despite similar influences, however, the countries of Europe are still remarkably localized, with special breads often found in only one town or region. I have often heard wonderful ribald stories of food professionals combing the hills and vales for a special bread, or have been asked to reproduce a recipe made in only one small country village for a certain yearly festival. Finding the breads, much less reproducing them, is often a matter of chance and luck.

Bread is a food that is an almost invisible yet necessary part of daily life. At the same time, it has long been endowed with layers of mystical and religious symbolism. The making of bread is intertwined with the skills of weather forecasting, fire making, gardening, and the preservation of foods. Bread has both helped man to survive and, as in the case of such cultures as the Minoan and Anasazi, brought on his decline due to blighted fields or droughts. It defines regions, provinces, and cultures. The type of bread a man eats shapes and defines his life.

In researching traditional and ethnic recipes, one thing is clear: bakers traditionally have respected the seasons, have made use of what is available. This challenge, especially in times of scarcity, has determined the evolution of the world's great cuisines. The family kitchen preserved and guided much of European and American regional baking traditions, and the abundance of the harvest, whether from a communal farm or individual kitchen garden, dictated eating habits. People had an awareness that guided baking and cooking, of how food grows and how it is brought to the table. It is an art of everyday life.

America is a paradise of fresh fruits, vegetables, and grains. We have potatoes, corn, chiles, tomatoes, squash, cocoa, and quinoa in our native cornucopia. The many ethnic groups that have settled on this land have created one of the most diverse baking traditions in history—everything from Chinese steamed buns to Mexican *pan dulce*; from Polish whole-wheat peasant bread to French *pain de campagne*; from Italian semolina *pane* to rustic Scandinavian loaves, such as the cardamom-spiked *nisua* or the leavened barley bread *ohraleipä*. The majority of breads are simple and hearty, and reflect authentic traditions that have nourished Americans for decades. New bakers are discovering the classics, developing new ones by adapting them to local ingredients, and offering them to a new generation of discerning and enthusiastic eaters.

Although bakers tend to remake family and personal favorites, I encourage you to experiment. Here is the chance to taste flavorings and flours you may have never eaten before, such as quinoa, toasted sesame seeds, nut oils, goat's milk, or buckwheat flour. A marvelous and ingenious cross-pollination of regional tastes has occurred in the last decade: roasted jalapeño chiles now turn up in a New England rye and Indian loaf, Tillamook cheese and roasted garlic go into a sourdough, quinoa is mixed into farmhouse white breads, blueberries stud an Alsatian *Kugelhopf,* and creamy goat cheese forms the base of a sweet filling for an eastern European holiday bread. The classic sensibility of the loaf is preserved, while new character and flavor emerge with each stunning variation.

You can also use such updated recipes to make breads that have graced the tables of continental royalty for hundreds of years, such as the *brioche.* Or you might bring together an unexpected combination of whole grains from around the world—wild rice, quinoa, millet, and polenta—to add flavor and texture to rustic country loaves. Experiment with a requested recipe from your favorite restaurant or bakery, scaled down to familiar cups and teaspoons from the pounds and ounces commonly used for measuring in commercial operations. Translate a dramatically simple European country bread recipe from the cryptic metric system to re-create a crusty Old World loaf. If you're looking for a way to add flair to your holiday meals, bake a symbolically shaped traditional bread, such as a *panettone* or a batch of rum babas, an art considered *de rigueur* in Europe.

"Life on earth has been a history of interaction between living things and their surroundings," wrote American scientist Rachel Carson decades ago, and her words seem more relevant than ever.

Environmentalists and sensitive writers remark often about "sacred rage," the anger grounded in the healthy, holy knowledge that all life is related, thereby questioning the modern practices that deny nature the respect she deserves. New generations of bread makers talk of the connection from the field to the mill, from the mill to your hands, from your hands to your family, from your family to the community, and finally, from the community back to the environment. Human traits of respect and gratitude are now ecologically viable principles. Sound grain-farming principles are the link with healthy future generations.

In a world where biotechnology, agrichemicals, irradiation, and genetic engineering are common food language, the interest in back-to-nature foods and the tenets of sustainable agriculture is at once old-fashioned and progressive. Historically, bread making in agricultural and pastoral communities was strictly women's work, a complementary task to the daily labor of men. It was an occasion for exchanging village news and socializing, an alliance based on trust and mutual dependence. The task, which often required the cooperation of several women at the communal ovens, helped strengthen ties between family and friends. Even children participated in the family work, by carrying twigs to feed the fire. Men, women, and children labored side by side in the sowing and harvesting of grain crops. Bread making did not become male-dominated until the onset of commercial bakeries. Then, in the last decade, all that has changed, with women working in bakery back rooms and men defining their own workplace in the home kitchen.

I have created a collection of recipes that interweave seasonal considerations with historical maxims, that juxtapose cross-cultural religious observances from the times when deities were considered local powers of life with myths and symbols drawn from the calendar of intrinsic agricultural cycles. The strong European baking traditions we take for granted are an evolution of religion and artistry, since the breaking of bread has long been regarded as basic nourishment for both the body and the soul. No other food except wine crosses the axiomatic boundaries so readily in so many cultures as daily bread. The refinement of ingredients, their widespread availability, and the increasingly adept skills of the baker only enhance existing traditions.

Enjoy my streamlined and updated versions of the classics: Irish Halloween bairmbrack; charming fez-shaped rum babas, favored by Polish nobility; and the austere Sun and Moon, a French version of the colonial favorite, Sally Lunn. Ideas on fresh produce and whole grains that are especially good incorporated into these breads, a streamlined repertoire of ethnic specialties, and a host of creative shapes are found under each seasonal rubric. This is a guide to the craft of creating excellent daily and celebration breads for the seasoned baker.

It has been said that recipes are one of the best ways to preserve the humanities. Every time you copy and practice a skill such as bread making, you inherit it and bring it alive. Bread is a tangible, living artifact. It is an acknowledgment of the ongoing rhythm of life. This is an opportunity to take an imaginative leap back through time, with your bread making the metaphorical key to a lineage of legendary cross-cultural practices and beliefs. Bake your country bread shaped into a ring to symbolize the continuity of life. Braid your challah to denote a ladder to heaven. Form your holiday bread into a crescent to symbolize the moon. Or lay a few whole eggs into an Easter sweet dough before sliding it into the oven to ensure the fertility of the earth and its wondrous ability constantly to renew itself.

Baking and the Seasonal Cycle   The honest endeavor of making a dough and the ethereal smell of its baking are as old as the first civilization. For these early cultures, the phenomenon of the seasons was all-important for survival. Seasons are very different in character from one another, but are, at the same time, connected. They affect crops, animals, and human behavior. The spring, summer, fall, and winter cycles are sometimes romantically labeled promise, fulfillment, harvest, and want, respectively, and are completely predictable throughout the generations of human

history. The rituals practiced at each part of the agricultural year were the means of connecting humans to their expression of the divine. In a world of strict dietary laws, scarcity, and ceaseless hard work, these occasions were a time of feasting and joyful merry-making. The great festivals from antiquity were also the principal times for animal and human sacrifices, often still reflected symbolically in present-day bread-making traditions. An integral part of these rituals, bread was transformed from a mere loaf to a symbolic bridge between the tangible and intangible worlds. The inner world gained a visible form. Breads are also intrinsically linked to the performance of liturgical and national community rituals, such as Jewish Passover and American Thanksgiving, that appear in some form in all cultures.

Religious sects long before Christ, who used bread in the form of the consecrated communion wafer at his last supper, have used bread making as a ritual sacrament. The Neolithic communities of the Balkans, the legendary peoples of Mesopotamia, the Eleusinian Bread Church of pre-Hellenic Greece, the pharaohic Egyptian dynasties, and the Incans of Cuzco are just a few of them. Archaeological sites in the Balkans show stone milling querns and ovens beside altars. The ancient Roman Festival of Ceres, celebrating the incarnation of an ancient female grain spirit and goddess of the harvest, was celebrated on New Year's Day, and Janus, the god of the double gate, was given an offering of bread and salt. The ancient polytheistic rituals of the Celts, the Teutons, early Romans, and Southwest Native Americans all used bread as one of their high sacral symbols, a lineage so strong that the rituals have become overlaid with present-day Christian festivals and saints' days, specifically Easter, All Souls' Day, and Christmas.

The story of the changing seasons is also a story of man's evolving sense of measuring time. The seasonal year was originally defined by twelve moon months, a system first recorded by the Babylonians and also practiced on the other side of the world by the Aztecs. The old Egyptian year was divided into three seasons of four months, each named for an agricultural activity: Flood, Planting, and Harvest, with their New Year beginning during the flood stage. Semitic Sabbath taboo days have been observed for thousands of years at the new, full, and quarter moons. The first of the month was when the first lunar crescent appeared. Time was related to the progression of the moon's journey, and daily time was told by the duration of the night rather than the day. The Jewish calendar is still based on lunar rhythms, with Rosh Chodesh, the first day of each month, the day the new moon appears. Many of the principal religious festivals of today continue to be calculated by the moon, such as the Christian Easter falling on the first Sunday after the spring equinox full moon.

Some secular festivals are movable feasts, changing in date from year to year, or can simply be held when a crop reaches ripeness. Each of these customs, often with ancient roots, has specialty breads at the heart of the feasting celebrations. The Gregorian calendar, used by the Christian world since the papal edict in 1582, replaced the Julian solar calendar, which had been in use since Julius Caesar in 46 B.C. The Eastern Orthodox church did not recognize the Gregorian calendar until 1923; hence there is still much inconsistency from region to region, especially in Eastern Europe and Russia, as to when religious festivals are held. Over the centuries, there often has been much overlapping and revision of the older celebrations due to migrations and changes in religions.

The agricultural year falls into a natural division of four quarters based on the action of the sun at the solstices and equinoxes. The summer and winter solstices in the Northern Hemisphere, June 22 and December 22, mark the sun at its farthest point from the celestial equator. The spring and fall equinoxes, March 21 and September 23, are times when day and night are of equal length. Historical records show early Israelites transforming the old seasonal festivals from the Canaanites of ancient Palestine and Phoenicia. Their spring festival of Unleavened Bread became Passover, and the fall harvest celebration, originally called In-gathering, became the Feast of the Tabernacles. Lent comes from the Anglo-Saxon word meaning "spring." Easter, the anniversary of resurrection, comes from the word *ost*, or "east," and the Saxon goddess of spring, Eostre (another form of the Mediterranean Astarte), rules the eastern rising sun with the moon-hare by her side. The early beginnings of the Yule season coincided with the birthday of Mithras the Unconquered Sun, an archaic celebration for the solar deity originating in the Mediterranean that spread northward throughout Europe and became the Roman midwinter festival of Kalends. Most pagan religions celebrated the birth of a divine child at the winter solstice, which would later become the basis for the Christian Christmas.

The pre-Roman Gaulish Coligny calendar was in use from the British Isles to Spain and Asia Minor, poetically counting days from moonrise to moonrise. Its Quarter Day folkfests straddling these heavenly passages are to this day a strong cultural imprint throughout Western Europe and were practiced up into the mid-nineteenth century by groups such as the Pennsylvania Dutch in America and the rural British Isles. In the Highlands of Britain, specific age-old recipes for rustic country oatcakes and barley bannocks were baked as a mandatory herald to each season, each overlaid with special significance. Imbolc (Candlemas, the return of longer days and lactating of the ewes), Beltane (May Day, coinciding with the sprouting of the first crops' spring shoots in the sun's warmth and the birth of farm animals), Lammas (First Fruits Festival, blessing of the first grains, and glorifying the sun), and Samhain (Summer's End or Winter's Eve, final gathering of the crops and time to bring the cattle in from the fields) are typical feasting festivals marking the nodal points of the seasonal cycle, midpoints between the solstice and equinox quarter marks.

The forty days after Christmas concludes on February 5, with the candlelight procession marking Candlemas, or Purification of the Blessed Virgin Mary. It symbolizes the "return of the light," or winter's end. The world may still be cold and snowy, but the energy shifts toward renewal. Sicilian convent bakers reverently make a yeasted almond dough in the shape of her breasts *(mammelle di vergine)* on this day. In Sweden, waffles are baked in a heart-shaped iron in remembrance of Mary's heart, and throughout Alsace, Italy, Switzerland, Austria, and Germany, the Feast of Saint Agatha, the patron saint of local bakers, is celebrated.

May Day is remembered for dancing around the tree or pole, also known as the *axis mundi,* with ribbons the colors of the rainbow honoring the May Queen and the Green Man. The ancient festival is symbolic of renewed life and the resurrection of spring. Bannocks were eaten with May wine summer punch, flavored with freshly picked sweet woodruff and fresh berries, a custom still practiced today. Often the Beltane bannock was deliberately burnt in one section. When the cake was divided to be eaten, whoever received the burnt portion suffered a forfeit, such as fire leaping or sacrifice.

During the week preceding Ash Wednesday, some locals in Russia still adhere to *maslenitsa,* or "butterweek." There is plenty of buckwheat *blini* and wheat *blinchiki* feasting, with offerings of bread and salt to a young girl dressed as spring. *Blini,* from the Russian word "milled," were ritually eaten at the Slavic and Thracian Maslenitsa sun festivals long before Christ.

The May King, the warrior Green Man who dominates Beltaine, appears again to preside over the Celtic bonfire festival of Saint John's Eve, midsummer's night. The hilltop bonfires predict the height the growing grain will reach by harvest. Wonderful shapes, such as the ear of wheat, the horse collar, and the mushroom, are preserved from early harvest festivals and are ancestors of creative Greek breads.

Lammas is from the Saxon "feast of the bread," or *Hlaf-mass,* ceremonializing the Celtic grain deities. (The words *lord* and *lady* are derived from the Anglo-Saxon *hlaford* and *hlaedige,* meaning "loaf ward" for the master and "giver of the loaf" or "loaf-kneader" for his wife, respectful gestures of rank.) Loaves of bread are made from the first harvested grain and taken to be consecrated at the local church that same day. Lammas is also referred to as Lughnasad, for the Celtic-Irish god Lugh who dies as the crops are harvested and will be reborn again at the spring planting, a symbol reminiscent of John Barleycorn and the yearly kings of Minoan Crete. Lammas eve is a time of great merrymaking and deep gratitude for nature's bounty, with loaves of fresh-baked barley bannocks marked with the ancient sun sign, the eight-armed cross. The Celtic

Ould Lammas Fair is still held during the last week in August at Bally Castle, the oldest surviving traditional harvest fair in Ireland.

A magical dimension to the pastoral festivities is the reverence for the last sheaf of grain gathered after threshing, practiced all over northern Europe. In Sweden, the stalk was pulled up by its roots and tightly tied into a bundle, inducing the *skördeanden,* the spirit of the harvest, to bring a good crop next season, as well as serving to decorate the house. An elaborately shaped cardamom egg bread, *såkaka,* was made from these grains. The loaf decorated the feast table and was then buried under stored grain until spring, when it would be pounded into crumbs and sowed back into the earth. The tradition is no longer enacted, but the bread is still served during the winter holidays.

The early November celebration of Samhain often coincided with honoring the souls of the deceased on All Saints' Day and with the old English Martinmas, marking the beginning of the rural new year. Old Indo-European warrior tribes practiced ancient burial customs. A wife cut off her hair to be buried with her deceased husband before being sacrificed. After the Visigoths accepted Christianity in the Middle Ages, this custom was outlawed and large braided breads such as *züpfe* and *pan de muerto* were baked and placed in the grave as part of the mourning ritual at Samhain. As part of the Feast of Saint Martin, some German Protestants still bake *Martinsweck,* braided-topped yeast buns, for the day.

With the growing influence of Christianity, the vibrant quarter-day folk festivals were transformed into the Ember Days, a time of self-denial and fasting. The monastic tradition of abstinence was often one characterized by "dry eating": only bread, salt, and water for various durations of time. Sacral unleavened loaves stamped with the image of Christ were infused with awesome qualities and distributed to the initiated. Since paganism was so tenacious, all the agricultural festivals were allowed to continue, but only under the patronage of a suitable canonized Christian saint. Saint-Honoré, still the patron saint of French bakers, was installed at this time, combining divine power and the practicality of providing food to communities.

Bread and wine are the two products of man's creative genius, while other foods, such as meat, fruit, and vegetables, are part of nature, and therefore hunted or gathered. The expression of gratitude to the gods for an abundant harvest has strong roots in every Western culture and is traditionally celebrated as part of everyday life. History is full of stories of the powerful deities, mystical festivals, and highly elaborate fertility rites that surround the growing of grain. Only in this century, with agribusiness and modern food-storage methods, has the immediate dependency upon Mother Nature seemed to decline.

Many of the fragile recipes of everyday, as well as special-occasion yeast breads and home-produced leavens, have survived the creation and destruction of civilizations completely intact, right down to their proportions. We owe thanks to hundreds of generations of unrecognized village artisans; baroque court bakers for their intricately decorated loaves; frugal matriarchs and their daughters for guarding their precious *madre* starters; monks and nuns for maintaining the old ways; and generations of slaves for the preservation of this ever-so-ordinary ancient culinary product. Bread continues to nourish and delight us in new, sophisticated ways with much gustatory pleasure.

Celebration Breads   Skillfully made yeast breads are baked into a rainbow of earth tones and decorated in an ornate fashion appropriate for special gift-giving occasions such as christenings, betrothals, weddings, namedays, birthdays, and religious holidays. It is a longstanding old-country tradition to bake these breads to mark the milestones of one's passage through life. Any stately loaf leavened with eggs or decorated with a luscious glaze makes an ideal special-occasion cakebread. It is a malleable, magical medium with infinite variations. In the past, yeasted cakebreads were popular preparations in country kitchens, as they could be successfully baked in the hot breath of intense wood-fire ovens, yet were still time-consuming and costly to prepare. It wasn't until the advent of home gas ovens in this century that the home baker could consistently make the more delicate cakes and pastries.

The first birthday parties are recorded by the Romans, lighting candles and eating together for protection from converging evil spirits that arrived specifically on birthdays. Polish *babkas* are classical, egg-rich loaves baked in deep, round cakes throughout the countryside and in the best bakeries. *Babka* translates to "old woman" in old Russian and Serbo-Croatian languages. They are often baked in fluted molds and said to resemble a grandmother's full skirt when baked. A single loaf destined for a celebration will sometimes contain up to twenty-four egg yolks and twelve ounces of butter in proportion to six cups of flour. Favorite recipes were passed down through generations of family bakers. The sweet white cakebreads are a welcome change from the strong-flavored dark daily breads. They may be served plain, or soaked with a liqueur-infused sugar syrup.

The Greeks bake bread rings decorated with hand-sculpted dough representations of birds, snakes, grapes, and even pomegranate seeds for marriages and births as well as decorating altars in the churches and monasteries on holidays. They make ring shapes for girls and horseshoe shapes for boys, often up to four feet in diameter, as good luck birthday charms. Lyon bakers make *pognons aux peurniaux*, my favorite special-occasion prune brioche, and the master Parisian baker Poilane has an oversized, dark-bake *pain au levain* topped with a stunning bound sheaf of wheat or scroll of dough with your name in bread-dough script. The Swiss excel in the art of *Gebildbrote*, elaborate and intricate picture breads that are sculpted artistic reproductions. The Alsatian *Bienenstich*, or "beesting," is a sponge-light yeast cake glazed with honey and often split and filled with vanilla pastry cream. Because the folded shape of the stollen is symbolic of the Christ child in swaddling clothes, it is perfect for christenings and baby showers. Along with the fluted tube *kugelhopf*, variations on the yeast-raised cake studded with almonds and raisins were central to birthday celebrations during the Middle Ages. The first tall, cone-shaped cakes were baked by the Romans. There was no "chimney," or tube, in the center of the deep, patterned cake mold, however, and the resulting shape was symbolic of the rotating sun. Both the stollen and the kugelhopf are still baked today for Christmas.

Ancient wedding cakes were often special spelt wheat or barley cakes. Early Roman couples practiced the custom of breaking the cake over the bride's head to acknowledge her fertility. (The favored time of the year for marriage was June, the month in the Julian calendar named after Juno, the goddess of marriage.) In England, small dense cakes of ground grain or waffles were piled into small towers as high as possible without toppling, and the new couple would kiss over the top of them. These rustic cakebreads were transformed over the centuries into the sweet, stacked wedding cake confection we recognize today. In many cultures the bride was crowned with a charming wreath of orange blossoms or whole woven grain in place of a veil, a custom popular since before the Holy Roman Empire, when the norm was to barter for, purchase, or even capture a bride.

Highland oatmeal "sautie" bannocks were baked with a ring inside for Shrove Tuesday. The recipient of the thin triangular slice containing the ring would be sure to marry within the new year. In later years, the Irish bairmbrack, made on Halloween, would continue the tradition with a wedding ring baked inside the fruit-studded loaf.

Colonial and English yeast cakes tended to be heavy and laced with spices. Queen Victoria was known personally to bake honey gingerbreads for her beloved Albert. Cornwall saffron breads appear in endless variations, a delicacy liberally permeated with mixed candied peels, currants, and Spanish saffron, a spice supposedly introduced to the area by the Phoenicians. Lardy cakes are yeasted egg doughs, such as Bath and Banbury cakes. Enriched with imported raisins, citrus peels, caraway confits, or precious Eastern spices, they were central to centuries of British family wedding celebrations and feast days. They were terrifically rich confections, with fresh lard and sugar rolled into layers like those of a *croissant,* and they have evolved into groom's cakes and English wedding cakes.

Large baked breads fashioned into pretzel twists, known as a *kringle* in Scandinavia, have also been referred to as the "marriage knot," to be broken or pulled apart during the ceremony for good luck. The Russians have a vodka-spiked vanilla-egg *krendel* that is shaped into a pretzel or figure-eight and is served at a variety of celebrations. A filling of fresh and dried fruits is encased inside the cylinders of dough before shaping, and each bite is full of flavor. Tower-shaped loaves of *panettone* are not uncommon wedding breads in Italy. *Brudlaupsking* is an oversized round, white German loaf, split and layered with a mixture of butter, soft fresh cheese, heavy cream, and sugar syrup, creating a unique marriage bread.

Bread and salt are traditional gifts to newlyweds in Eastern Europe, as they symbolize prosperity. In the Ukraine, stately three-tiered braids with lots of butter, eggs, and raisins are served as wedding cakes. *Kolach* is a braided milk-and-egg ring decorated with poetic symbols of the sun and moon or studded with whole nut meats. *Korovai* wedding loaves, also known as *Korowei* to the Swiss-German Mennonites, are simple round breads made with heavy cream and slowly risen at least three times for a very fine texture. They are decorated with doves shaped from dough or crushed candy corn and are served on lovely hand-embroidered linens. These loaves are traditionally kissed by the bride and groom after the ceremony.

Celebration breads are typically made quite large, so coordinate the size of your oven with the yield of your recipe if you plan to bake one.

More is written about the season of spring than any other. It opens officially on March 21, the date of the vernal equinox, and although it is often a brief period of time, life responds instantly. Earthbound flora and fauna respond to the increasing warmth. There is a release of water from frozen, chilly nights. Moods lift and appetites awaken. ❦ Seeds that have lain underground for months sprout with new life, and wild greens flourish. Asparagus tips pierce the still-wet soil and wild mushrooms abound in untrampled woody areas. Wild flowers appear, tracing the progression of spring with a show of miniature blossoms. Fruit trees burst into masses of delicate blossoms. The flowers soon dissolve into falling petals, replaced by the first green shoots that will form into fruits. The ground is ready for sowing. ❦ The baroque peasant breads of Europe show themselves in full regalia at this time, looking very much like they belong in a fairy-tale citadel on a long banquet table served up by a magician's apprentice. They are based on the addition of eggs, which impart a rich flavor, a subtle sunny color, and a delicate texture. The spherical egg, often referred to as the Cosmic Egg since the time of the ancient Greeks, is the symbol that has reigned supreme over the centuries in every religion as the affirmative springtime symbol, the mysterious beginning of creation and resurrection. Since no eggs could be eaten during Lent, agricultural communities ended up with piles of eggs that were featured in Easter foods. The doughs are also rich in animal fat, which marks a release from the austerity defined by fasting laws. Loaves are fashioned into a myriad of shapes, such as spirals, braids, coronas, and serpentines, to reflect the passionate pre-Christian religious symbology of hope and rebirth. The simplest and most common shape, however, is the round, symbolizing the sun and the universe. ❦ San Juan Capistrano Mission, on the El Camino

Real in Southern California, celebrates Saint Joseph's Day on March 19. Memorialized in a famous song, the swallows return to their old nests in Capistrano, Orange County, from their winter home six thousand miles away in Goya, Argentina. The feast, based on the stories the Indians told the Spanish, is celebrated yearly with chanting, Mexican dancing, and singing. Old adobe ovens are fired up for baking the round wheat loaves so beloved by Californians and Franciscan fathers for hundreds of years. ❦ The cycle of the seasons, based on life and death, is acted out with Lenten, Easter, Passover, and Whitsuntide rituals. Purim, which falls a full month before Passover, celebrates the deliverance of the Jews from the massacre plotted by Haman in ancient Persia. Delicate individual yeast pastries known as hamantashen ("Haman's pockets") are shaped like triangular hats and filled with fruit or poppy seeds. Passover, a dramatic reenactment marking the Hebrews' liberation from bondage in Egypt three thousand years ago, is a time when the restrictions of winter are lifted and the planting season begins. No hametz, or leavened grain (from wheat, barley, spelt, oats, or rye), which would symbolize a connection with last year's grain, can be consumed for eight days, and three types of unleavened wheat matzos are the table centerpieces in each home during this time. ❦ Carnival, the festival street party of parades and feasting particularly famed in New Orleans and Rio de Janeiro, is acted out on Shrove Tuesday, before the quiet Lenten period commences. Pain de boulanger, New Orleans' special bakers' bread, is a must on every table, for every meal. Join the celebration by baking a batch of Cajun French Quarter Rolls (page 27), spiked with the alchemic mixture of red pepper and herbs that somehow creeps into all Louisiane food. ❦ Pre-Lenten festivities throughout Europe find people eating a myriad of spherical pancakes and jelly donuts, often made-to-order at outdoor stalls. German Pfannkuchen, Hungarian palacsintas, dainty yeasted Swedish tarkedli sandwiched with jam, dollar-sized Dutch poffertijes with butter and powdered sugar, and the ultrathin Breton buckwheat krampouz are beautifully heliomorphic, delicious symbols of the sun. ℂ Greeks who practice the Eastern Orthodox tradition take the Easter purification rites seriously. Their flat, sesame-crusted bread, known as lagána, is baked to mark the first day of Lenten fasting. It is never cut with a knife, but broken apart with the hands. Tsouréki, translated from the Turkish "that which is kneaded," is a sweet bread eaten to break the fast and appears here as Byzantine Easter Bread (page 35). Ropes of the egg-and-olive-oil dough representing the Holy Trinity are fashioned into a spiral or three-strand braid and are gently scented with favorite Mediterranean sweet spices. ℂ Missionaries introduced Russian Orthodoxy to Kodiak, Alaska, in 1794, and a great number of Alaskan native communities, from Sitka to Ketchikan, are still faithful to the religious customs, including the carrying of bread and wine to the church for blessing. In old Russia, family matriarchs carried breads wrapped in linen, often adorned with a single red taper, to the cathedral to be blessed at the midnight Resurrection service, a custom still practiced on Good Saturday at Russian Orthodox churches today. The Russian Easter bread called kulich is embellished with fruits, nuts, and a flavored vodka and baked in a stately mold reminiscent of the gold onion–domed kiosks that mark the city skylines. Long wedges of this wonderful sugar-glazed bread are often served spread with creamy pashka, a combination of fresh cheese and dried fruits molded into a unique truncated pyramid with a planed tip, a form representing Mount Golgotha. ℂ The Italians create a myriad of unique and delicious breads for Easter. Among the best known are an anise loaf from Lombardy, the ornamental Easter dove known as la colomba di Pasqua, and the orange-scented berlingaccio from Tuscany. The Istrians of northern Italy make Slavic-inspired thick coils of nut-filled gubana and potica, reflecting their long association with the Austro-Hungarian empire and Yugoslavia. ℂ German and Austrian bakers do not celebrate the Easter season to the degree of many of their neighbors, but nonetheless have beautiful and imaginative breads to mark the occasion. My favorite is the wonderful Osterkarpen, or "Easter carp," fashioned from the silky and lusciously subtle leichter Hefeteig sweet dough, with the big fish glazed with sliced almonds for scales. The fish, which is a symbol of early Christianity, is a shape often baked throughout Europe in the spring, along with the Eir Im Nest, individual wreaths nesting a vegetable-dyed egg. ℂ English hot cross buns decorated with tasty icing crosses, one of the oldest symbols of nourishment and resurrection, have been served on Good Friday and Easter throughout Great Britain and Ireland since Victorian times. Originally the buns were an imitation of unleavened Passover bread and later were baked from the dough used for making the Eucharist. Since early Christianity, the cross has been a common decorative mark on breads and rolls, reaching a zenith in popularity with the Elizabethans. Eating a cross-decorated loaf protects you for a year and wards off the evil spirits that can prevent the bread's rising during baking. ℂ The Merrie Monarch Festival is a yearly hula competition in Hilo, Hawaii, during the week beginning with Easter Sunday. Hula dancers were integral parts of the expressive Hawaiian religious ceremonies, makahiki (harvest), and mourning rituals. Hawaiian food is traditionally baked in umus (earth ovens). The Hawaiians have no bread-making traditions of their own, but early missionaries and Portuguese immigrants brought their breads from home and many have become part of the Hawaiian diet, including the famed Hawaiian sweet bread (also known as Portuguese sweet bread). Today, creative bakers are originating an assortment of innovative breads that utilize the islands' diverse pantry: coconuts, mangoes, passion fruit, macadamia nuts, Kona coffee, dried bananas and papaya, pineapples, exotic flower honeys, and the new Big Island crop of chocolate. ❧ April is the time to travel to St. Albans, Vermont, for the classic New England Vermont Maple Festival. Depending on the sun and rain, warm and cool winds, the syrup gathered from the Acer saccharum sugar maples varies from year to year. You know spring has arrived when it is time to tap the trees. Nova Scotia Germans prepare a yeasted deep-fried bread called Fanikaneekins, hauntingly similar to Navajo fry bread, drizzled with maple syrup. Food writer Leslie Land describes maple syrup as the most "poetic of sweets, with the distinctive yet delicate undertones of wood, wildness, and smoke." The addition of maple syrup or sugar to bread doughs is my first preference in sweetening. ❧ May Day eve marks the beginning of the luminous time, the halfway point between the spring equinox and summer solstice. ❧ In Ireland, the towns of Cork and Belfast are known for their pastoral spring fairs. Excellent soda breads (arán sóide) and fresh churned buttermilk scones (bonnóga blathaí) are plentiful. There are also breads shaped into fat shamrocks, which look like swollen crosses. Peat, a main source of fuel in Ireland, is still harvested by hand-held spade along the Atlantic coastal bogs. The strong, musky scent of the slow-burning peat is very much a part of Irish baking, giving the local bastable potoven- and griddle-baked goods a unique flavor. ❧ On the first Saturday in May, the Kentucky Derby is held at Churchill Downs in Louisville. A southern tradition for two hundred years, the ritual includes mint juleps made from good Kentucky bourbon served in silver cups. Ninety percent of all U.S. bourbon is made in this genteel country, with Southern Comfort (a bourbon liqueur with peaches and oranges) and Jack Daniel's among the most famous brands. Either one is a fine addition to Bourbon Dinner Rolls (page 46). ❧ Mother's Day, celebrated on the second Sunday in May, has been a holiday in over one hundred countries since 1914, and is a "public expression of our love and reverence for our mothers." It is a good time to remember the guardianship that is contained in the natural forces known as Mother Earth and Mother Nature, and it draws upon the long-practiced European tradition of honoring the goddess at ancient springtide festivals. ❧ On Memorial Day weekend, the Basques, dressed in their predominately red-and-green Old World regalia, hold their annual picnics. They are descendants of shepherds who came to the United States and settled in the agricultural communities of the California Sierras, Idaho's Rocky Mountains, and the Nevada foothills. Known for their exceptional wheat and corn fields in the semiarid regions in Spain, they are also known for their corn breads baked inside cabbage leaves and talo, a flatbread baked on a special iron griddle called a talo burni. On this last day of May, they fire up their barbecues and cauldrons to prepare some of the same foods enjoyed for centuries by their ancestors in the Spanish Pyrénées. The air is filled with the scent of roasted spring lamb, the aroma of crusty rounds of peasant bread (euskaldun ogia) slow cooked in iron pots submerged in ember-lined pits, traditional songs, and the cries from the vigorous pelota ball games. ❧

Tuscan Peasant Bread

For centuries, Tuscan cooks have been making their saltless peasant loaf. Traditionally baked once a week in wood-fired ovens, pane sciocco, or "tasteless bread," is a crisp-crusted, practical staple for a cuisine high in such salty foods as prosciutto. It has a spongelike interior and does not mold (since there is no salt to hold excess moisture), but it turns dry quickly. Break or slice off pieces of the chewy loaf for eating throughout a meal. For the freshest texture and flavor, eat within twelve hours; leftovers can be stored in plastic at room temperature up to two days for use as toast or in recipes.

YIELD: ONE LARGE LOAF

2½ teaspoons active dry yeast
2 cups warm water (105° to 115°)
3¼ to 3½ cups unbleached all-purpose flour
½ cup coarse-grind whole-wheat flour
Pinch of salt
Pinch of sugar

1. In a large bowl or in the work bowl of a heavy-duty electric mixer fitted with the whisk attachment, sprinkle the yeast over the warm water. Mix by swirling to dissolve. The mixture will look milky. Add 1 cup of the unbleached flour and all of the whole-wheat flour. Beat hard with a whisk until combined, about 1 minute. Cover with plastic wrap or a clean cotton towel and let stand 1 hour, or until bubbly.

2. Using a wooden spoon or switching to the flat paddle attachment of the mixer, beat in the salt, sugar, and 1 cup more of the flour until smooth, about 1 minute. Add the remaining flour, ½ cup at a time, beating vigorously between additions to form a soft dough that just clears the sides of the bowl.

3. Turn out the dough onto a lightly floured work surface and knead vigorously until a soft, smooth, yet quite pliable dough is formed, at least 5 to 8 minutes, adding only 1 tablespoon of flour at a time as necessary to prevent sticking. Vigorous kneading is important for developing the gluten and keeping the dough moist to produce the light, moist interior that is characteristic of this bread. Place on a floured work surface, dust the top with flour, and cover with plastic wrap or a clean cotton towel. Let rise at room temperature until doubled in bulk, 1 to 1½ hours.

4. Flatten gently and form the dough into one tight round, known as a *ruota*, or into an oblong loaf. Place on a lightly floured parchment-lined baking sheet or pizza pan (no greased pans, please). Dust the tops with additional flour. Let rest 20 minutes. At the same time, line the lowest and highest rack settings with baking stones or unglazed terra-cotta tiles and preheat the oven to 425°.

5. Using a serrated knife, score a tic-tac-toe pattern on the round loaf or score the oblong loaf with 3 diagonal slits, no deeper than ¼ inch. Bake on the lowest rack of the preheated oven until very crusty and deep brown, 55 to 65 minutes. The loaf will look done at around 45 minutes, but needs the extra few minutes to bake the interior thoroughly. Remove the *pane tuscano* to a rack to cool completely, about 2 hours, before serving.

TUSCAN PEASANT BREAD WITH OLIVES
This is a nontraditional variation, but one of my favorites.

Add 1½ teaspoons salt and ⅓ cup *each* finely chopped, pitted green and black olives to the dough during the mixing in step 2, after you have added all the flour. Proceed as directed.

Overnight Pain Ordinaire

*Light beer, imported French hard apple cider, or non-alcoholic sparkling apple cider is added
to the dough to give it a special flavor not unlike that imparted by the long-fermenting starters typical in European
country breads. The bread will have a distinctly different taste depending on which liquid you use. If you prefer a whole-grain
bread, substitute 1/4 cup barley flour and 1 cup whole-wheat flour for an equal amount of the unbleached flour.*

*Plan to make, rise, and shape the dough one day and bake it the next. Serve the bread toasted with jam and tea for breakfast,
use it to make great Monterey Jack cheese sandwiches for lunch, or tear it into pieces at the table for supper.*

YIELD: 3 ROUND LOAVES OR LONG BAGUETTES

1¼ tablespoons (1¼ packages) active
    dry yeast
Pinch of sugar
1 cup warm water (105° to 115°)
2 teaspoons salt
About 5 cups unbleached all-purpose flour
1½ cups (12-ounce bottle or can) light beer or
    hard apple cider, heated slightly to burn off
    some of the alcohol and cooled to 105° to
    115°, or non-alcoholic sparkling apple cider
Yellow cornmeal, polenta, or farina,
    for sprinkling
2 tablespoons vegetable or olive oil,
    for brushing
¼ cup water mixed with ¼ teaspoon salt,
    for brushing

1. In a small bowl, sprinkle the yeast and sugar over the water. Stir to dissolve. Let stand until foamy, about 10 minutes.

2. In a large bowl or in the work bowl of a heavy-duty electric mixer fitted with the paddle attachment, place the salt and 1 cup of the unbleached flour. Add the yeast mixture and the warm beer or hard cider. Beat hard by hand with a whisk for 2 minutes or on low speed until smooth. Add the remaining flour, ½ cup at a time, until the dough forms a shaggy mass that just clears the sides of the bowl, switching to a wooden spoon as necessary if making by hand.

3. Turn out the dough onto a lightly floured work surface. Using a plastic dough scraper, knead the dough by lifting one side of the dough up and over to the opposite side. When the dough is no longer sticky and begins to smooth out, switch to kneading with your hands. Continue to knead until the dough is soft, silky, and resilient, about 3 minutes, adding flour only 1 tablespoon at a time as necessary to prevent sticking. Place the dough in a flour-dusted container. Cover with plastic wrap and let rise at room temperature until tripled in bulk, 1½ to 2 hours. Do not rush the rising.

4. Turn out the dough onto the work surface and divide it into 3 equal portions. Knead in more flour now if the dough seems sticky. To make round loaves, or *boules,* form each portion into a tight round ball. To make *baguettes,* flatten each portion into a rectangle and, using your thumbs, roll it up tightly to form a long sausage shape. Roll back and forth with your palms to adjust the length. Place the loaves, seam side down and 4 inches apart, on a greased or parchment-lined baking sheet heavily sprinkled with cornmeal, polenta, or farina. Using a serrated knife, make diagonal cuts no deeper than ¼ inch every 4 inches down the length of the *baguettes* and 3 cuts on the *boules.* Brush the surface of the loaves with oil to prevent surface sticking. Cover loosely with 2 layers of plastic wrap, allowing plenty of room for expansion yet pressing tight around the edges to keep air out. Refrigerate 6 to 12 hours, as desired.

5. When ready to bake, place a baking stone on the lowest rack in the oven and preheat the oven to 425° for at least 20 minutes; if not using a stone, preheat the oven to 425°. Remove the loaves from the refrigerator and uncover. Brush the surfaces gently with the salt water. Redefine the slashes, if necessary. Immediately place the pan in the oven on the lowest rack. Bake until brown, crusty, and hollow sounding when tapped, 30 to 35 minutes. For crustier loaves, brush the surface of the loaves once more with the salt water 10 minutes after placing them in the oven. Eat immediately or cool on a rack.

GARLIC PAIN ORDINAIRE

Simple garlic bread is a natural accompaniment to all types of meals.

SERVES 6 TO 8

1 Overnight Pain Ordinaire *baguette* (preceding)
⅓ cup good-quality olive oil
3 cloves garlic, minced or pressed, or to taste
¼ cup minced fresh Italian (flat-leaf) parsley
⅔ cup grated Parmesan cheese

1. Preheat the oven to 400° or prepare a charcoal fire. Slice the bread in half lengthwise. In a small bowl, combine the olive oil and garlic and brush onto the cut surfaces of the bread, allowing it to soak in well. In another small bowl, combine the parsley and Parmesan cheese. Sprinkle evenly over the cut surfaces. Combine the two halves to form a whole loaf again. Wrap in aluminum foil.

2. Place in the oven or on a grill rack over a charcoal fire until heated through, about 15 minutes. Cut into sections to serve.

Toasted Pine Nut Adobe Bread

Here is a home loaf of my own design that will produce a bread with a moist texture and strong, rustic flavor, even though it is made in your indoor kitchen oven. The secret? A combination of white and whole-wheat flours coupled with ground toasted pine nuts. Serve with roast turkey dusted with red chile powder and a pumpkin seed–green chile sauce or your own arroz con pollo casserole made with a generous measure of peas and olives studding the chicken and rice.

Yield: 2 round loaves

1½ cups pine nuts
1¾ tablespoons (2 packages) active dry yeast
2 tablespoons brown sugar
1¼ cups warm water (105° to 115°)
2¼ cups whole-wheat flour
1 cup warm milk or goat's milk (105° to 115°)
2 tablespoons vegetable oil or unsalted butter, melted
2½ teaspoons salt
3 to 3½ cups unbleached bread flour

1. Preheat oven to 325°. Place the pine nuts in a single layer on an ungreased baking sheet. Toast in the center of the oven until pale golden, 10 to 12 minutes, stirring once to redistribute the nuts for even toasting. Do not bake until dark in color, or the flavor will be too strong. Remove from the oven and let cool.

2. In a small bowl, sprinkle the yeast and a pinch of the brown sugar over ¼ cup of the warm water. Stir to dissolve. Let stand until foamy, about 10 minutes. Meanwhile, in a blender or a food processor, combine the nuts and 1 cup whole-wheat flour and process to the consistency of coarse meal. Set aside.

3. In a large bowl with a whisk or in the work bowl of a heavy-duty electric mixer fitted with the paddle attachment, combine the remaining 1 cup warm water, the remaining sugar, the warm milk, oil or melted butter, salt, and the remaining 1¼ cups whole-wheat flour. Beat until smooth, about 1 minute. Add the yeast and nut-flour mixtures. Beat 1 minute longer. Add the unbleached flour, ½ cup at a time, until a soft dough is formed that just clears the sides of the bowl.

4. Turn out the dough onto a lightly floured work surface and knead until firm yet still springy, about 3 minutes, adding only 1 tablespoon flour at a time as necessary to prevent sticking. Because whole-grain flour is used, the dough will retain a slightly tacky quality. Do not add more flour than required, as the dough will get hard and the bread will be too dry. Place in a greased deep container, turn once to coat the top, and cover with plastic wrap. Let rise at room temperature until almost tripled in bulk, 2 to 2½ hours. Do not worry if it takes a bit longer.

5. Turn out the dough onto the work surface, and divide into 2 equal portions. Form each portion into a tight round. Place the loaves, seam side down, on a greased or parchment-lined baking sheet, dust with flour, and cover loosely with plastic wrap. Let rise at room temperature until doubled in bulk, about 50 minutes. Twenty minutes before baking, preheat the oven to 425°, with a baking stone on the center rack, if desired.

6. *Using a serrated knife,* slash the surface of each loaf decoratively no more than ¼ inch deep. Place the loaves in the oven and immediately reduce the oven thermostat to 400°. Bake in the preheated oven until brown, crusty, and hollow sounding when tapped, 40 to 45 minutes. Remove immediately to a rack to cool completely before slicing.

Yeasted Sweet Cheese Strudel

The blend of fresh goat cheese and cream cheese that fills this sweet strudel is, to my palate, much like the homemade curd cheese pastry fillings of rural Hungarian country cooking known as túrós töltelék. This dough is rolled up jelly-roll fashion to create compact cylinders, then topped with a brandy-spiked almond crust that looks crackled after baking. It is a delightful sweet bread for brunch, decorated with some just-picked violets if you have a garden. Serve with fresh orange juice and sliced fresh Hawaiian pineapple and pink grapefruit.

YIELD: 3 LOAVES

2½ teaspoons active dry yeast
½ cup sugar
½ cup warm water (105° to 115°)
½ cup sour cream
6 tablespoons unsalted butter, at room
    temperature, cut into pieces
2 eggs
Grated zest of 1 large lemon
1½ teaspoons salt
3¾ cups unbleached all-purpose flour
    (exact measure)

Sweet Cheese Filling
8 ounces fresh goat cheese, such as domestic
    chabi or imported Montrachet, at room
    temperature
8 ounces cream cheese, at room temperature
⅔ cup sugar
1 egg
2 teaspoons pure vanilla extract
Grated zest of 1 large lemon

Brandied Almond Crust
1 egg yolk
1 teaspoon good-quality brandy
2 tablespoons light brown sugar
¼ teaspoon ground allspice
½ cup slivered or sliced almonds

1. *In a small bowl*, sprinkle the yeast and a pinch of the sugar over the warm water. Stir to dissolve. Let stand until foamy, about 10 minutes. Warm the sour cream on the stove top or in a microwave oven to about 105°, then add the butter pieces. Stir to melt.

2. *In a large bowl* with a whisk or in the work bowl of a heavy-duty electric mixer fitted with the paddle attachment, combine the remaining sugar, the eggs, lemon zest, salt, and 1 cup of the flour. Add the warm sour cream and yeast mixtures. Beat until smooth, about 1 minute, switching to a wooden spoon as necessary if making by hand. Add the remaining flour, ½ cup at a time. The dough will be rather soft and have a silky, translucent quality. Scrape down the sides of the bowl with a spatula. Cover the bowl with 2 layers of buttered plastic wrap and let rise in the refrigerator overnight.

3. *The next day*, make the sweet cheese filling. In a bowl, using an electric mixer, blend together the cheeses, sugar, egg, vanilla, and lemon zest until smooth and well combined. Cover and refrigerate until needed.

4. *Using a large plastic* dough scraper, scrape the chilled batter onto a lightly floured work surface. Divide into 3 equal portions. Roll out each portion into an 8-by-12-inch

rectangle, dusting lightly with flour as necessary to prevent sticking. Spread each rectangle with one-third of the sweet cheese filling, leaving a ½-inch border around the edges. Starting from a long side, roll up jelly-roll fashion and pinch the seam together to seal. Pinch both ends to seal and tuck them under. Place on a greased or parchment-lined baking sheet, at least 3 inches apart. Using a serrated knife, score each finished cylinder in 5 places across the top, no more than ¼ inch deep. Cover loosely with plastic wrap and let rise at room temperature until doubled in volume, 45 minutes to 1 hour. Twenty minutes before baking, preheat the oven to 350°.

5. *Bake in the center* of the preheated oven 10 minutes. Meanwhile, prepare the brandied almond crust. In a small bowl, combine the egg yolk, brandy, brown sugar, and allspice and beat briskly with a whisk. Using a pastry brush, spread the crust mixture gently over the tops of the partially baked strudels. Immediately sprinkle each strudel with one-third of the almonds. Quickly return the pan to the oven and bake until the strudels are golden, sound hollow when tapped, and a cake tester inserted into the center comes out clean, another 15 to 20 minutes. Using a spatula, carefully transfer the strudels from the baking sheet to a rack to cool completely.

Cinnamon-Walnut Sweet Bread

This sweet yeast cake is elegant and delicate in the grand European baking tradition. It matches a spiced walnut coating and dried cherries with an extravagant, gently sweet dough, baking them into a beautifully glazed bread. It is known as arany galuska, or "golden dumpling coffeecake," in Hungary and can be sliced or pulled apart with your fingers.

YIELD: ONE 10-INCH RING LOAF, OR TWO 8-BY-4-INCH RECTANGULAR LOAVES

⅔ cup (4 ounces) pitted dried cherries
Boiling water, as needed
1 tablespoon (1 package) active dry yeast
⅓ cup sugar
¾ cup warm water (105° to 115°)
4½ to 5 cups unbleached all-purpose flour
Zest and juice of 1 large lemon
1 teaspoon salt
1 egg
¾ cup thick plain yogurt
4 tablespoons (½ stick) unsalted butter,
   at room temperature

Spicy Walnut Coating
½ cup (1 stick) unsalted butter
1 cup sugar
1½ tablespoons ground cinnamon
1½ cups (6 ounces) finely chopped walnuts

1. *In a small bowl,* combine the dried cherries with boiling water to cover. Set aside to cool to room temperature. In another small bowl, sprinkle the yeast and a pinch of the sugar over the warm water. Stir; let stand until foamy, about 10 minutes.

2. *In a large bowl* with a whisk or in the work bowl of a heavy-duty electric mixer fitted with the paddle attachment, combine 1 cup of the flour, the remaining sugar, the lemon zest and juice, salt, egg, yogurt, and the yeast mixture. Beat hard until creamy, about 1 minute. Add the room-temperature butter in 3 additions, beating after each addition until incorporated. Add the remaining flour, ½ cup at a time, until a soft, shaggy dough is formed that just clears the sides of the bowl, switching to a wooden spoon as necessary if mixing by hand.

3. *Turn out the dough* onto a lightly floured work surface and knead until very soft yet quite springy, about 1 minute, adding only 1 tablespoon flour at a time as necessary to prevent sticking. Place in a greased deep container, turn once to coat the top, and cover with plastic wrap. Let rise at warm room temperature until doubled in bulk, 1 to 1½ hours.

4. *Meanwhile,* make the spicy walnut coating. Melt the butter and set aside. In a small bowl, combine the sugar, cinnamon, and walnuts. Drain the dried cherries and pat dry.

5. *Generously butter* one 10-inch tube pan, or two 8-by-4-inch loaf pans. Turn out the dough onto a very lightly floured work surface and pull off pieces each about the size of a golf ball. Roll each piece between your palms to form an even ball. Dip the balls, one at a time, into the melted butter, and then roll them in the walnut mixture to coat thickly all over. Place the balls in the prepared pan(s), leaving about ½ inch between them. When you have arranged a full layer, sprinkle evenly with all of the dried cherries. Repeat to make a full second layer and sprinkle the top with any remaining walnut mixture and melted butter. Cover with plastic wrap and let rise at room temperature until doubled in bulk, 1 to 1½ hours. Twenty minutes before baking, preheat the oven to 375°.

6. *If using a tube pan* with a removable bottom, place it on a sheet of aluminum foil. Bake in the center of the preheated oven until the sweet bread(s) is golden brown and sounds hollow when tapped, 40 to 45 minutes for the tube pan and 30 to 35 minutes for the rectangular loaves. Cover the top loosely with foil if browning too quickly. Remove from the oven and let stand 2 minutes (no longer, as the sugar mixture will tighten as it cools and make unmolding difficult), then invert onto a wire rack to cool. Let cool at least 20 minutes before serving warm or at room temperature.

Sun and Moon

This is just one member of a large family of rich breakfast breads that includes the brioche.
Also known as Sally Lunn in English and early colonial American baking, and as soleilune in French,
sun and moon was originally made as muffin-sized cakes with characteristic golden tops
and white bottoms that were hawked by street vendors. It is a favorite breakfast bread in New Orleans, where it
is affectionately called pain à la vielle tante. *Serve slices of the bread perfectly plain with*
fresh fruit salads, poached or baked fruits, ice cream, or dessert mousses for your equinox libations. The
next day, toast it and serve with a good berry jam or Spiced Applesauce Butter (page 160).

YIELD: ONE 10-INCH BUNDT OR ANGEL FOOD CAKE

1 tablespoon (1 package) active dry yeast

¼ cup sugar

½ cup warm water (105° to 115°)

1 cup milk

6 tablespoons unsalted butter, at room temperature, cut into pieces

½ cup whole-wheat pastry flour

3½ cups unbleached all-purpose flour (exact measure)

1 teaspoon salt

1 tablespoon grated lemon zest, or ¼ teaspoon *each* ground allspice and mace

3 eggs, at room temperature

2 teaspoons pure vanilla extract

Glaze

2 tablespoons milk

2 tablespoons sugar

1. In a small bowl, sprinkle the yeast and a pinch of the sugar over the warm water. Stir to dissolve. Let stand until foamy, about 10 minutes. Warm the milk on the stove top or in a microwave oven, then add the butter. Stir to melt and cool to 105° to 110°.

2. In a large bowl with a whisk or in the work bowl of a heavy-duty electric mixer fitted with the paddle attachment, combine the whole-wheat pastry flour, unbleached flour, the remaining sugar, salt, and lemon zest or spices. Add the warm milk mixture, eggs, vanilla, and yeast mixture. Beat until smooth, about 1 minute, switching to a wooden spoon as necessary if making by hand. The batter will be very soft and sticky. Cover with buttered plastic wrap. Let rise at room temperature until doubled in bulk and bubbly, about 1½ hours.

3. Using a large plastic dough scraper, scrape the batter into a heavily buttered 10-inch bundt or angel food cake pan, filling about half full. Cover loosely with buttered plastic wrap and let rise at room temperature until doubled in volume, 45 minutes to 1 hour. Twenty minutes before baking, preheat the oven to 350°.

4. Remove the buttered plastic wrap. Bake in the center of the preheated oven until the bread is golden, sounds hollow when tapped, and a cake tester inserted into the center comes out clean, 30 to 35 minutes. Turn out of the pan onto a wire rack.

5. To prepare the glaze, in a small saucepan, bring the milk and sugar to a boil, stirring to dissolve the sugar. Brush the warm bread with the glaze. Cool almost completely before slicing with a serrated knife.

ORANGE SUN AND MOON
Substitute 1 cup orange juice for the milk in step 1 and substitute grated orange zest for the lemon zest in step 2. Mix, rise, and bake as above.

Cajun French Quarter Rolls

The piquant spice mixture of herbs, red and black peppers, and garlic and onion powders is one that frequently jazzes up Cajun and Creole cooking. Here, elegant little French rolls are dressed up with the same distinctive flavors. This unique recipe was liberally adapted from the delightful King Arthur's Flour Winterbake recipe pamphlet. Plan to make the sponge the day before baking, as it must sit overnight to develop a tangy flavor. Serve the rolls with seafood or crisp salads, and spread them with Crawfish Butter (page 160), a seasonal delicacy that appears around Mardi Gras and continues until the locals have had their fill.

YIELD: 10 FRENCH ROLLS

Sponge
1 tablespoon (1 package) active dry yeast
Pinch of sugar
1¾ cups warm water (105° to 115°)
1 cup (8 ounces) plain yogurt
2½ cups unbleached all-purpose or bread flour

Dough
2½ teaspoons salt
3¼ to 3½ cups unbleached all-purpose or
   bread flour

Cajun Spice Mixture
1½ teaspoons garlic powder
1½ teaspoons onion powder
1½ teaspoons Hungarian sweet paprika
1½ teaspoons cayenne pepper or your favorite
   red chile powder
1½ teaspoons freshly fine-ground black pepper
¾ teaspoon dried thyme, crushed
¾ teaspoon dried oregano, crushed
Pinch *each* of ground allspice and mace

Yellow cornmeal or farina for sprinkling

1. Prepare the sponge: In a 3- or 4-quart plastic container or bowl, sprinkle the yeast and sugar over the warm water. Stir to dissolve. Let stand until foamy, about 10 minutes. Add the yogurt and flour, and, using a whisk, beat until smooth. Cover loosely with plastic wrap and let stand at room temperature 4 to 6 hours. (This sponge can be stored 1 day in the refrigerator before using, if necessary.)

2. Prepare the dough: Add the salt and ½ cup of the flour to the sponge. Beat hard with a whisk 3 minutes. Alternatively, transfer to a heavy-duty electric mixer fitted with the paddle attachment and beat 1 minute. Add the remaining flour, ½ cup at a time, until a soft dough is formed that just clears the sides of the bowl, switching to a wooden spoon as necessary if making by hand.

3. Turn out the dough onto a lightly floured work surface and knead vigorously to create a soft, moist, elastic dough, 2 to 3 minutes, adding flour only 1 tablespoon at a time as necessary to prevent sticking. Use a plastic dough scraper to clean off the film of dough that accumulates on the work surface as you go along. Place the dough in a greased deep container, turn once to coat the top, and cover with plastic wrap. Let rise at room temperature until tripled in bulk, about 2 hours.

4. To make the Cajun spice mixture, in a small bowl, stir together all the ingredients until well mixed. You should have about 3 tablespoons. Sprinkle the work surface with 1 tablespoon spice mixture. Turn out the dough onto the work surface and pat it into a 10- by 18-inch rectangle. Sprinkle evenly with another tablespoon of the spice mixture. Fold the two long edges in to meet in the center. Dust the surface again with the remaining spice mixture and fold in half lengthwise. This will create a swirl effect in the finished rolls. Pinch the seams together to seal and roll the log with your palms to stretch it until it is about 30 inches long. With your dough scraper or a sharp knife, cut the cylinder in half to form 2 logs, each about 15 inches long. Cut each log into 3-inch-long sections to form 5 fat rectangles. Set the 10 rolls on a greased or parchment-lined baking sheet sprinkled with cornmeal or farina. Cover loosely with plastic wrap and let rise at room temperature until doubled in bulk, about 30 minutes. Twenty minutes before baking, preheat the oven to 425°, with a baking stone, if desired.

5. Using a serrated knife, slash the top of each roll in 1 or 2 places, no more than ¼ inch deep. Slide the baking sheet onto the hot stone, if used. Bake until crusty and brown, 20 to 25 minutes. Cool slightly and eat warm.

White Whole-Wheat Cinnamon Twist with Maple Syrup

*Cinnamon twists are just too popular not to make them at least every other time you bake. And this is no ordinary
loaf: it is rolled up with a spicy filling studded with plump raisins and pecans. The flour ground from hard white wheat is
a new product available to the home consumer that offers a gentler, sweeter flavor than other commercial bread flours. It is the
predominate wheat grown today in Australia and produces a whole-wheat bread that is a significantly lighter amber.*

YIELD: TWO 9-BY-5-INCH LOAVES

Sponge
1½ tablespoons (1½ packages) active
    dry yeast
¾ cup warm water (105° to 115°)
1 cup warm buttermilk (105° to 115°)
⅓ cup pure maple syrup
3 cups white whole-wheat flour

Dough
¼ cup sunflower seed oil or melted
    unsalted butter
3 eggs
1 tablespoon salt
3½ to 4 cups white whole-wheat flour

Cinnamon Smear
¾ cup (1½ sticks) unsalted butter, at
    room temperature
1 cup firmly packed light brown sugar
1 tablespoon ground cinnamon or pumpkin
    pie spice blend

1 cup raisins
½ cup unsweetened apple juice
1 cup chopped pecans
1 teaspoon cornstarch, for glaze

1. To prepare the sponge: In a large bowl with a whisk or in the work bowl of a heavy-duty electric mixer fitted with the whisk attachment, sprinkle the yeast over the warm water. Stir to dissolve. Add the warm buttermilk, maple syrup, and flour. Beat hard until smooth, about 1 minute. Cover with plastic wrap and let stand at room temperature until bubbly, about 30 minutes.

2. To prepare the dough: Add the oil or butter, eggs, salt, and 1 cup of the flour to the sponge. If using an electric mixer, switch to the paddle attachment. Beat vigorously until creamy, about 1 minute. Add the remaining flour, ½ cup at a time, until a soft dough is formed that just clears the sides of the bowl, switching to a wooden spoon as necessary if making by hand.

3. Turn out the dough onto a lightly floured work surface and knead until smooth and elastic, about 3 minutes, adding only 1 tablespoon flour at a time as necessary to prevent sticking. The dough will retain a nubby, tacky quality. Place in a greased deep container, turn once to coat the top, and cover with plastic wrap. Let rise at room temperature until doubled in bulk, 1½ to 2 hours.

4. Meanwhile, make the cinnamon smear. Place the butter, brown sugar, and cinnamon in the bowl of an electric mixer. Beat with the paddle attachment until creamy and evenly combined. Set aside at room temperature. In a small saucepan, place the raisins and the apple juice and bring to a boil. Immediately remove from the heat and let stand at least 15 minutes to plump.

5. Turn out the dough onto a very lightly floured work surface and divide into 2 equal portions. Roll out or pat each portion into a thick rectangle about 6 by 12 inches. Do not use any more flour unless the dough is sticking mercilessly, as it will make the dough too dry. The dough should feel a bit sticky to work with. Spread half the cinnamon smear over each rectangle of dough, leaving a ½-inch border around the edges. Drain the raisins, reserving the apple juice. Sprinkle 1 rectangle with all of the drained raisins. Sprinkle the other rectangle with all of the chopped pecans. Cut each portion in half lengthwise to make 4 equal strips. Starting from a long side, tightly roll up each section, finishing at the clean border; pinch all seams to seal. Tuck the ends under. Twist 1 raisin-filled roll together with 1 pecan-filled roll to form a 2-strand twist. Place in a greased 9-by-5-inch loaf pan. Repeat to form a twist with the remaining 2 portions. Cover loosely with plastic wrap and let rise at room temperature until 1 inch above the rims of the pans, 1 to 1½ hours. Twenty minutes before baking, preheat the oven to 375°.

6. Place the loaves in the center of the preheated oven to bake. Meanwhile, add enough water or more apple juice to the raisin soaking liquid to measure ¼ cup. In a small saucepan, combine the cornstarch and liquid with a small whisk and bring to a boil. Boil, stirring constantly, until translucent, about 1 minute.

Remove the breads from the oven after 20 minutes and brush the tops evenly with the glaze. Return them immediately to the oven for an additional 10 to 15 minutes, or until they are light brown and sound hollow when

tapped, 30 to 35 minutes total. Do not over-bake, or the loaves will be dry. Turn out of the pans to cool on racks completely before slicing.

Hungarian Nut Roll

Recipes for Hungarian rolls have graced many a handwritten cookbook, reflecting the subtle and exquisite baking tradition of the Viennese Empire. They are tremendously popular in Hungary, appearing for spring and winter holidays filled with ground nuts or poppyseeds and raisins; both fillings make standard sweets in the pastry shops. Every home has its own recipe for these rolls. As holiday gifts they are much anticipated. The cinnamon in the filling may be replaced with 1 tablespoon of unsweetened cocoa powder, and pecans, pistachios, chestnuts, or hazelnuts can be used instead of walnuts.

YIELD: 4 ROLLS

1 tablespoon (1 package) active dry yeast
Pinch of sugar
1 cup warm milk (105° to 115°)
½ cup (1 stick) unsalted butter, at room
    temperature
½ cup sugar
1 egg
Grated zest of 1 lemon
½ teaspoon salt
3¾ to 4¼ cups unbleached all-purpose flour

Walnut-Cinnamon Paste
4 cups (1 pound) walnuts
½ cup sugar
1½ teaspoons ground cinnamon
2 tablespoons Cognac
About ⅓ cup hot milk

1 whole egg, beaten, for glaze

1. In a small bowl, sprinkle the yeast and the pinch of sugar over ⅓ cup of the warm milk. Stir to dissolve. Let stand until foamy, about 10 minutes

2. In a large bowl with a wooden spoon or in the work bowl of a heavy-duty electric mixer fitted with the paddle attachment, beat together the butter and sugar until fluffy. Add the egg and beat vigorously for 1 minute. Beat in the remaining ⅔ cup milk, the lemon zest, salt, and 1 cup of the flour. Then add the remaining flour, ½ cup at a time, until a soft dough is formed that just clears the sides of the bowl.

3. Turn out the dough onto a lightly floured work surface and knead until smooth and pliable, about 3 minutes, adding only 1 table-spoon flour at a time as necessary to prevent sticking. The dough will be very soft but not sticky. Place in a greased deep container, turn once to coat the top, and cover with plastic wrap. Let rise at cool room temperature for 4 to 6 hours, deflating once or twice, or as long as overnight in the refrigerator.

4. Turn out the dough onto the work sur-face and divide into 4 equal portions. Form each portion into a thick rectangle, set on some lightly floured parchment paper, cover loosely with a clean tea towel, and let rest 30 minutes.

5. *Meanwhile,* make the walnut-cinnamon paste. Combine the walnuts, sugar, and cinnamon in a food processor fitted with the metal blade. Process until finely ground. Add the Cognac to the milk and, with the motor running, add the mixture through the feed tube in a slow, steady stream, processing until a thick, spreadable paste is formed. (If made ahead, store in the refrigerator.)

6. *Using a floured rolling pin* on a clean or very lightly floured work surface to minimize sticking, roll or pat out each dough portion into a rectangle about 13 by 7 inches and ⅛ inch thick. Evenly spread the surface of each portion with one-fourth of the nut paste. Working with 1 rectangle at a time and starting from a long side, fold over a 2-inch section. Continue to fold the dough in this manner to create a flattish oval (rather than round) log of dough. Pinch the seams together and tuck under the ends. Place seam side down on a greased or parchment-lined baking sheet. I fit all 4 rolls horizontally with about 2 inches in between. Brush with the egg glaze and prick all over with a fork. Let rest, uncovered, at room temperature about 20 minutes. Meanwhile, preheat the oven to 350°.

7. *Brush once more* with the beaten egg and bake in the center of the preheated oven until golden, 30 to 40 minutes. (If using 2 baking sheets, change the rack positions halfway through baking.) Let rest on the baking sheet 10 minutes, then, using a large spatula, transfer to a rack to cool completely. Handle the hot breads carefully, as they are quite delicate.

Italian Anise Easter Bread

*Here is a special family recipe from my friend Lisa Warren. The austere bread is infused with the
strongly scented oil of anise, a plant also known for its soothing digestive qualities. Lisa's original recipe triples
the ingredients listed here, using a full five pounds of flour, to make six to eight braids for gift giving. Note that the dough
rises slowly at room temperature before a final rise and shaping. After baking, the hairline crust is dark and glossy,
studded decoratively with fennel seeds. You may add a cup or two of golden raisins to the dough
if your palate desires, but it is quite perfect made simply as follows.*

YIELD: THREE 9-BY-5-INCH OR FREESTANDING BRAIDED LOAVES

1 cup milk
1 cup sugar
6 tablespoons unsalted butter
2 teaspoons active dry yeast
Pinch of sugar
¼ cup warm water (105° to 115°)
6 to 6½ cups unbleached all-purpose flour
1½ teaspoons salt
2 teaspoons baking powder
4 eggs
2 tablespoons pure anise extract
1 egg, beaten, for glaze
1 tablespoon fennel seeds, for sprinkling

1. *In a medium saucepan* or microwave-proof bowl, combine the milk, the 1 cup sugar, and butter. Heat, stirring occasionally, until the butter is melted. Let the mixture stand until warm, 105° to 115°. In a small bowl, sprinkle the yeast and the pinch of sugar over the warm water. Stir to dissolve. Let stand until foamy, about 10 minutes.

2. *In a large bowl* with a whisk or in the work bowl of a heavy-duty electric mixer fitted with the paddle attachment, place 3 cups of the flour, salt, and baking powder. Make a well in the center and break the 4 eggs into the well. Gradually mix a few tablespoons of the flour into the eggs, add the anise extract and yeast and milk mixtures, and mix until a soft, smooth, sticky dough is formed, about 2 minutes. Add the remaining flour, ½ cup at a time, until a soft dough is formed that just clears the sides of the bowl, switching to a wooden spoon as necessary if making by hand.

3. *Turn out the dough* onto a lightly floured work surface and knead until smooth and elastic, 2 to 3 minutes, adding only 1 tablespoon flour at a time as necessary to prevent sticking. It is important that this dough remain very soft and springy. Place in a greased deep container, turn once to coat the top, and cover tightly with plastic wrap. Let rise at cool room temperature until doubled in bulk, about 12 hours or as long as overnight.

4. *Gently deflate* the dough and let rise again at room temperature until doubled in bulk, 1 to 1½ hours. Gently deflate and divide the dough into 9 equal portions. On a lightly floured work surface, roll each portion into a rope 12 inches long. Using 3 ropes for each braid, braid the ropes together, tuck under the ends, and place each braid into a greased 9-by-5-inch loaf pan. Alternatively, place the loaves on a greased or parchment-lined baking sheet. Cover loosely with plastic wrap and let rise at room temperature until doubled in bulk or 1 inch above the rims of the pans, 45 minutes to 1 hour. Twenty minutes before baking, preheat the oven to 350°.

5. *Brush the tops* with the egg glaze, taking care not to let it drip down the sides of the pan. Sprinkle with the fennel seeds. Bake in the center of the preheated oven until deep golden brown, 35 to 40 minutes. Remove from the oven and immediately turn out onto a rack to cool completely. This bread freezes well.

Pain Hawaiian

There is magic in the transformation of a simple dough with the addition of the gloriously flavored macadamia nut.
This is not a sweet bread, but uniquely rich and crunchy with nuts. Pain Hawaiian is fantastic with a wedge of good cheese or
in a basket to accompany your indoor or outdoor meals. I like it with a platter of roasted vegetables.
It makes wonderful toast and freezes well.

YIELD: 3 ROUND LOAVES

Sponge
1 tablespoon (1 package) active dry yeast
Pinch of sugar
1½ cups unbleached all-purpose or bread flour
2 cups warm water (105° to 115°)

Dough
4 to 4½ cups unbleached all-purpose or
    bread flour
3 tablespoons nut oil, such as almond
    or walnut
½ teaspoon salt
1½ cups coarsely chopped salted
    macadamia nuts

1. To prepare the sponge: In a large bowl with a whisk or in the work bowl of a heavy-duty electric mixer fitted with the paddle attachment, sprinkle the yeast, sugar, and flour over the warm water. Beat well until smooth and creamy, about 1 minute. Cover loosely with plastic wrap and let stand at room temperature until bubbly, 30 minutes to 1 hour.

2. To prepare the dough: Add ½ cup of the flour, the oil, salt, and nuts to the sponge, and beat until smooth, about 1 minute. Add the remaining flour, ½ cup at a time, until a soft, sticky dough is formed that just clears the side of the bowl, switching to a wooden spoon as necessary if making by hand.

3. Turn out the dough onto a lightly floured work surface and knead vigorously until smooth and springy, about 2 minutes, adding only 1 tablespoon flour at a time as necessary to prevent sticking. The dough will be soft and smooth. Push back any nuts that fall out during the kneading. Place in a greased deep container, turn once to coat the top, and cover with plastic wrap. Let rise at room temperature until doubled in bulk, 1½ to 2 hours.

4. Turn out the dough onto a lightly floured work surface and divide into 3 equal portions. Form each portion into a tight round, dusting the entire round of dough with a bit of flour, and place seam side down at least 4 inches apart on a greased or parchment-lined baking sheet. Dust the tops with flour. Cover loosely with plastic wrap and let rise at room temperature until puffy, about 45 minutes. Meanwhile, place a baking stone on the bottom rack of the oven and preheat the oven to 450°; if not using a stone, preheat the oven to 400°.

5. Using kitchen shears, gently snip three Vs into the top of each loaf at a 45-degree angle down the center or at the four corners. Place the loaves in the preheated oven, reduce the oven thermostat to 400° if using a baking stone, and bake the loaves until they are crusty, brown, and sound hollow when tapped, 30 to 35 minutes. Transfer to a rack to cool completely before serving.

Almond and Ginger Kulich

Kulich, a Russian brioche served at Orthodox Easter celebrations, has a tall shape rather like a puffy mushroom. It is served by cutting the top puff off horizontally and placing it on a serving plate. Then the body is sliced in half vertically and each half is cut into 1/2-inch-thick half-circle slices that are arranged around the top. Serve the bread on a Chinese-red tablecloth alongside an assortment of stuffed eggs, sliced cold meats, an icy flavored vodka, and plenty of hot coffee. Decorate the snowy top with a small, perfect fresh rose from your garden or a rose fashioned from white or dark chocolate (available by mail order from Consuming Passions, 707-571-8380).

YIELD: TWO 7-INCH ROUND LOAVES

¼ cup golden raisins

¼ cup pitted dried sweet cherries

¼ cup finely chopped dried apricots or
   unsweetened, unsulfured dried papaya

¼ cup orange brandy, Triple Sec, or
   flavored vodka

Sponge

1 tablespoon (1 package) active dry yeast

¼ cup tepid water (100°)

½ cup tepid milk or light cream (100°)

1 cup unbleached all-purpose flour

Dough

3 eggs

2 teaspoons pure vanilla extract

2 teaspoons salt

½ cup sugar

2¾ to 3¼ cups unbleached all-purpose flour

4 tablespoons (½ stick) unsalted butter, at
   room temperature, cut into pieces

½ cup chopped almonds, lightly toasted

⅓ cup (about 1½ ounces) crystallized ginger,
   finely chopped

1 tablespoon unsalted butter, melted,
   for brushing

Powdered sugar, for dusting

1. In a small bowl, combine the raisins, cherries, and apricots or papaya with the liquor. Cover and macerate at room temperature while preparing the sponge, about 1 hour.

2. To prepare the sponge: In a large bowl with a whisk or in the work bowl of a heavy-duty electric mixer fitted with the paddle attachment, combine the yeast, warm water and milk or cream, and flour. Beat hard until smooth, about 1 minute. Cover with plastic wrap and let rest at room temperature until bubbly, about 1 hour.

3. To prepare the dough: Add the eggs, vanilla, salt, sugar, and 1 cup of the flour to the sponge. Beat until smooth. Add the butter, a few pieces at a time, and beat until incorporated. Stir in the macerated fruit and its liquor. Add the remaining flour, ½ cup at a time, until a soft dough is formed that just clears the sides of the bowl, switching to a wooden spoon as necessary if making by hand.

4. Turn out the dough onto a lightly floured work surface and knead until smooth, shiny, and soft, about 2 minutes, adding only 1 tablespoon flour at a time as necessary to prevent sticking. It is important that this dough remain very soft and pliable. Place in a greased deep container, turn once to coat the top, and cover with plastic wrap. Let rise at room temperature until doubled in bulk, 1½ to 2 hours.

5. Turn out the dough onto the work surface and pat into a fat rectangle. Sprinkle with the almonds and ginger. Fold the dough over and knead gently to distribute evenly. Divide the dough into 2 equal portions. Place each portion in a greased 7-inch charlotte mold, 5-pound honey tin, or 2-pound coffee can. Cover loosely with buttered plastic wrap and let rise until about ½ inch above the rims of the pans, about 40 minutes. Twenty minutes before baking, preheat the oven to 350°.

6. Bake on the lowest rack of the preheated oven until golden brown and a cake tester inserted into the center comes out clean, 35 to 40 minutes. If the tops brown too quickly, cover loosely with a piece of aluminum foil. Immediately remove the baked loaves from their molds to a rack. Brush the warm tops with melted butter and dust with powdered sugar. Cool completely and serve at room temperature. If made ahead, wrap the undecorated breads airtight and freeze up to 3 months. Thaw in their wrappings and rewarm in a 350° oven for 20 minutes, then decorate.

Byzantine Easter Bread

The Greek religious festival bread, tsouréki, and the Armenian braided choreg are favorite eastern Mediterranean spring egg breads. They may be flavored in a number of ways—lemon, orange, vanilla, bay, allspice, aniseed, or petimezi (grape-must syrup)—and are sprinkled with a thick crust of sesame seeds or almonds. The exotic spices used in this loaf are mastic, a resiny spice, and mahlepi seeds, from the crushed pits of St. Lucy's cherries (named for the convent where the trees were first planted). Both are native to Asia Minor, and they are readily available, along with the black cumin seeds called for, at Middle Eastern or Greek markets. Springtide motifs, such as flowers, leaves, or berries, fashioned from excess dough will transform these rich religious festival loaves into objects of art. Serve with fresh goat cheese.

Yield: 4 round loaves

1 cup warm milk (105° to 115°)
¾ cup (1½ sticks) unsalted butter
1½ tablespoons (1½ packages) active
    dry yeast
1¼ cups sugar
6 eggs
⅓ cup good-quality olive oil
1 tablespoon pure vanilla extract
1 tablespoon salt
2 teaspoons black cumin seeds (*nigella*)
1 teaspoon lightly crushed *mahlepi* seeds, or
    2 teaspoons lightly crushed aniseeds and
    1 teaspoon ground cinnamon
¾ teaspoon mastic granules, pulverized in
    a mortar with ½ teaspoon sugar, or
    1 teaspoon ground allspice
6 to 6½ cups unbleached all-purpose or
    bread flour
1 egg beaten with 1 tablespoon honey and
    1 tablespoon milk, for glaze
⅓ cup sesame seeds

1. *In a medium saucepan* or microwave-proof bowl, combine ½ cup of the milk and the butter. Heat on the stove top or in the microwave oven, stirring occasionally, until the butter is melted. Let the mixture stand until warm, 105° to 115°. In a small bowl, sprinkle the yeast and a pinch of the sugar over the remaining ½ cup warm milk. Stir to dissolve. Let stand until foamy, about 10 minutes.

2. *In a large bowl* with a whisk or in the work bowl of a heavy-duty electric mixer fitted with the paddle attachment, beat the 6 eggs and the remaining sugar until light colored, about 1 minute. Add the olive oil, vanilla, salt, black cumin seeds, spices, warm milk-butter mixture, yeast mixture, and 2 cups of the flour. Beat until a soft, sticky, smooth dough is formed, about 2 minutes. Add the remaining flour, ½ cup at a time, until a soft dough forms that just clears the sides of the bowl, switching to a wooden spoon as necessary if making by hand.

3. *Turn out the dough* onto a lightly floured work surface and knead until smooth, translucent, and elastic, about 2 minutes, adding only 1 tablespoon flour at a time as necessary to prevent sticking. It is important that this dough remain soft and springy. Place in a greased deep container, turn once to coat the top, and cover tightly with plastic wrap. Let rise at cool room temperature about 6 hours, deflating 3 times or as necessary.

4. *Gently deflate* the dough and divide into 4 equal portions. Form each portion into a smooth, tight, round loaf. Place on 2 greased or parchment-lined baking sheets (these loaves will rise to almost triple in bulk during baking). Cover loosely with plastic wrap and let rise at room temperature until doubled in bulk, 45 minutes to 1 hour. Twenty minutes before baking, preheat the oven to 350°.

5. *Brush the loaves* with the egg glaze and sprinkle with the sesame seeds. Bake both trays as close to the center of the preheated oven as possible, switching positions halfway during baking, until browned and a cake tester inserted into the center comes out clean, 35 to 40 minutes. Alternatively, bake only 1 sheet at a time and keep the other baking sheet refrigerated for 30 minutes before baking. Remove to a rack to cool completely before slicing.

To Decorate Easter Bread in the Traditional Manner

The Greek lambrópsomo, *a traditional braided bread eaten to break the Lenten fast, is made from the same dough. It is uniquely decorated with eggs dyed a Byzantine crimson (symbolizing rebirth, fertility, and the blood of Christ) embedded into the surface in the shape of a cross.*

YIELD: 2 BRAIDS

1 tablespoon red food coloring
6 eggs, at room temperature
2 tablespoons olive oil
1 recipe Byzantine Easter Bread dough
   (preceding)
²/₃ cup slivered blanched almonds
1 egg beaten with 1 tablespoon honey and
   1 tablespoon milk, for glaze

1. *Fill a medium saucepan* half full with water. Add the food coloring and the eggs. Bring to a boil. Boil gently for 10 minutes. Turn off the heat and let the eggs cool in the water. When cool, remove them with a spoon and set on a plate to dry. When dry, dip a paper towel in the olive oil and rub each egg all over with the oil.

2. *Turn the risen dough* out onto a clean work surface and divide into 6 equal portions. Roll each portion into a fat strip and lay 3 strips side by side. Braid the 3 strips together and taper the ends. Pinch the ends together and tuck them under. Repeat to make a second loaf. Place the loaves on a greased or parchment-lined baking sheet. Press 3 dyed eggs down the center of each braid. Cover loosely with plastic wrap and let rise at room temperature until puffy, about 1½ hours. Twenty minutes before baking, preheat the oven to 350°. Gently repress the eggs into place, if necessary.

3. *Brush the loaves* with the egg glaze and sprinkle with the almonds. Bake as directed. Discard the decorative dyed eggs when the bread is cut.

Golden Rum Babas

Babas are named for Ali Baba, the hero of Arabian Nights fame. Here is the classic version with rum, but other popular variations call for framboise, orange and peach brandy, or Kirsch. Babas and their relatives, the savarin and brioche, are light and spongy, moist and delicate. They are remarkably easy to prepare, as they require no kneading. Babas are baked in small, round molds three inches in diameter and three inches tall (also known as dariole or castle pudding molds). Each mold looks like the Turkish cap called a fez and they are readily available in specialty cookware stores. If possible, top each baba with a crystallized flower (recipe follows).

YIELD: 12 BABAS

½ cup dried currants or pitted dried
    sour cherries
3 tablespoons golden rum

Dough
1 tablespoon (1 package) active dry yeast
Pinch of granulated sugar
¼ cup warm water (105° to 115°)
2 cups unbleached all-purpose flour
4 eggs
1 tablespoon granulated sugar
1 teaspoon salt
½ cup (1 stick) unsalted butter, cut into
    16 pieces

Soaking Syrup
2 cups water
1¼ cups granulated sugar
½ cup golden rum

Apricot Glaze
1 cup good-quality apricot jam
2 tablespoons water
1 tablespoon golden rum

Vanilla Whipped Cream
¾ cup heavy (whipping) cream, chilled
1 tablespoon powdered or superfine sugar
½ teaspoon pure vanilla extract

Garnish
12 commercial or homemade crystallized
    violets (following) or strips of bittersweet
    citrus peel, or 24 almond slices or com-
    mercial marzipan decorations, such as
    miniature carrots

1. Place the currants or dried cherries in a small jar or bowl and add the rum. Let stand 1 hour to as long as overnight at room temperature to macerate.

2. To prepare the dough: In a small bowl, sprinkle the yeast and the pinch of sugar over the warm water. Stir to dissolve. Let stand until foamy, about 10 minutes.

3. Place the flour in a large bowl and make a well in the center. Add the eggs, sugar, and salt to the well. Gradually mix a few table-spoons of the flour into the eggs, add the yeast mixture, and stir with a whisk until a soft, sticky dough is formed. Beat vigorously until smooth, about 3 minutes. Place in a greased container and sprinkle the butter pieces over the top. Cover with plastic wrap and let rise at room temperature until doubled in volume, about 1 hour.

4. Using a wooden spoon, fold the butter into the dough and then gently slap the dough against the sides of the bowl until completely incorporated. The dough and butter will be about the same temperature during the mix-ing. Add the macerated fruit with its liquid and fold in. The baba dough may also be mixed in the work bowl of a heavy-duty elec-tric mixer fitted with the paddle attachment.

5. Generously butter twelve ½-cup baba molds or 2½- to 3-inch muffin cups. Spoon in enough batter to fill each mold one-third to one-half full (about 3 tablespoons). Do not overfill or the babas will not rise and expand properly during baking. Press the dough lightly into the bottom of each mold. If using baba molds, arrange them on a baking sheet about 2 inches apart. Let the dough rise, uncovered, at room temperature until even with the rims of the molds, about 45 minutes. Twenty minutes before baking, preheat the oven to 375°.

6. Place the baking sheet on the center rack of the preheated oven and bake the babas until a cake tester inserted into the center comes out clean and the sides are brown and have shrunk from the molds slightly, about 15 minutes. Unmold the babas onto a rack and let cool completely. (The cakes may be wrapped and stored at room temperature up to 2 days at this point before glazing and decorating.)

7. *To prepare the soaking syrup:* In a medium, heavy saucepan, combine the water and sugar. Heat slowly over low heat until the sugar dissolves, swirling occasionally. Raise the heat and bring to a boil. Immediately remove from the heat and pour into a heat-proof bowl. Place a cooled baba into the hot syrup and ladle the syrup gradually over the cake to moisten the surface evenly. Do this only for about 5 seconds or the baba will be soggy. Using a slotted spoon, transfer to a rack placed over a baking sheet to catch the drips. Repeat with the remaining babas, reheating the syrup, if necessary, as the hot syrup is more easily absorbed. Let the babas stand at room temperature for 30 minutes to dry.

8. *Place the babas* on a large plate and spoon about 2 teaspoons rum over each one. Replace on the rack to dry. Meanwhile, prepare the apricot glaze by puréeing the apricot jam in a blender or a food processor fitted with a metal blade until smooth. Transfer to a small, heavy saucepan and add the water and rum. Heat just until warm. Using a small brush, apply the glaze over the entire surface of each baba to seal in the liquor. Place the babas on a serving platter as each one is finished. Refrigerate, tightly covered, at this point until serving.

9. *One hour before serving,* make the vanilla whipped cream. In a small bowl, whip the cream with the sugar and vanilla until soft peaks form. Scoop into a pastry bag fitted with a large star tip. Pipe a large rosette of cream on top of each baba. Garnish each baba as desired. Babas are best served the day they are made, but will keep refrigerated up to 2 days.

Crystallized Flowers or Herbs

A special touch for a celebration bread is to decorate it with small, fresh crystallized blossoms and leaves. Sweet violets (not inedible African violets), geraniums, baby rosebuds, lilacs, lemon blossoms, acacia blooms, some small orchids, and mint leaves are exceptionally easy to work with because of their broad flat petals and vibrant colors, both of which stay intact. Often the scent is also preserved. Use only freshly harvested, pesticide-free blossoms and herbs. Flowers from a florist may be treated with chemicals and should therefore be avoided. Keep the stems intact to use as handles during the preparation, but discard them once the decorating is completed, as they are usually unpalatable. Prepare the blossoms and herbs for coating by rinsing in cool water and patting dry with soft facial tissues.

1 egg white
¼ teaspoon water
½ cup superfine sugar
Small flowers or herb leaves (see introduction)

1. *In a small bowl,* beat together the egg white and water until foamy. Spread the sugar out on a small plate. Using a clean, tiny water-color paint brush, coat the top and underside of each flower blossom or herb leaf. Place the flower or leaf immediately into the sugar. Lift the sugar-coated blossom or herb with tweezers or sprinkle with a spoon if necessary to coat both sides. Place the sugar-coated bits on a double layer of paper towels. Let dry overnight at room temperature until dried and brittle.

2. *Store in an airtight container* with waxed paper separating the layers. The crystallized blossoms and leaves are fragile, so handle carefully.

Cheddar Cheese Bread with Toasted Sesame Seeds

The combination of toasted sesame seeds and a nutty-tasting sharp Cheddar cheese is a gustatory delight.
The cheese sets into a marbled pattern that is quite beautiful when sliced. This is a recipe adapted from Betsy Oppenneer,
a talented Georgia baker who reminded me of how dramatic cheese-enhanced country breads are. They are perfect
warm from the oven in fat slices au naturel. Serve with meat or poultry salads, chunky vegetable soups,
as a superior sandwich bread, or with fresh apples and a glass of cold cider.

YIELD: TWO 9-BY-5-INCH OR SIX 6-BY-4-INCH LOAVES

⅓ cup sesame seeds

1 tablespoon (1 package) active dry yeast

Pinch of sugar

2 cups warm water (105° to 115°)

2 tablespoons vegetable oil

2 teaspoons salt

2 eggs

5½ to 6 cups unbleached all-purpose or bread flour

3 cups (12 ounces) shredded sharp Cheddar cheese, such as Oregon Tillamook, Vermont Colby, or Wisconsin longhorn

1. *To toast the sesame seeds*, place them in a small skillet over medium heat. Cook until golden brown, shaking the pan often, about 2 minutes. Immediately remove from the skillet to a small bowl to cool completely.

2. *In a small bowl*, sprinkle the yeast and sugar over ½ cup of the warm water. Stir to dissolve. Let stand until foamy, about 10 minutes.

3. *In a large bowl* with a whisk or in the work bowl of a heavy-duty electric mixer fitted with the paddle attachment, combine the remaining 1½ cups warm water, oil, salt, eggs, sesame seeds, 2 cups of the flour, and the yeast mixture. Beat hard until smooth, about 1 minute. Add half of the shredded cheese and the remaining flour, ½ cup at a time, until a shaggy dough is formed, switching to a wooden spoon as necessary if making by hand.

4. *Turn out the dough* onto a lightly floured surface and knead until smooth and silky, about 3 minutes, adding only 1 tablespoon flour at a time as needed to prevent sticking. Place the dough in a greased deep container, turn once to coat the top, and cover with plastic wrap. Let rise at room temperature until doubled in bulk, 1½ to 2 hours.

5. *Turn out the dough* onto the work surface and pat into a thick, 12-inch-long rectangle. Sprinkle with the remaining cheese, fold the dough around the cheese, and knead gently a few times to distribute throughout the dough, which will produce the marble effect. Cover with a tea towel or piece of plastic wrap to prevent drying and let rest 5 to 10 minutes on the work surface to relax the dough. Divide the dough into 2 equal portions and shape each portion into a rectangular loaf. Place each loaf in a greased 9-by-5-inch standard loaf pan, seam side down. Alternatively, divide the dough into 6 equal portions and shape into loaves. Place each loaf in a 6-by-4-inch miniloaf pan, seam side down. Cover loosely with plastic wrap and let rise at room temperature until doubled in bulk or 1 inch above the rims of the pans, about 45 minutes. Twenty minutes before baking, preheat the oven to 375°.

6. *Using kitchen shears*, gently snip the top of each loaf 5 or 6 times at a 45-degree angle a full 2 inches deep and the length of the loaf, to create a pronounced off-center jagged pattern. Bake in the center of the preheated oven until the loaves are golden brown and sound hollow when tapped, 40 to 45 minutes for the standard loaf pans and 25 to 30 minutes for the miniloaf pans. Remove from the pans to a rack to cool completely before slicing.

Shepherd's Bread

Shepherd's bread is traditionally baked in a cast-iron pan submerged in a small, ember-lined pit covered with dirt.
It is easily adapted to conventional home ovens by baking it in a contemporary clay cloche (a miniature brick oven also
known as a forneau de campagne), cast-iron Dutch oven with a tight-fitting flanged lid, or on a pizza stone.
This venerable Basque bread is a relative of the simple Spanish and Greek peasant loaves of Europe. For a whole-wheat
version, substitute an equal amount of whole-wheat grain flour for the 2 cups of flour in the sponge and 1 1/2 cups
whole-wheat flour for an equal amount in the dough, making a slightly denser finished loaf.
Eat this bread the same day it is made.

YIELD: 1 LARGE LOAF

Sponge
2 teaspoons active dry yeast or ¾ ounce
   compressed fresh yeast
2 cups tepid water (90° to 100°)
2 cups unbleached all-purpose or bread flour
½ cup sugar

Dough
1 teaspoon active dry yeast or ¼ ounce
   compressed fresh yeast
1 cup warm water (105° to 115°)
1 tablespoon salt
½ cup good-quality olive oil
5½ to 6 cups unbleached all-purpose or
   bread flour

¼ cup unbleached all-purpose or bread flour

1. *To prepare the sponge:* In a large bowl, sprinkle the dry yeast or crumble the fresh yeast over the tepid water. Using a large whisk, add 1 cup of the flour and the sugar. Add the remaining 1 cup flour and beat hard until very smooth, 2 minutes. Scrape down the sides of the bowl and cover with plastic wrap. Let stand at room temperature until soft, spongy, and pleasantly fermented, 2 hours.

2. *To prepare the dough:* Using a wooden spoon, beat down the sponge. Alternatively, beat down the sponge in the work bowl of a heavy-duty mixer fitted with the paddle attachment. In a measuring cup, stir the yeast into the warm water to dissolve. Add the yeast, warm water, salt, and olive oil to the sponge and beat well. Add the flour, ½ cup at a time, beating vigorously until a soft dough is formed that just clears the sides of the bowl.

3. *Turn out the dough* onto a well-floured work surface and knead until a smooth and firm yet springy and resilient dough is formed, about 5 minutes, adding only 1 tablespoon flour at a time to prevent sticking. Place the dough in a floured deep container, dust the top with flour, and cover with plastic wrap. Let rise at cool room temperature until tripled in bulk, 2½ to 3 hours.

4. *Turn out the dough* onto a clean work surface. It will be slightly sticky from the long rise. Knead in about ¼ cup more flour to make a firmer dough, about 1 minute. Shape into a tight round ball. Pull the ends tightly to the center of the loaf to form a smooth bottom and sides. Mist the surface with some water. Using about 2 tablespoons of flour, heavily coat the top surface. Using a serrated knife, slash the top surface with 4 gashes to form a large square no more than ¼ inch deep to allow steam to escape and to allow room for the dough to expand. Using butter or solid vegetable shortening, grease the inside of the lid and the bottom and sides of a 12-inch (6-quart) seasoned cast-iron Dutch oven cooking pot. The bottom may also be lined with a round of foil, if desired, to prevent sticking. Dust the bottom lightly with flour. Add the formed loaf, seam side down. Cover the pot with its well-greased lid and let the dough rise in a sheltered area until doubled in bulk, about 1 hour, or until the dough pushes the lid up.

5. *Meanwhile,* burn a wood, charcoal, or combination fire until you have a good supply of coals. Sweep the coals into a shallow depression in the ground dug next to the fire, saving some larger coals.

6. *Set the pot on a grill* or balance it on three stones ½ inch above a ring of 6 to 8 evenly spaced hot coals. Using a short-handled shovel, set 12 to 16 of the larger coals directly on the pot lid around the edges and in the middle for even heat distribution from the top as well as the bottom of the pot. Check the bread after 35 minutes; keep in mind that the handle will be very hot. Use a pair of pliers or a short fireplace poker shaped into a hook to lift the lid, and wear leather gloves to avoid burns. Bake, fanning the coals periodically, until the bread is golden brown, crisp, and sounds hollow when tapped, 45 minutes to 1 hour. Using heavy gloves, move the Dutch oven from the cooking site by carrying it by its wire bail. Use a whisk broom to sweep the ashes off the lid, if necessary. Using oven mitts, remove the loaf from the hot pan with care. Serve immediately. When the Dutch oven is cool, wipe it or rinse with water to clean.

7. *Alternatively,* line a conventional home oven with unglazed terra-cotta tiles (or use a baking stone if possible) and preheat the oven to 425°. Sprinkle a greased or parchment-lined baking sheet with flour and place the ball of dough on it, seam side down. (When using the baking sheet, 2 loaves can be made.) Using a serrated knife, slash the top surface with 4 gashes to form a large square no more than ¼ inch deep. Dust the top with flour. Cover loosely with plastic wrap and let rise at room temperature 35 minutes.

8. *If using a cloche,* sprinkle the dish with flour and place the dough ball in the center of the dish. Move the dough around to cover the bottom and up the sides a bit with flour. Using a serrated knife, slash the top decoratively. Cover with the cloche bell and let rest at room temperature 15 minutes. Before placing in the oven, rinse the inside of the cloche bell with water, draining off excess drips. Place back over the bread and place in the preheated oven.

9. *Place the baking sheet* or cloche in the center of the preheated oven and bake 10 minutes. Lower the thermostat to 400° and bake until the bread is golden brown, crisp, and sounds hollow when tapped, 25 to 35 minutes. If using the cloche, remove the bell after 30 minutes of baking to allow the loaf to brown thoroughly. Remove the loaf from the oven to a rack to cool 15 minutes before serving.

NOTE: If using a cloche, to clean it, tap out the excess flour once the dish has cooled completely. Using a dry brush, scrub off any bits of dried dough stuck to the clay. Rinse with plain water only, as any soap will be absorbed into the porous clay, giving the next loaf a soapy aftertaste.

Sesame Whole-Wheat Bread

High in fiber and nutrition, this loaf is a favorite bread with the health-conscious. It tastes good, is easy to make, and has a great moist texture due to the addition of eggs. You may glaze the crust with beaten egg, but I prefer the matte finish with the sesame seeds peeking out. In the early days of my restaurant baking, we made this popular old-fashioned recipe often, filling the bakery with a grain-sweet aroma. The free-form loaves should be quickly shaped and compact for the best results. Substitute graham flour for the whole-wheat flour, if you desire, or add 1/4 cup barley flour for more sweetness.

YIELD: 3 OVAL LOAVES

1 tablespoon (1 package) active dry yeast
Pinch of light brown sugar
1½ cups warm water (105° to 115°)
1 cup warm milk (105° to 115°)
¼ cup light brown sugar
¼ cup light molasses
2¼ cups whole-wheat flour
¼ cup vegetable or sesame oil
¼ cup sesame seeds
¼ cup medium-grind yellow cornmeal
2½ teaspoons salt
3 eggs
5 to 5½ cups unbleached all-purpose or
 bread flour
Extra cornmeal and sesame seeds,
 for sprinkling

1. In a large bowl or in the work bowl of a heavy-duty electric mixer fitted with the paddle attachment, sprinkle the yeast and the pinch of sugar over the warm water. Stir to dissolve. Let stand until foamy, about 10 minutes. Add the milk, the ¼ cup sugar, molasses, and whole-wheat flour. Whisk until smooth. Cover with plastic wrap and set aside at room temperature until bubbly, about 1 hour.

2. Add the oil, sesame seeds, cornmeal, salt, eggs, and 1 cup of the flour to the whole-wheat batter. Beat until smooth, about 2 minutes. Add the remaining unbleached flour, ½ cup at a time, until a soft dough is formed that just clears the sides of the bowl, switching to a wooden spoon when necessary if making by hand.

3. Turn out the dough onto a lightly floured work surface and knead gently until just past sticky, smooth on the surface, and soft, about 2 minutes, adding only 1 tablespoon flour at a time as necessary to prevent sticking. It is important that this dough remain soft and pliable or it will be too dry. If it is kneaded too long, the dough will continue to absorb flour and make a much firmer loaf, so stop even

though it is slightly sticky. Place in a greased deep container, turn once to coat the top, and cover with plastic wrap. Let rise at room temperature until doubled in bulk, 1½ to 2 hours.

4. Turn out the dough onto the work surface and divide into 3 equal portions. Form each portion into a fat rectangular loaf. Place seam side down (I stagger the 3 loaves) on a greased or parchment-lined baking sheet sprinkled with cornmeal. Cover loosely with plastic wrap and let rise until almost doubled in bulk, about 1 hour. Twenty minutes before baking, preheat the oven to 350°.

5. Using a serrated knife, slash 3 parallel gashes down the sides of each loaf to form a herringbone effect. Bake in the center of the preheated oven until the loaves are evenly golden brown and sound hollow when tapped on the bottom, 35 to 40 minutes. Do not overbake. Remove from the pans by pulling the loaves apart, and let cool completely on a rack before slicing.

Lemon Saffron Tea Bread

Saffron is often used in spring breads, as its marigold-yellow threads are the embodiment of seasonal light.
Serve this tea bread for brunch spread with fromage blanc, a fresh goat cheese often used as a substitute for butter
in Europe, or as an unusual dessert with the first strawberries of the season crushed with a bit of sugar and orange liqueur.
This is a yeasted batter bread, so it only rises once in the pan before baking. Serve fresh on your best pedestal
cake plate decorated with unsprayed spring flowers. It is great toasted the next day.

YIELD: ONE 10-INCH COFFEE CAKE

⅛ teaspoon saffron threads, crumbled
½ cup milk
1 tablespoon (1 package) active dry yeast
1 cup sugar
½ cup warm water (105° to 115°)
3¾ cups unbleached all-purpose flour
   (exact measure)
½ cup blanched almonds
½ cup (1 stick) unsalted butter,
   at room temperature
4 eggs
Grated zest of 1 lemon
⅓ cup fresh lemon juice
1½ teaspoons salt

1. In a small saucepan, sprinkle the saffron over the milk. Heat just until tiny bubbles form along the edge of the pan and then remove from the heat. Let stand at room temperature about 30 minutes, until lukewarm. Meanwhile, in a medium bowl, sprinkle the yeast and a pinch of the sugar over the warm water. Stir to dissolve and then stir in ½ cup of the flour with a whisk. Cover the batter loosely with plastic wrap and let stand at room temperature until bubbly, about 30 minutes. In a food processor fitted with the metal blade or in a nut grinder, combine ½ cup of the flour with the blanched almonds and process until a smooth flour is formed. Set aside the nut flour.

2. In a large bowl with a whisk or in the work bowl of a heavy-duty electric mixer fitted with the paddle attachment, beat together the butter and the remaining sugar until smooth. Add the eggs one at a time, beating well after each addition. Beat in the lemon zest and juice, salt, and ½ cup of the flour. Add the yeast mixture, saffron-milk mixture, and nut flour. Beat until smooth, about 1 minute. Add the remaining unbleached flour, ½ cup at a time, until a thick, fluffy batter is formed, about 2 minutes.

3. Grease a 10-inch fluted tube pan, preferably nonstick. Using a large spatula, scrape the batter into the prepared pan. Cover with plastic wrap and let rise until even with the top of the pan (about doubled in bulk), 1½ to 2 hours. Twenty minutes before baking, preheat the oven to 350°.

4. Bake in the center of the preheated oven until golden brown and a cake tester inserted into the center comes out clean, 40 to 45 minutes. Cool in the pan 10 minutes, then invert onto a rack to cool completely before serving.

Bourbon Dinner Rolls

Soft crescent dinner rolls are spiked with the legendary American drink, bourbon whisky. I am partial to Southern Comfort, a silky-sweet bourbon liqueur mythically invented by the Louisiana pirate, Jean Lafitte, but any good brand you have in your bar will do. Be sure to heat the whisky with the milk, so as to burn off some of the alcohol. Serve for Kentucky Derby weekend with molded vegetable salads and curried country captain over steamed white rice, and keep this recipe around for the Thanksgiving holidays to serve with roast poultry and baked sweet potatoes.

YIELD: 18 CRESCENT ROLLS

1 tablespoon (1 package) active dry yeast
Pinch of light brown sugar
½ cup warm water (105° to 115°)
½ cup milk
½ cup bourbon whisky or bourbon liqueur
2 tablespoons light brown sugar
2 tablespoons unsalted butter, cut into pieces
1 teaspoon grated orange zest
2 teaspoons salt
4 to 4½ cups unbleached all-purpose or
　　bread flour
3 tablespoons melted, unsalted butter mixed
　　with 3 tablespoons bourbon, for brushing
Plain or honey-crunch wheat germ,
　　for sprinkling

1. In a small bowl, sprinkle the yeast and the pinch of sugar over the warm water. Stir to dissolve. Let stand until foamy, about 10 minutes.

2. In a saucepan, scald the milk and bourbon. Add the 2 tablespoons brown sugar and the butter. Stir until the butter is melted, remove from the heat, and cool until warm, 105° to 115°. In a large bowl with a whisk or in the work bowl of a heavy-duty electric mixer fitted with the paddle attachment, combine the milk mixture, orange zest, salt, and 2 cups of the flour. Add the yeast mixture and beat until smooth and creamy, about 2 minutes. Add the remaining flour, ½ cup at a time, until a soft dough is formed that just clears the sides of the bowl, switching to a wooden spoon as necessary if making by hand.

3. Turn out the dough onto a lightly floured work surface and knead until satiny and elastic, about 2 minutes, adding only 1 tablespoon flour at a time as necessary to prevent sticking. This should be a very smooth dough. Place in a greased deep container, turn once to coat the top, and cover with plastic wrap. Let rise at room temperature until doubled in bulk, 1 to 1½ hours.

4. Turn out the dough onto a lightly floured work surface and divide the dough into 3 equal portions. Roll out each portion into an 8-inch circle. Brush lightly with the butter-bourbon mixture. With a knife or pastry wheel, cut each circle into 6 equal wedges. Beginning at the wide end, firmly roll up each wedge toward the point. Place, point side down, on the prepared baking sheet and curve the ends inward. Brush the tops with more of the butter-bourbon mixture and sprinkle the surfaces with wheat germ. Cover loosely with plastic wrap and let rise until doubled in bulk, about 20 minutes. Meanwhile, preheat the oven to 375°.

5. Bake in the center of the preheated oven until golden brown, 18 to 22 minutes. Using a spatula, immediately remove from the baking sheet and serve warm or place on racks to cool.

REFRIGERATOR BOURBON DINNER ROLLS
Brush the tops of the formed rolls with the butter-bourbon mixture as directed in Step 4. Cover loosely with 2 layers of plastic wrap, leaving some room for expansion, but taking care to wrap all the edges tightly to prevent drying. Immediately refrigerate from 2 to 24 hours. When ready to bake, uncover and let stand at room temperature no more than 20 minutes while preheating the oven to 375°. Glaze and bake as directed.

Irish Freckle Bread

A Celtic bread with a new twist, this Irish Freckle Bread, bairmbrack, or bairín breac, has
roots in medieval baking. Any loaf with the word breac is "speckled," and this loaf is dotted with golden raisins,
currants, dried pineapple, and freshly grated carrots, but the loaf can also be as simple as a potato bread studded with raisins.
It is known as a lardy cake in the British Isles, where it, and its close cousins, the Selkirk bannock from Scotland and
the Welsh bara brith, were prepared with plenty of tenderizing animal fat for seasonal celebrations.

YIELD: THREE 8-BY-4-INCH LOAVES

1 medium-sized russet potato (about 6 ounces),
    peeled and cut into chunks
1½ tablespoons (1½ packages) active
    dry yeast
⅓ cup sugar
5 to 5½ cups unbleached all-purpose or
    bread flour
2 teaspoons salt
2 eggs
¼ cup vegetable oil
¾ cup golden raisins
½ cup dried currants
1 cup grated carrot or parsnip
½ cup finely chopped dried pineapple

1. Place the potato chunks in a saucepan and add water to cover. Bring to a boil, reduce the heat to a simmer, and cook until tender, about 20 minutes. Drain, reserving the liquid; add water as needed to make 1¾ cups liquid. Mash the potato (no lumps please) to yield ½ cup and set aside. Cool both the potato water and the mashed potato to 105° to 115°.

2. In a large bowl with a whisk or in the work bowl of a heavy-duty electric mixer fitted with the paddle attachment, sprinkle the yeast over the potato water. Stir to dissolve. Add the sugar, mashed potato, and 1 cup of the flour. Beat until smooth and cover with plastic wrap. Let rest at room temperature until bubbly, about 45 minutes.

3. Add the salt, eggs, oil, and 1 more cup flour to the batter and beat until smooth, about 1 minute. Add the raisins, currants, carrot or parsnip, and pineapple. Add the remaining flour, ½ cup at a time, until a soft dough is formed that just clears the sides of the bowl.

4. Turn out the dough onto a lightly floured work surface and knead until smooth, shiny, and soft, about 2 minutes, adding only 1 tablespoon flour at a time as necessary to prevent sticking. Push back any fruits that may fall out during kneading. It is important

that this dough remain soft and pliable, or it will be too dry. Place in a greased deep container, turn once to coat the top, and cover with plastic wrap. Let rise at room temperature until doubled in bulk, 1½ to 2 hours.

5. Turn out the dough onto the work surface and divide into 3 equal portions. Form each into a fat rectangular loaf. Place each portion into a greased 8-by-4-inch loaf pan. Cover loosely with plastic wrap and let rise at room temperature until doubled in bulk, or about 1 inch above the rims of the pans, 45 minutes to 1 hour. Twenty minutes before baking, preheat the oven to 375°.

6. Bake in the center of the preheated oven until the loaves are golden brown and sound hollow when tapped, 30 to 35 minutes. Remove immediately from the pans to a rack to cool completely before slicing.

Rosemary Raisin Bread

Rosemary leaves add a distinctive herbal tinge to this full-bodied bread. It is an eggy panmarino that calls for only one rise and is rich with good olive oil and big dark raisins. Use the moist, jumbo Monukka raisins, if you can find them, as they are a fall treat. This is an often-requested recipe in my teaching repertoire and is exceptionally easy for such a classic yeast bread. The usually pungent rosemary is a subtle rather than dominating accent, so even a finicky eater will swoon. Serve fresh with brunch eggs or salads, or offer it toasted to accompany a cup of tea.

YIELD: 2 ROUND LOAVES

1 tablespoon (1 package) active dry yeast
Pinch of sugar
1 cup warm water (105° to 115°)
5¼ to 5¾ cups unbleached all-purpose or
     bread flour
2 heaping teaspoons dried rosemary leaves,
     or to taste
⅔ cup nonfat dry milk powder
½ cup sugar
1 tablespoon salt
½ cup good-quality olive oil
4 eggs
2 cups dark raisins
Extra olive oil, for brushing

1. In a small bowl, sprinkle the yeast and the pinch of sugar over the warm water. Stir to dissolve. Let stand until foamy, about 10 minutes. In a food processor fitted with the metal blade, combine 1 cup of the flour and the rosemary. Process until the rosemary is pulverized into small bits.

2. In a large bowl with a whisk or in the work bowl of a heavy-duty electric mixer fitted with the paddle attachment, combine the rosemary flour, dry milk, the ½ cup sugar, salt, the ½ cup oil, and eggs. Beat until smooth, about 1 minute. Add the yeast mixture and 1½ more cups flour. Beat 1 minute longer. Let stand 20 to 30 minutes. Add the raisins and the remaining flour, ½ cup at a time, until a soft dough is formed that just clears the sides of the bowl, switching to a wooden spoon as necessary if making by hand. This dough can soak up a lot of excess flour during the mixing, so take care to stop adding the flour when the mixture clears the sides of the bowl and is no longer wet looking.

3. Turn out the dough onto a lightly floured work surface and knead until smooth and springy, about 3 minutes, adding only 1 tablespoon flour at a time as necessary to prevent sticking. When finished kneading, immediately divide the dough into 2 equal portions. Form each portion into a tight round loaf and place on a greased or parchment-lined baking sheet. Brush the tops with a bit of olive oil and cover loosely with plastic wrap. Let rise at room temperature until doubled in bulk, 2 to 2½ hours. The loaves will spread and look slightly flat while rising, but they will dome during baking. Twenty minutes before baking, preheat the oven to 350°, with a baking stone, if desired.

4. Using a serrated knife, slash the tops decoratively with an X no deeper than ¼ inch. Bake in the center of the preheated oven until the loaves are dramatically domed, evenly golden brown, and sound hollow when tapped, 35 to 40 minutes. Remove to a rack to cool completely before slicing.

When I drive by meadows and see spires of blue lupines, I know the onset of summer is here. It is the season of light, a time of outdoor activity and open-air eating. Barbecue-roasted meats, cooling salads, fresh fruits and vegetables, and ice cream are staples under a yard's shade tree or an urban balcony. Crusty bread, either from your own kitchen or picked up at a corner deli bakery, is an important accompaniment. Rustic and stuffed picnic breads travel well and are easily eaten with your fingers. ❧ June 21 is the Summer Solstice and the Native American moon calendar marks June, July, and August Shawnodese, or Spirit Keeper of the South, the time when the earth's power flowers and fruits in a last rapid spurt of growth before slowing down. ❧ Barley is harvested in Washington state and oats in the Dakotas. The winter soft wheat is ready for harvest in New York state and in the Midwest and Northwest. Freshly ground rye flour is the product of Canadian fields. The small crop of Kansas hard winter white wheat, a golden tan in contrast to the normal russet bran layer, is harvested and then freshly ground for use in whole-grain breads. ❧ Ripe plums and peaches abound, as do rosy apricots and cherries, home-grown figs, and imported mangoes, masses of berries, heady fresh green chile peppers, bushels of fresh garlic in their papery coats, and sweet corn. Trailing summer squash vines take over the garden, with an abundance of bulky-looking appendages scattered on the ground, changing in size and shape from week to week as they grow. There is so much fresh food that the markets overflow with produce and empty fields and parking lots are transformed into Saturday morning farmer's markets. ❧ Old-time state fairs are still a family affair, especially across the Midwest. In regional rural communities, there are celebrations honoring the local crops, such as northern Maine's potato-growing Aroostook

County, where the Potato Bloom Festival is held. In between the prize-winning heifer judging and the pie-eating contests, there is often a section reserved for the yeast bread competition. I love being asked to judge some of these, as the breads are wonderful creations of proud bakers. To win a baking sweepstakes is a great feather in any home baker's cap. ℂ This is the season when stuffed breads are accompanied by homemade pickles, chutneys, jams, and the remarkable summertime treat, homemade ketchup. I fondly remember peeling a lug of ripe tomatoes and simmering them all day until they formed a thick paste, filling the kitchen with an enticingly spicy aroma. Although the ketchup was destined for pint jars, half of the batch was unabashedly devoured that very night, still slightly warm, alongside wedges of a double-crust French-Canadian meat pie known as tourtière (page 71). ℂ In France, Bastille Day, which falls on July 14, celebrates the end of royalist rule two hundred years ago. The long struggle was supposedly sparked by Marie Antoinette's now famous comment, "qu'ils mangent de la brioche." In other words, let the peasants eat the highly taxed white bread. After the Revolution, legions of unemployed ancien régime palace chefs opened the first restaurants and bakeries. With a new law, butter-rich brioches and the first thin, pointed cylinders of white bread, predecessors of the baguette classique, became available to the public. ℂ August 14 is Victory Day in Paris. It is a splendid celebration that observes the liberation of Paris and the end of the world at war in 1945. The city's boulevards and bridges over the Seine are packed with crowds waiting for the display of fireworks to begin. Then the bistros à vin fill with late-night snackers who sample half-inch-thick slices of Gruyère cheese sandwiched between lengths of buttered baguette or a tartine, thick slices of fresh sour country bread spread with soft goat cheese or house-made pâté. Many boulangeries are closed for the month of August, since the native Parisians are great vacationers and head for the country en masse. But there is still plenty of good pain français for the food cognoscenti: petits pains au lait, rustic pain aux noix, pain de campagne, and the dark, oversized le roi du pain, a wood-fired round that looks as much like a field stone as a loaf of bread. ❦ After Paris, proceed through the Tyrolean Alps on the way to the Salzburg Music Festival and discover the hearty breads of Austria and Germany. They rival those of Italy and France in sheer variety and tend to be more compact and substantial than typical American breads, with an earthy, deeply appetite-satisfying quality. The word Brot describes breads made with a proportion of rye or wheat flour, and Weissbrot (white wheat bread), Sonnenblumenbrot (rye with sunflower seeds), Schwarzbrot (black rye bread), and Bauernbrot (mixed rye made with the distinctive Saurteig starter that varies from region to region) are just a few of the many peasant-style breads available. ❦ August 15 is the Feast of the Madonna in Calabria, Italy, also known as the Christian Feast of the Assumption. Pan pepato, an unusual pepper-and-chocolate-spiced bread also seen at New Year's in Emilia-Romagna, is baked in the shape of body parts for the occasion, and is at once hot, spicy, and sweet in flavor. Sardinian breads are descended from ones learned from the Phoenicians (who scored their loaves with a horned symbol to deify them), with their unique brick-oven pane carasau, or "music paper bread," a large, thin wheat flat bread not so different than the American Southwest piki. Mediterranean pita is a widely available close substitute in America, as the Sardinian bread does not bake properly in a gas or electric oven, although family recipes adapting it have been recorded. ❦ Homemade Italian country bread doughs, especially flat hearth breads, are still made in a madia, a kneading and rising chest with a lid. Simple unleavened disks of la piadina, similar to a fine wheat tortilla but made with olive oil, are baked in Romagna for local festas on hot stones or a round clay bakestone with handles known as a testo. In lieu of the authentic testo, I use a Vermont-made soapstone griddle for my Italian flat breads with great success. Eat hot, wrapped around oven-dried marinated plum tomatoes and small chunks of melting Gorgonzola cheese. (Spanish countryside breads are perfect for summer entertaining. Among the seasonal favorites are large, round finely-crumbed loaves of pan de pueblo, the lean country bread made with milk and water, and pan de payes, the coarser peasant bread. They appear topped with toma-toes and sprinkled with olive oil or grilled and rubbed with garlic, and are served as snacks or to mop up the strong flavors of chorizo sausage, serrano ham, salami, and sardines so loved in Spanish cuisine. In Portugal, the traditional thick-crusted and chewy-textured country daily bread called broa is made with cornmeal and olive oil. (The Central Navajo Nation Fair and Rodeo is held in Chinle, Arizona, with plenty of cast-iron cauldrons set up and filled with hot fat for cooking fry breads. The breads are folded around beans and cheese or drizzled with honey. This outdoor food reminds me of the Hungarian zsiros kenyér, thick slices of peasant rye bread topped with grilled slabs of smoked bacon, sliced fresh green peppers, onions, tomatoes, and cucumbers. The bacon and vegetable bread is good served with crunchy wedges of dill pickles, a variation on a rustic country meal that is enjoyed throughout Europe during the warm weather months.

Celtic Farmhouse Bread

Here is my re-creation of a hearty peasant loaf of the chilly hinterlands. If you have an
outdoor wood-fired oven, or a baking stone for your indoor oven to simulate one, please use it for this
bread. The cracked barley and millet are readily available in natural foods stores. They add superb flavor and
crunchy texture to a humble loaf. Serve in thick slices for midsummer toast or for sandwiches. Accompany
with vanilla yogurt and a fruit salad of the season's first cherries and plums.

YIELD: 3 MEDIUM ROUND OR TWO 9-BY-5-INCH LOAVES

1½ cups boiling water
½ cup barley grits
½ cup millet grits
1 tablespoon (1 package) active dry yeast
Pinch of sugar
½ cup warm water (105° to 115°)
3 tablespoons honey
3 tablespoons corn oil or other vegetable oil
1 egg
1 tablespoon salt
2 tablespoons unprocessed wheat bran or
  wheat germ
¼ cup barley flour
⅓ cup rolled oats
⅓ cup stone-ground yellow cornmeal
1¼ cups whole-wheat flour
2½ to 3 cups unbleached all-purpose or
  bread flour

1. In a small bowl, pour the boiling water over the barley and millet grits. Let stand 30 minutes to soften and cool to room temperature.

2. In a small bowl, sprinkle the yeast and sugar over the warm water. Stir to dissolve. Let stand until foamy, about 10 minutes.

3. In a large bowl with a whisk or in the work bowl of a heavy-duty electric mixer fitted with the paddle attachment, combine the soaked grits, honey, oil, egg, salt, wheat bran or germ, barley flour, rolled oats, cornmeal, and whole-wheat flour. Beat hard until smooth, about 1 minute. Beat in the yeast mixture. Add the unbleached flour, ½ cup at a time, until a soft, sticky dough is formed that just clears the sides of the bowl, switching to a wooden spoon as necessary if making by hand.

4. Turn out the dough onto a lightly floured work surface and knead until a soft and springy dough is formed, about 3 minutes, adding only 1 tablespoon flour at a time as necessary to prevent sticking. The dough will have a nubby and slightly tacky quality. Place in a greased deep container, turn once to coat the top, and cover with plastic wrap. Let rise at room temperature until doubled in bulk, 1½ to 2 hours.

5. Turn out the dough onto a clear work surface. Divide into 3 equal portions for round loaves or 2 equal portions for rectangular loaves. Place the round loaves on a greased or parchment-lined baking sheet and the rectangular loaves in greased 9-by-5-inch clay or metal loaf pans. Cover loosely with plastic wrap and let rise at room temperature until doubled in bulk, 30 to 40 minutes. Twenty minutes before baking, preheat the oven to 375°, with a baking stone, if desired.

6. Bake in the center of the preheated oven or place the pans directly on the hot stone until the loaves are golden brown and sound hollow when tapped, 35 to 40 minutes. Immediately turn out onto a rack to cool completely before slicing.

Jewish Seeded Dill Rye

My friend Rose Levy Beranbaum's favorite bread is her famous New York rye,
baked in an earthenware domed platter called a cloche. It is a technique that produces a chewy,
crisp crust similar to that found in the bakery-made Jewish ryes. Here is my favorite savory summertime herbed rye,
studded with caraway and dill, made in the manner of Rose's childhood loaf.

YIELD: 1 ROUND HEARTH LOAF

Sponge

1 tablespoon (1 package) active dry yeast
3 tablespoons light brown sugar
1 cup medium rye flour
2 cups warm water (105° to 115°)
1½ cups unbleached all-purpose or bread flour

Dough

½ cup medium rye flour
½ cup nonfat dry milk powder or goat's milk powder
1 tablespoon dried dill
1 tablespoon dill seeds
2 heaping teaspoons caraway seeds
2½ teaspoons salt
3 tablespoons canola oil
2 to 2½ cups unbleached all-purpose or bread flour
White cornmeal or farina, for sprinkling

1. To prepare the sponge: In a large bowl with a whisk or in the work bowl of a heavy-duty electric mixer fitted with the paddle attachment, sprinkle the yeast, brown sugar, and rye flour over the warm water and let stand 5 minutes. Add the unbleached flour and beat hard until well moistened and creamy. Cover with plastic wrap and let stand at room temperature until bubbly, about 4 hours or as long as overnight.

2. To prepare the dough: Add the rye flour, dry milk, dried dill, dill seeds, caraway seeds, salt, and oil to the sponge. Beat hard about 1 minute. Add ½ cup of the unbleached flour and beat until smooth. Add the remaining unbleached flour, ½ cup at a time, until the dough just pulls away from sides of bowl, switching to a wooden spoon as necessary if making by hand.

3. Scrape out the dough onto a lightly floured work surface and knead until smooth and elastic, about 3 minutes, adding only 1 tablespoon flour at a time as necessary to prevent sticking. The dough will retain a slight stickiness due to the rye flour. Place in a greased bowl, turn once to coat the top, and cover with plastic wrap. Let rise at room temperature until doubled in bulk, 1½ to 2 hours.

4. Turn out the dough onto a lightly floured work surface and shape into a round by kneading and pulling the ends together lightly on the bottom to create surface tension. Sprinkle the cloche dish with cornmeal or farina. Place the dough on the clay dish, seam side down. Move the dough around to cover the entire bottom and part of the sides of the dish with the cornmeal or farina. It is okay to have extra meal left in the bottom of the dish that is not adhering to the surface of the dough. Using a serrated knife, slash the top with 3 parallel lines no more than ¼ inch deep. This will allow steam to escape and give the dough room to expand. Cover with the bell dome and let rest 20 minutes, no more. (This loaf can also be baked on a greased or parchment-lined baking sheet sprinkled with cornmeal or farina. Let rise until doubled in bulk, about 50 minutes.) Twenty minutes before baking, preheat the oven to 450°.

5. Before placing the bread in the oven, rinse the inside of the domed cloche cover with water. Drain off excess drips. A bit of dripping water does not matter. Replace the cover and place the dish in the center of the preheated oven. After 10 minutes, reduce the oven thermostat to 400° and set a timer for 20 minutes. After 20 minutes, remove the cover and allow the loaf to brown thoroughly, 20 to 30 minutes longer. The loaf should sound hollow when tapped and the crust should be crackly crisp. Remove the loaf to a rack to cool completely before serving.

NOTE: To clean a cloche, see note page 42.

Semolina Sesame Seed Twist

When I was a child, the supermarkets were closed on Sundays, so after church,
my mother and I would stop by the neighborhood Jewish delicatessen. One of my favorite loaves was
a thick, oblong Italian bread coated with sesame seeds. This bread shows itself in many traditional forms, such
as a crown or serpentine. Use the creamy-colored semolina flour milled for pasta making for this loaf, not
the coarse variety, or substitute canary-yellow durum flour, which contains the bran and germ.
The bread is best eaten the day it is made, and should be frozen if kept beyond that point.

YIELD: 2 LARGE TWISTS

Sponge
1 tablespoon (1 package) active dry yeast
3 cups tepid water (100°)
2 cups fine semolina flour
2 cups unbleached all-purpose or bread flour

Dough
1 tablespoon salt
3 tablespoons good-quality olive oil
1 cup semolina flour
2½ to 3 cups unbleached all-purpose or
   bread flour

Semolina flour, for sprinkling
1 egg beaten with 1 teaspoon water, for glaze
¼ cup hulled or unhulled sesame seeds
3 tablespoons good-quality olive oil,
   for drizzling

1. To prepare the sponge: In a large bowl or plastic bucket, whisk together the yeast, tepid water, and flours. Beat hard until smooth, about 30 seconds. Cover loosely with plastic wrap and let the sponge rise at room temperature until bubbly and at least doubled in bulk, about 3 hours.

2. To prepare the dough: In a large bowl with a whisk or in the work bowl of a heavy-duty electric mixer fitted with the paddle attachment, combine the salt, olive oil, semolina flour, ½ cup of the unbleached flour, and the sponge. Beat until smooth, 1 minute. Add the remaining flour, ½ cup at a time, until a soft dough is formed that just clears the sides of the bowl, switching to a wooden spoon as necessary if making by hand.

3. Turn out the dough onto a lightly floured work surface and knead vigorously for about 3 minutes to form a springy smooth dough, adding only 1 tablespoon flour at a time as necessary to prevent sticking. It is important that this dough be quite soft and springy, yet not sticky, and able to hold its own shape. Place in a deep container brushed lightly with olive oil, turn once to coat, and cover with plastic wrap. Let rise at room temperature until tripled in bulk, 2 to 3 hours. Gently deflate the dough and let rise again until doubled, about 1 hour.

4. Turn out the dough onto the work surface and divide into 2 equal portions. With your palms, roll 1 portion into a log about a yard long. Twist the entire log and leave on the work surface as the base. Twist a second portion and attach the 2 twisted logs at one end. Loop one log around the other 4 or 5 times to form a fat, twisted loaf. Pinch the end to seal. Transfer to a greased or parchment-lined baking sheet sprinkled with semolina flour, tucking the ends under to make a high, tightly twisted loaf. Repeat with the remaining portions to form the second loaf. Cover loosely with plastic wrap and let rise at room temperature until almost doubled in bulk, about 1 hour. Twenty minutes before baking, preheat the oven to 425°, with a baking stone, if desired.

5. Gently brush the surfaces with the egg glaze and sprinkle heavily with the sesame seeds. Using a serrated knife, slash the top of each loaf about ½ inch deep in a few places along its length. Drizzle each gash with olive oil. Bake in the center of the preheated oven for 15 minutes. Then reduce the oven thermostat to 375° and bake until golden brown and crusty, 25 to 30 minutes longer. Remove to a rack to cool completely before slicing.

Oatmeal Rye with Millet and Dried Apricots

Rye and oats were cultivated from the wild grasses that originally grew in the cold climates and high altitudes of old Europe, especially Russia, Germany, England, and the alpine areas. Here, they are paired with millet and brown rice to create a whole-grain hearth loaf with a nutty sweetness. Serve as hearty summer breakfast toast or alongside a mixed green salad with a balsamic vinegar dressing and leek vegetable soup.

YIELD: 3 LARGE ROUND OR 9-BY-5-INCH LOAVES

Sponge

1 tablespoon (1 package) active dry yeast
2 tablespoons light or dark brown sugar
⅔ cup cooled cooked brown rice
2¼ cups warm water (105° to 115°)
¾ cup medium rye flour
1 cup unbleached all-purpose or bread flour

Dough

1¼ cups regular rolled oats
¼ cup oat bran
¼ cup whole raw millet
¼ cup light or dark brown sugar
3 tablespoons vegetable oil
1 tablespoon salt
1 cup finely chopped dried apricots
3¼ to 3½ cups unbleached all-purpose or
   bread flour

1. To prepare the sponge: In a large bowl with a whisk or in the work bowl of a heavy-duty electric mixer fitted with the paddle attachment, sprinkle the yeast, brown sugar, and brown rice over the warm water and let stand for 5 minutes. Add the rye and unbleached flour and beat hard until well moistened and creamy. Cover with plastic wrap and let stand at room temperature until bubbly, about 1 hour.

2. To prepare the dough: Add the rolled oats, bran, millet, brown sugar, oil, and salt to the sponge. Beat hard about 1 minute. Stir in the dried apricots. Add ½ cup of the flour and beat for 1 minute longer, until stretchy and well moistened. Add the remaining flour, ½ cup at a time, until the dough just pulls away from the sides of the bowl, switching to a wooden spoon as necessary if making by hand.

3. Scrape out the dough onto a lightly floured work surface and knead until the dough is smooth and elastic, about 3 minutes, adding only 1 tablespoon flour at a time as necessary to prevent sticking. Place the dough in a greased deep container, turn once to coat the top, and cover with plastic wrap. Let rise at room temperature until doubled in bulk, 1½ to 2 hours.

4. Turn out the dough onto a clean work surface and divide into 3 equal portions. Shape each portion into a round or rectangular loaf and place on two greased or parchment-lined baking sheets, or in 3 well-greased 9-by-5-inch loaf pans. Cover loosely with plastic wrap and let rise at room temperature until doubled in bulk, about 45 minutes. Twenty minutes before baking, preheat the oven to 375°.

5. Using a serrated knife, slash the tops of the loaves decoratively no more than ¼ inch deep. If unable to fit both baking sheets in the oven at one time, refrigerate one until baking, so it will not rise too much. Bake in the preheated oven until the loaves are browned and sound hollow when tapped, 25 to 35 minutes. Let cool in the pans for 5 minutes, then turn out onto racks to cool completely.

Greek Feta Buns

Tiropeta spitikia ("housemaking buns") are savory little rolls filled with creamy feta cheese.
The recipe was created by food writer Lou Pappas after enjoying them as a morning snack from an Athens
bakery during a visit to Greece in 1965. Use an imported Greek or French sheep's milk feta for a tangy Mediterranean
flavor, although I have had excellent success with an American goat's milk feta made by the Corralitos Cheese
Company in Watsonville, California. Lou likes to tuck a few leaves of fresh oregano, or sage, or a sprig of rosemary in with
the cheese before baking. Serve the feta buns with a big salad of spinach leaves tossed with black olives
and red tomatoes and a plate of chilled steamed asparagus.

YIELD: 16 BUNS

2 teaspoons active dry yeast
Pinch of sugar
¼ cup warm water (105° to 115°)
¾ cup warm milk (105° to 115°)
⅓ cup good-quality olive oil
1 tablespoon sugar
¼ teaspoon salt
3 eggs
3¼ to 3¾ cups unbleached all-purpose flour
8 ounces feta cheese
2 tablespoons good-quality olive oil,
    for brushing
2 tablespoons black sesame seeds or *nigella*
    for sprinkling
2 tablespoons white sesame seeds,
    for sprinkling

1. In a small bowl, sprinkle the yeast and the pinch of sugar over the warm water. Stir to dissolve. Let stand until foamy, about 10 minutes.

2. In a large bowl with a whisk or in the work bowl of a heavy-duty electric mixer fitted with the paddle attachment, combine the warm milk, the ⅓ cup oil, sugar, salt, eggs, and 1 cup of the flour. Beat until smooth and add the yeast mixture. Beat hard until creamy, about 2 minutes. Add the remaining flour, ½ cup at a time, and beat until a soft dough is formed that just clears the sides of the bowl, switching to a wooden spoon as necessary if making by hand.

3. Turn out the dough onto a lightly floured work surface and knead until smooth, springy, and no longer sticky, about 1 minute, adding only 1 tablespoon flour at a time as necessary to prevent sticking. Place in a greased deep container, turn once to coat the top, and cover with plastic wrap. Let rise at room temperature until doubled in bulk, about 1½ hours.

4. Turn out the dough onto a lightly floured work surface and divide into 16 equal portions. Cut the cheese into 16 equal chunks, each about 2 tablespoons. Form each portion of the dough into a 2½-inch ball, then, using your palm, flatten each ball into a 6-inch round. Crumble a portion of cheese into the center of each round and bring up the two opposite sides over the cheese. Pinch to close the seams and roll to taper the ends. Place, seam-side down, about 2 inches apart on a greased or parchment-lined baking sheet. Brush the tops with the 2 tablespoons olive oil and sprinkle heavily with the black sesame or *nigella* seeds and the white sesame seeds. Cover loosely with plastic wrap and let rise in a warm place until doubled in bulk, about 30 minutes. Twenty minutes before baking, preheat the oven to 375°.

5. Prick each bun several times with a wooden skewer or large toothpick to allow steam to be released during baking. Bake on the middle rack of the preheated oven until golden brown and firm to the touch, 15 to 20 minutes. Remove to a rack to cool completely before serving.

Panetti with Prosciutto and Olives

*Panetti are savory little Italian buns perfect for serving as dinner rolls or with cheese and your
best pasta salad. I think these rolls were originally made with ciccioli, or pork cracklings, the by-product of
a rural Italian kitchen. In today's more urbanized Italy, prosciutto is the more likely ingredient. These rolls may be made,
risen, formed in disposable cake pans, and then immediately frozen up to 1 month. To bake, defrost at room
temperature and let rise, about 4 hours total, then bake as directed.*

YIELD: 24 SMALL ROLLS

1½ tablespoons (1½ packages) active
   dry yeast
Pinch of sugar
2¾ cups warm water (105° to 115°)
1 small white onion, minced
4 tablespoons pure olive oil
1 cup semolina flour
4½ to 5 cups unbleached all-purpose or
   bread flour
1 teaspoon salt
3 ounces thinly sliced prosciutto, minced
½ cup chopped, pitted black olives
⅓ cup chopped, drained oil-packed sun-dried
   tomatoes
1 egg white beaten with 1 teaspoon water,
   for glaze
⅓ cup freshly grated Parmesan cheese

1. *In a small bowl,* sprinkle the yeast and sugar over ½ cup of the warm water. Stir to dissolve. Let stand until foamy, about 10 minutes. In a small skillet, sauté the onion in 2 tablespoons of the olive oil a few minutes, or until just wilted. Set aside to cool.

2. *In a large bowl* with a whisk or in the work bowl of a heavy-duty electric mixer fitted with the paddle attachment, combine the remaining 1½ cups warm water, the remaining 2 tablespoons olive oil, the semolina flour, 1 cup of the unbleached flour, salt, and yeast mixture. Beat 1 minute. Add the sautéed onions, prosciutto, olives, tomatoes, and 1½ cups more unbleached flour. Then add the remaining unbleached flour, ½ cup at a time, until a soft dough forms that just clears the sides of the bowl, switching to a wooden spoon as necessary if making by hand.

3. *Turn out the dough* onto a lightly floured work surface and knead until just past being sticky, about 2 minutes, adding only 1 tablespoon flour at a time as necessary to prevent sticking. The dough will be smooth and springy. Place in a greased deep container, turn once to coat the top, and cover with plastic wrap. Let rise at room temperature until doubled in bulk, about 1½ hours.

4. *Turn out the dough* onto the work surface and divide into 4 equal portions. Divide each portion into 6 pieces and form each portion into a small ball, pulling the surface tight and pinching the seams on the bottom. Place the rolls barely touching in 2 greased 10-inch pie plates, springform pans, or earthenware baking dishes to form a solid flat round of rolls. There will be 12 rolls in each pan. Cover loosely with plastic wrap and let rise at room temperature until doubled in bulk, about 40 minutes. Twenty minutes before baking, preheat the oven to 400°, with a baking stone, if desired.

5. *Brush the tops* of the rolls with the egg white glaze. Bake in the center of the preheated oven for 20 minutes. Carefully remove the pans from the oven and sprinkle the tops with the Parmesan cheese. Return to the oven and continue to bake until browned, an additional 15 minutes. Slide out of the pan onto a rack to cool. Eat warm or at room temperature, pulling the rolls apart to serve.

Spicy Jamaican Half-Moons

On the Caribbean island of Jamaica, stuffed meat pies are sold by street vendors. Serve them throughout the summer and for Kwanzaa, an African-American winter harvest celebration held on December 24 and 25. Pass a habanero or chipolte hot-pepper sauce or a jalapeño catsup for guests to splash liberally on the pies.

YIELD: TEN 6-INCH TURNOVERS

Turnover Dough

2¾ to 3¼ cups unbleached all-purpose flour
½ cup whole-wheat flour
2 teaspoons active dry yeast
1 teaspoon salt
1½ cups hot water (120°)
2 tablespoons vegetable oil

Meat Filling

1 pound ground turkey
¼ pound ground beef or veal
1 teaspoon ground red chile or good-quality chili powder
¾ teaspoon medium-hot paprika
½ cup minced celery
½ cup minced red bell pepper
½ cup minced yellow onion
One 4-ounce can roasted whole mild green chiles, undrained, coarsely chopped
1 clove garlic, crushed
Salt to taste
½ cup fine dried bread crumbs
1 tablespoon unbleached all-purpose-flour
1 egg beaten with 1 tablespoon milk, for glaze

1. *To prepare the turnover dough:* In a mixing bowl, combine 1 cup of the unbleached flour, the whole-wheat flour, yeast, and salt. Add the hot water and oil. Beat hard with a whisk until smooth, about 1 minute. Add the remaining unbleached flour, ½ cup at a time, until a soft dough is formed, switching to a wooden spoon when the whisk becomes clogged.

2. *Turn out the dough* onto a lightly floured work surface and knead until just smooth and springy. The dough will remain quite soft. Place in a small greased container, turn once to coat the top, cover with plastic wrap, and let rise at room temperature until doubled in bulk, about 45 minutes.

3. *Meanwhile,* make the meat filling. In a large sauté pan over medium heat, brown the turkey and beef or veal. When the fat is released, add the ground chile or chili powder, paprika, minced vegetables, green chiles, and garlic. Cook, stirring occasionally, until the vegetables are tender, 5 to 8 minutes. Add the salt, bread crumbs, and flour, stirring to mix thoroughly and bind the mixture. Remove from the heat and set aside to cool to room temperature. (Cover and refrigerate the mixture if it cools before it is needed.)

4. *Turn out the dough* onto the work surface and divide into 10 equal portions. Roll out each portion into a 6-inch round. Place about ¼ cup of the meat filling on the center of each round. Lift up two parallel sides of each round and bring them together over the center of the filling. Moisten the inside of one edge with water and pinch or crimp the edges to seal with a center seam. Place at least 2 inches apart on a parchment-lined baking sheet. Let rest 15 minutes at room temperature while preheating the oven to 425°.

5. *Brush the turnovers* with the egg glaze and place in the center of the preheated oven. Immediately reduce the oven thermostat to 375°. Bake until golden brown, 20 to 25 minutes. Serve warm or at room temperature. Refrigerate any leftovers and reheat for 2 minutes in a microwave oven or for about 7 minutes in a 350° oven. The turnovers also freeze nicely up to 2 months.

Rye and Indian Bread with Jalapeños

Also known as colonial bread, the combination of rye, wheat, and cornmeal is a well-loved blend of grains for an American loaf. There are lots of recipes for rye and Indian bread, with varying amounts of each flour, that have survived intact over the centuries. Topped with goat cheese and sliced tomatoes, the hearty bread makes memorable summertime grilled cheese sandwiches. The dough can also be shaped into outstanding hamburger or sandwich buns.

YIELD: TWO 8-BY-4-INCH LOAVES OR 14 BUNS

1½ cups boiling water

⅓ cup light brown sugar

2 teaspoons salt

⅔ cup yellow cornmeal, preferably stone-ground

1 cup milk

⅓ cup corn oil

One 3-ounce can fire-roasted diced jalapeño chiles, drained

2 tablespoons (2 packages) active dry yeast

1½ cups medium rye flour

4¼ to 4½ cups unbleached all-purpose or bread flour

1. *In a small mixing bowl*, place the boiling water, sugar, salt, and cornmeal. Stir with a whisk and add the milk, corn oil, and jalapeños. Cool to 120° to 130°.

2. *In a large mixing bowl* with a whisk or in the work bowl of a heavy-duty electric mixer fitted with the paddle attachment, combine the yeast, rye flour, and 1 cup of the unbleached flour. Add the cornmeal mixture and beat hard 1 minute to combine. Continue to add the unbleached flour, ½ cup at a time, until a shaggy dough is formed that just clears the sides of the bowl, switching to a wooden spoon as necessary if making by hand.

3. *Turn out the dough* onto a lightly floured work surface and knead until springy and just past sticky, about 2 minutes, adding only 1 tablespoon flour at a time as necessary to prevent sticking. There will be a nubby texture due to the cornmeal, but the dough will feel soft yet hold its shape. Place in a greased deep container, turn once to coat the top, and cover with plastic wrap. Let rise at room temperature until doubled in bulk, 1½ to 2 hours.

4. *Gently deflate* the dough and turn it out onto the work surface. Divide the dough into 2 equal portions. Shape into rectangular loaves and place in 2 greased 8-by-4-inch clay or metal loaf pans. For burger or sandwich buns, divide the dough in half and then divide each half into 7 equal pieces. Form each piece into a tight round ball. Place seam side down and at least 2 inches apart on 2 greased or parchment-lined baking sheets. Flatten each ball with your palm. Cover lightly with plastic wrap and let rise at room temperature until fully doubled in bulk, 30 to 45 minutes. Twenty minutes before baking, preheat the oven to 375°.

5. *Using a serrated knife*, score the top of each loaf with 2 or 3 slashes no more than ¼ inch deep. Bake in the center of the preheated oven until the loaves are browned, sound hollow when tapped, and pull away from the pans, 40 to 45 minutes. Bake the buns 20 to 25 minutes. Turn out of the pans or remove from the baking sheet to cool completely on racks before slicing or serving.

Savory Three-Cheese Spirals

*The spiraled sweet roll is a common enough sight, but a savory dough flecked with fresh herbs
and encasing a highly flavorful triple-cheese filling is every bit as enticing. The dough is easy to handle and the
aroma of the baking rolls is irresistible. The rolls are formed into a double snail by cutting each fat section almost in half, and
then twisting the halves to form a double swirl pattern rather like a loose figure eight. Serve with pasta salad, roasted
vegetables with a balsamic vinaigrette, or chilled gazpacho for a truly unique cheese sandwich.*

YIELD: 12 LARGE ROLLS

1 tablespoon (1 package) active dry yeast

6 to 6¼ cups unbleached all-purpose or
bread flour

1 tablespoon salt

½ cup hot milk (120°)

1 cup hot water (120°)

⅓ cup good-quality olive oil

¼ cup chopped fresh basil or marjoram

3 eggs

Three-Cheese Filling

3 cups (12 ounces) shredded Monterey
Jack cheese

1¼ cups (5 ounces) finely shredded
Parmesan cheese

12 ounces fresh goat cheese, such as
domestic chabi or imported Montrachet,
at room temperature

3 to 4 tablespoons milk or olive oil, if needed

1. *In a large bowl* with a whisk or in the
work bowl of a heavy-duty electric mixer
fitted with the paddle attachment, combine
the yeast, 3 cups of flour and the salt. Add the
hot milk, hot water, and oil. Beat hard until
creamy, about 1 minute. Add the basil or
marjoram and eggs. Beat again until smooth,
about 1 minute. Add the remaining flour,
½ cup at a time, until a shaggy dough is
formed that just clears the sides of the bowl,
switching to a wooden spoon as necessary if
making by hand.

2. *Turn out the dough* onto a lightly floured
work surface and knead until smooth and
springy, about 2 minutes, adding only 1 tablespoon flour at a time as necessary to prevent
sticking. Place in a greased container, turn
once to coat the top, and cover with plastic
wrap. Let rise at room temperature until
doubled in bulk, 1 to 1½ hours.

3. *To make the three-cheese filling,* in a
medium bowl, combine the Jack and Parmesan
cheeses. In a separate bowl, mash the goat
cheese to a spreading consistency, adding
1 tablespoon of the milk or oil, if necessary
to achieve a smooth consistency.

4. *Turn out the dough* onto a lightly floured
work surface. Divide the dough into 2 equal
portions for easiest handling. Roll out each

portion into a large 12-by-18-inch rectangle
½ inch thick. Spread each rectangle evenly
with half of the goat cheese. Then sprinkle
each with half of the shredded cheeses.
Starting from a long side, roll up jelly-roll
fashion. Pinch all seams together to seal.
Repeat with the second roll. Using a serrated
knife, cut each roll into six 3-inch-thick slices.
Then, using a gentle sawing motion, cut into
the center of each slice only two-thirds of the
way through to form a roll that falls open into
a double snail with two spiral-cut fans facing
up. Place the double snails at least 2 inches
apart on 1 or 2 parchment-lined baking sheets
(parchment is important to prevent sticking).
Cover loosely with plastic wrap. Let rise
at room temperature until doubled in bulk,
45 minutes to 1 hour. Twenty minutes before
baking, preheat the oven to 350°.

5. *Bake in the center* of the preheated oven
until golden brown and puffy, 20 to 25 minutes. Using a spatula, remove to a rack to cool
completely before serving. The cheese spirals
may be frozen in freezer bags up to 2 months,
if desired.

Greek Island Bread

Related to the earthy shepherd's breads eaten throughout the Greek islands, this is a special
village loaf known as psomi. *Serve this bread with whatever looks good at the market: tomatoes and tender salad greens;*
cucumbers, feta, and Kalamata olives; eggplant and zucchini marinated in red wine vinegar. It is also good with
fragrant Summer Cheese (page 160) or with fig jam for breakfast.

YIELD: 2 LARGE ROUND LOAVES

Starter
1 tablespoon (1 package) active dry yeast
½ cup whole-wheat flour
½ cup tepid water (90° to 100°)

Sponge
2 cups tepid goat's milk (90° to 100°)
¼ cup unprocessed wheat bran
½ cup barley grits or couscous
1 cup unbleached all-purpose or bread flour
1¼ cups whole-wheat flour

Dough
¼ cup orange blossom honey or other
    mild honey
½ cup oat bran
2½ to 2¾ cups unbleached all-purpose or
    bread flour
4 teaspoons salt

Topping
1 egg
2 teaspoons water
½ cup sesame seeds

1. *Day One:* To prepare the starter, in a deep bowl or a 4-quart plastic bucket with a lid, place the yeast and whole-wheat flour. Add the tepid water and whisk hard until a smooth batter is formed. Cover loosely with a double layer of cheesecloth and let stand at room temperature for 12 to 24 hours. The starter will bubble and begin to ferment.

2. *Day Two:* To prepare the sponge, add the tepid goat's milk to the starter. Whisk to combine. Alternately add the wheat bran, barley grits or couscous, and unbleached and whole-wheat flours, ½ cup at a time, until a smooth batter is formed, changing to a wooden spoon as necessary. The sponge will be very wet. Scrape down the sides of the bowl, cover loosely, and let rise again at room temperature for about 12 hours, but no longer than 24.

3. *Day Three:* To prepare the dough, stir down the sponge with a wooden spoon or in the work bowl of a heavy-duty electric mixer fitted with the paddle attachment. Add the honey, oat bran, 1 cup of the unbleached flour, and the salt. Gradually beat in most of the remaining unbleached flour, ½ cup at a time, until a shaggy dough forms that clears the sides of the bowl.

4. *Turn out the dough* onto a lightly floured work surface and knead until smooth, slightly tacky, and springy, about 2 minutes, adding only 1 tablespoon flour at a time as necessary to prevent sticking. The dough will form little blisters under the surface when ready to rise. Place in a greased deep container, turn once to coat the top, and cover with plastic wrap. Let rise at room temperature until fully doubled in bulk, 2 to 2½ hours.

5. *Turn out the dough* onto a lightly floured work surface and divide into 2 equal portions. Shape each portion into a tight round. Place the loaves on a greased or parchment-lined baking sheet. (Or shape to fit round cloth-lined baskets lightly dusted with flour to rise before turning out onto a prepared baking sheet or onto a hot baking stone.) Cover loosely with floured plastic wrap and let rise at room temperature until doubled in bulk, about 1 hour. Twenty minutes before baking, preheat the oven to 425°, with a baking stone placed on the lowest rack, if desired.

6. *To prepare the topping,* in a small bowl, combine the egg and water and whisk until frothy. Brush all loaf surfaces. Sprinkle heavily with the sesame seeds. Using a serrated knife, slash the loaf decoratively. Reduce the oven thermostat to 350° and bake in the preheated oven for 15 minutes; reduce it to 325° and bake until the loaves are browned, crisp, and sound hollow when tapped, an additional 40 to 50 minutes. Remove to a rack to cool completely before slicing.

Garlic and Mozzarella Stromboli

I don't need a special occasion to pack a homemade Stromboli roll, sliced cucumbers and crisp red peppers,
fresh fruit, and a chilled Pellegrino mineral water in my old basket and head up to the local winery to enjoy the day. It is
important to allow the cheese roll to rest for at least an hour after baking, for the easiest and neatest slicing.

YIELD: 1 ROLLED BREAD; 4 TO 6 SERVINGS

2 teaspoons active dry yeast
Pinch of sugar, or 1 teaspoon honey or
   barley malt
½ cup whole-wheat pastry flour
1 cup warm water (105° to 115°)
1 egg
2 tablespoons good-quality olive oil
½ teaspoon salt
2 to 2½ cups unbleached all-purpose flour

Garlic-Cheese Filling
1 cup (4 ounces) shredded whole-milk
   mozzarella cheese
½ cup (2 ounces) shredded smoked
   mozzarella cheese
½ cup freshly grated Parmesan cheese
3 tablespoons minced Italian (flat-leaf) parsley
1 large clove garlic, minced
1 egg

Good-quality olive oil, for brushing

1. In a small bowl, sprinkle the yeast, sugar or other sweetener, and 1 tablespoon of the whole-wheat flour over the warm water. Stir to dissolve. Let stand until foamy, about 15 minutes.

2. In a large bowl with a whisk or in the work bowl of a heavy-duty electric mixer fitted with the paddle attachment, place the egg, oil, salt, the remaining whole-wheat flour, 1 cup of the unbleached flour, and the yeast mixture. Whisk hard until smooth, about 1 minute. Add the remaining unbleached flour, ¼ cup at a time, until a soft, sticky dough is formed that just clears the sides of the bowl, switching to a wooden spoon as necessary if making by hand.

3. Turn out the dough onto a lightly floured surface and knead vigorously, about 1 minute, to form a springy ball, adding only 1 teaspoon flour at a time as necessary to prevent sticking. The dough should be quite soft, smooth, and very springy. Shape into a flattened ball. Place in a greased container, turn once to coat the top with an extra tablespoon of olive oil, and cover with plastic wrap. Let rise at room temperature until tripled in bulk, about 1 hour.

4. Meanwhile, make the filling: In a bowl, place all the filling ingredients and mix until evenly combined and coated with the egg. Set aside in the refrigerator until needed.

5. Turn out the dough onto a very lightly floured work surface and roll out into a 12-by-16-inch rectangle. Dust with a bit of flour, if necessary, to prevent sticking. Position the dough so that the shorter ends are to either side. Spread the filling in an even layer over the dough, leaving a full 1-inch border around the edges. (Any holes poked will leak filling.) Starting from a long side, roll up jelly-roll fashion. Pinch together the seams; tuck under the ends, pinching them into tapered points. Using 2 spatulas, carefully transfer to a parchment-lined baking sheet, seam side down. Position the roll on the diagonal if necessary to fit. Cover lightly with plastic wrap and let rest 30 minutes. If you wish a thinner, crispier outer crust and a less breadlike interior, bake immediately. Meanwhile, preheat the oven to 400°, with a baking stone, if desired.

6. Brush the top of the roll with olive oil and prick all over with a fork to allow steam to escape. Bake in the center of the oven for 15 minutes, then reduce the oven thermostat to 375°. Bake until golden brown and crusty, an additional 20 to 25 minutes. Let rest on the baking sheet 10 minutes, then transfer to a rack to cool completely before slicing. The Stromboli is excellent at room temperature, cold or warm. To serve it warm, reheat the slices on a baking sheet at 350° for about 10 minutes. If not eaten the same day it is made, store wrapped in plastic in the refrigerator.

Herb-Yogurt Rye

Fresh summer herbs lavishly fleck this flavorful rye bread.
The yogurt tenderizes the whole grains, giving the loaf a moist, even texture. It is best eaten
on the day that it is baked, perhaps with some Lappi or Jarlsberg cheese.

YIELD: 2 ROUND OR 9-BY-5-INCH LOAVES

1½ tablespoons (1½ packages) active
    dry yeast
Pinch of sugar
½ cup warm water (105° to 115°)
2¼ cups plain yogurt, at room temperature
¼ cup olive oil
1 tablespoon salt
1 egg
2 teaspoons caraway seeds
1 tablespoon minced fresh basil
1 tablespoon minced fresh thyme
¼ teaspoon freshly ground black or
    white pepper
½ cup whole-wheat flour
1 cup medium rye flour
4 to 4½ cups unbleached all-purpose or
    bread flour

1. In a small bowl, sprinkle the yeast and sugar over the warm water. Stir to dissolve. Let stand until foamy, about 10 minutes.

2. In a large bowl with a whisk or in the work bowl of a heavy-duty electric mixer fitted with the paddle attachment, combine the yogurt, olive oil, salt, egg, caraway, basil, thyme, pepper, and the whole-wheat and rye flours. Add the yeast mixture. Beat hard until smooth, about 1 minute. Add the unbleached flour, ½ cup at a time, switching to a wooden spoon if making by hand, until a shaggy dough is formed that clears the sides of the bowl.

3. Turn out the dough onto a lightly floured surface and knead until the dough is smooth and satiny, about 2 minutes, adding only 1 tablespoon flour at a time as necessary to prevent sticking. Place in a greased deep container, turn once to coat the top, and cover with plastic wrap. Let rise at room temperature until doubled in bulk, 1 to 1½ hours.

4. Gently deflate the dough, turn it out onto the work surface, and divide it into 2 equal portions. Form into round free-form or rectangular loaves. Place on a greased or parchment-lined baking sheet or in 2 greased 9-by-5-inch clay or metal loaf pans. Cover lightly with plastic wrap and let rise in a warm place until fully doubled in bulk, 30 to 45 minutes. Twenty minutes before baking, preheat the oven to 375°.

5. Using a serrated knife, score the tops with 2 or 3 slashes no more than ¼ inch deep. Bake in the center of the preheated oven until the loaves are browned, sound hollow when tapped, and if rectangular, pull away from the sides of the pans, 40 to 45 minutes. Remove from the pans to racks to cool completely before slicing.

Tourtières

French-Canadian tourtières are flavored with a blend of savory herbs and sweet spices. It is customary to serve these pies for Christmas Eve supper and other festive occasions, but they are also delicious as summer picnic food with a side of homemade tomato ketchup (page 161) or a prune chutney, cold cider or Champagne, and mixed greens dressed with vinaigrette.

YIELD: TWO 8-INCH PIES; EACH PIE SERVES 4 OR 5

Dough
1 tablespoon (1 package) active dry yeast
Pinch of sugar
½ cup warm water (105° to 115°)
1 cup whole-wheat flour
1 teaspoon salt
½ cup sour cream, warmed
3 eggs
About 3 cups unbleached all-purpose flour
6 tablespoons unsalted butter, at room
    temperature, cut into small pieces

Meat Filling
3 large russet potatoes, peeled and
    cut into chunks
2 tablespoons unsalted butter
1 pound ground pork
1½ pounds ground turkey
1 large yellow onion, chopped
2 to 3 cloves garlic, pressed
2 shallots, minced
2 teaspoons dried savory, crumbled
2 teaspoons dried thyme, crumbled
½ teaspoon ground cinnamon
½ teaspoon ground clove
2 tablespoons Dijon mustard
⅓ cup chopped celery leaves
⅓ cup chicken broth (canned or homemade)
Salt and freshly ground pepper to taste

1. To prepare the dough: In a large mixing bowl with a whisk or in the work bowl of a heavy-duty electric mixer fitted with the paddle attachment, sprinkle the yeast and sugar over the warm water. Stir to dissolve. Let stand until foamy, about 10 minutes. Add the whole-wheat flour and salt. Beat until creamy, about 30 seconds.

2. Beat in the sour cream and the eggs, one at a time, until incorporated. Add the flour, ½ cup at a time, until a soft dough is formed that just clears the sides of the bowl, switching to a wooden spoon as necessary if making by hand. Beat in the butter, 1 tablespoon at a time, beating well after each addition. The dough will be soft and sticky.

3. Scrape out the dough onto a lightly floured work surface, and knead about 6 times to form a smooth ball. Use only a few teaspoons more flour if the dough is very sticky; it is important that the dough be moist and springy for easy handling. Place in a greased deep container, turn once to coat the top, and cover with plastic wrap. Let rise at room temperature until doubled in bulk, about 1 hour.

4. Meanwhile, prepare the meat filling: Place the potato chunks in a saucepan with water, to cover. Bring to a boil, reduce the heat to a simmer and cook uncovered until tender, about 20 minutes. Drain and mash the potatoes. Add the 2 tablespoons of butter. Set aside.

In a large skillet or sauté pan over medium heat, combine the pork, turkey, onion, garlic, and shallot. Sauté until soft and beginning to brown. Stir in the herbs, spices, mustard, and celery leaves. Add the broth and simmer until the liquid evaporates, about 20 minutes. Remove from the heat and set aside to cool to warm. Add the mashed potatoes and salt and pepper and stir to combine evenly.

5. Preheat the oven to 425°. Turn out the dough onto a lightly floured work surface. Do not punch down or knead, as the dough will be too stiff to roll out properly. Divide the dough into 2 equal portions. Then divide each portion into 1 large and 1 small portion, about two-thirds and one-third respectively of each dough portion. Roll out each of the larger portions into a thin 12-inch round. Transfer each round to a greased 8-inch springform pan, deep fluted quiche pan, or earthenware or metal *tourtière* pan. Press the dough up and over the sides of the pan, letting the excess hang over the edge. Spoon half of the meat filling into each pastry shell and fold in the overhanging dough. Roll out the remaining 2 dough portions into 9-inch rounds. Cover each pie with the dough, turn under the edges, and gently crimp to seal. Prick the tops in several places in a decorative manner to form vents for releasing the steam during baking.

6. *Immediately place the pans* in the center of the preheated oven and bake 15 minutes. Reduce the oven thermostat to 350° and bake until browned, an additional 35 to 45 minutes. Cool in the pan on a rack for 10 minutes before removing the pan sides. Let stand for 30 minutes before cutting into wedges. Serve hot or warm. Or let cool completely and store in the refrigerator. To reheat, place the cold pie in a preheated 350° oven until warmed through, about 20 minutes.

Orange-Raisin Bagel Bread

The silky dough used to make bagels is outstanding baked into this loaf studded with raisins,
one of the first breads I learned to make from master baker and cooking teacher Connie Pfieffer. The dough is easy to
work with because of the extra leavening power of the eggs. If you love dried prunes, as I do, substitute an equal amount
of chopped prunes for the raisins to create another winning spice–dried fruit combination.
Serve the bread toasted, of course, with plenty of sweet butter.

YIELD: THREE 9-BY-5-INCH LOAVES

1 large russet potato (about 12 ounces), peeled and cut into large chunks
2½ cups water
1½ tablespoons (1½ packages) active dry yeast
1½ tablespoons honey or sugar
1½ tablespoons salt
2 teaspoons ground cardamom
Grated zest of 2 oranges
7½ to 8 cups unbleached all-purpose or bread flour
¼ cup vegetable oil
4 eggs
2 cups golden or dark raisins
1 egg beaten with 1 teaspoon water, for glaze

1. In a medium saucepan, combine the potato chunks with the water. Bring to a boil, reduce the heat to a simmer, and cook, uncovered, until the potato is tender, about 20 minutes. Drain the potato, reserving 2 cups of the potato water. Let the water cool to 120°. Reserve the potato for another use.

2. In a large bowl with a whisk or in the work bowl of a heavy-duty electric mixer fitted with the paddle attachment, combine the yeast, honey or sugar, salt, cardamom, orange zest, and 2 cups of the flour. Add the reserved potato water and oil. Beat until smooth, about 2 minutes. Add 1 cup of the flour and the eggs. Beat again for 2 minutes. Mix in the raisins. Add the remaining flour, ½ cup at a time, until a soft dough is formed that just clears the sides of the bowl, switching to a wooden spoon as necessary if making by hand.

3. Turn out the dough onto a lightly floured work surface and knead until smooth, firm, and springy, about 2 minutes, adding only 1 tablespoon flour at a time as necessary to prevent sticking. Place in a greased deep container, turn once to coat the top, and cover with plastic wrap. Let rise at room temperature until doubled in bulk, 1 to 1½ hours.

4. Turn out the dough onto a lightly floured work surface and divide it into 3 equal portions. Form into rectangular loaves and place in 3 greased 9-by-5-inch loaf pans. Cover loosely with plastic wrap and let rise at room temperature only until level with the rims of the pans (these loaves will rise a lot in the oven), about 40 minutes. Twenty minutes before baking, preheat the oven to 375°.

5. Brush the tops gently with the egg glaze and, using kitchen shears, carefully snip the top of the dough at 2-inch intervals about ½ inch deep to make a zigzag pattern. Bake in the center of the preheated oven until the loaves are crusty, golden brown, and sound hollow when tapped, 40 to 45 minutes. Turn out of the pans onto racks and let cool completely before slicing.

Orange-Blueberry Sweet Rolls

This is one of my favorite sweet doughs. It is light, sweet, and citrus-perfumed throughout, creating a sumptuous and seductively flavored spiral roll. The shape is most certainly a slice of the alternating rhythms of the expanding and contracting universe, as well as a symbol of the cyclic seasons. The sunshine color reflects the cool summer mornings. In an era of convenience foods, the delight of a homemade bun is very special. Serve these oversized berry-studded sweet rolls with sliced fresh fruit and cups of hot Darjeeling tea.

YIELD: 2 DOZEN SPIRAL ROLLS

4 teaspoons active dry yeast
½ cup sugar
½ cup warm water (105° to 115°)
6 tablespoons (¾ stick) unsalted butter,
   cut into pieces
¾ cup warm milk (105° to 115°)
½ cup fresh orange juice
1½ teaspoons salt
2 eggs
5 to 5½ cups unbleached all-purpose flour

Orange Butter Filling
6 tablespoons (¾ stick) unsalted butter,
   at room temperature
¾ cup sugar
Grated zest of 1 large lemon
Grated zest of 1 orange

Orange Crumb Topping
½ cup sugar
⅓ cup unbleached all-purpose flour
¼ teaspoon ground cardamom or nutmeg
Grated zest of 1 orange
3 tablespoons unsalted butter, cold, cut into
   small pieces

3 cups fresh or frozen (unthawed) blueberries

1. *In a small bowl*, sprinkle the yeast and a pinch of the sugar over the warm water. Stir to dissolve. Let stand until foamy, about 10 minutes.

2. *In a large bowl* with a whisk or in a heavy-duty electric mixer fitted with the paddle attachment, combine the butter and warm milk. Stir until the butter is almost melted. Add the orange juice, the remaining sugar, salt, eggs, yeast mixture, and 1 cup of the flour. Whisk hard 1 minute to combine. Add the remaining flour, ½ cup at a time, until a shaggy dough is formed that just clears the sides of the bowl, switching to a wooden spoon as necessary if making by hand.

3. *Turn out the dough* onto a lightly floured surface and knead until smooth and satiny, about 2 minutes, adding only 1 tablespoon flour at a time as necessary to prevent sticking. Place in a greased deep container, turn once to coat the top, and cover with plastic wrap. Let rise at room temperature until doubled in bulk, 1 to 1½ hours.

4. *Meanwhile,* prepare the orange butter filling. In a small bowl with a wooden spoon or with an electric mixer, beat together the butter, sugar, and citrus zests until creamy. Set aside at room temperature until needed. Then prepare the orange crumb topping: In a small bowl, combine the sugar, flour, cardamom or nutmeg, and orange zest. Using your fingers or a fork, cut in the pieces of butter until coarse crumbs are formed. Set aside in the refrigerator until needed.

5. *Turn out the dough* onto a lightly floured work surface and roll with a rolling pin into a 12-by-24-inch rectangle. Smear the surface evenly with the orange butter filling and sprinkle with all of the blueberries. Starting from a long edge, roll up jelly-roll fashion and pinch the seam to seal. Using a serrated knife or a piece of dental floss, cut gently into twenty-four 1-inch-thick slices. Place in 3 greased 9-inch springform or cake pans, a 12-by-16-by-1½-inch baking sheet, or a 12-inch springform or cake pan, as desired. Cover loosely with plastic wrap and let rise at room temperature until puffy, about 40 minutes. There will be blueberry juice in the pan if you have used frozen berries. This is okay, as the juice will caramelize during baking. Twenty minutes before baking, preheat the oven to 350°.

6. *Sprinkle the surface* of the rolls with the orange crumb topping and bake in the center of the preheated oven until golden brown and the rolls have pulled away from the sides of the pan, 35 to 40 minutes for the smaller pans and 10 to 15 minutes longer for the larger pans. Remove the rolls from the oven and let stand 5 minutes before transferring to a rack, crumb side up, to cool.

7. *To store leftover rolls*, place each roll in a sandwich-sized plastic freezer bag, and freeze up to 1 month. To reheat, remove from the freezer and let thaw in the bag at room temperature. Remove the roll from the bag, place, uncovered, on a heatproof plate, and microwave for no more than 30 seconds or warm in a preheated 350° oven for about 7 minutes. Serve immediately.

Whole-Wheat Mountain Bread

Here is one of my favorite summer whole-wheat hearth breads, made with cornmeal, sesame seeds, and olive oil.
It is a delight for the baker who is concerned about fat intake, yet it can be transformed into a positively outrageous extravagance
when spread with homemade Orange–Passion Fruit Curd (page 161), a true delicacy.

YIELD: 4 ROUND LOAVES

Sponge

1 cup cold water
½ cup yellow cornmeal, preferably
    stone-ground
1½ cups boiling water
1¼ tablespoons (1½ packages) active
    dry yeast
½ cup mild honey or light molasses
½ cup warm water (105° to 115°)
¾ cup dry buttermilk powder
½ cup unprocessed wheat bran
2 cups whole-wheat flour

Dough

⅓ cup olive oil
1 tablespoon salt
2 tablespoons sesame seeds
½ cup whole-wheat flour
3½ to 4 cups unbleached all-purpose or
    bread flour

Unprocessed wheat bran and yellow cornmeal,
    for sprinkling

1. To prepare the sponge: In a large bowl or in the work bowl of a heavy-duty electric mixer fitted with the whisk attachment, whisk together the cold water and the cornmeal. Let soak 5 minutes. Add the boiling water gradually, beating with a whisk. Let stand 10 minutes. Meanwhile, in a small bowl, sprinkle the yeast and 1 teaspoon of the honey or molasses over the warm water. Stir to dissolve. Let stand until the mixture just begins to bubble, about 5 minutes.

2. Add the buttermilk powder, the remaining honey or molasses, bran, and the whole-wheat flour to the cornmeal mixture and beat until smooth. Add the yeast mixture and beat to combine. Scrape down the sides of the bowl with a spatula and cover with plastic wrap. Set in a warm place for about 1 hour. The sponge will double in bulk and be bubbly. Gently stir it down with a wooden spoon.

3. To prepare the dough: Sprinkle the oil, salt, sesame seeds, and whole-wheat flour over the sponge and, using a wooden spoon or switching to the paddle attachment, beat hard until smooth, about 1 minute. Add the unbleached flour, ½ cup at a time, until a soft dough is formed that just clears the sides of the bowl.

4. Turn out the dough onto a lightly floured work surface and knead until smooth and springy yet slightly sticky, about 2 minutes, adding only 1 tablespoon flour at a time as

necessary to prevent sticking. Do not add too much flour, as the dough must retain a definite sticky quality, which will smooth out during the rising process. The dough will also have a slightly abrasive, nubby quality due to the whole grains. Place in a deep container brushed with olive oil, turn once to coat the top, and cover with plastic wrap. Let rise at room temperature until doubled to tripled in bulk, 2½ to 3 hours.

5. Turn out the dough onto the work surface and divide it into 4 equal portions. Shape into 4 tight round balls, roll them in some bran to coat the top, and place at least 4 inches apart on 2 greased or parchment-lined baking sheets that have been sprinkled with cornmeal. Cover loosely with plastic wrap and let rise until not quite doubled in bulk, about 45 minutes. Twenty minutes before baking, preheat the oven to 400°.

6. Gently tuck the sides of the loaves under to make higher round loaves, being careful not to deflate them. Bake in the center of the preheated oven for 10 minutes. Reduce the oven thermostat to 350°, and bake until the loaves are deep brown and sound hollow when tapped, an additional 25 to 30 minutes. Switch the position of the baking sheets at the halfway point to ensure even baking. Also, place a piece of aluminum foil over the tops to control browning, if necessary. Remove to racks to cool completely before slicing.

Tomato Bread with Fresh Basil

For everyone I know, the lure of ripe tomatoes reaches its peak during August. Whether picked from your own garden or bought by the lug from a corner vegetable stand, ripe tomatoes readily perfume the kitchen. Use this bread for wonderful double tomato sandwiches with lettuce and your own mayonnaise or alongside large mixed-vegetable salads.

YIELD: TWO 9-BY-5-INCH LOAVES

8 slices dry-packed sun-dried tomatoes
2 cups Fresh Tomato Juice (following) or
    canned tomato juice
2 tablespoons regular or sun-dried
    tomato paste
2 tablespoons brown sugar
3 tablespoons olive oil
1 tablespoon (1 package) active dry yeast
4¾ to 5¼ cups unbleached all-purpose or
    bread flour
¼ cup chopped fresh basil leaves
2 teaspoons salt
Coarse-grind yellow cornmeal or semolina
    for dusting
1 egg beaten with 1 tablespoon water, for glaze

1. In a small bowl, place the sun-dried tomatoes and add hot water to cover. Let stand for 15 minutes to soften. Meanwhile, in a nonreactive saucepan, heat the tomato juice, tomato paste, brown sugar, and oil to about 120°. Drain the sun-dried tomatoes and chop coarsely. Set aside.

2. In a large bowl with a whisk or in the work bowl of a heavy-duty electric mixer fitted with the paddle attachment, combine the yeast, 2 cups of flour, the basil leaves, and salt. Add the tomato juice mixture and the chopped sun-dried tomatoes. Beat hard until smooth, about 1 minute. Add the remaining flour, ½ cup at a time, until a thick, shaggy mass is formed that just clears the sides of the bowl, switching to a wooden spoon as necessary if making by hand.

3. Turn out the dough onto a lightly floured work surface and knead until smooth and springy, 1 to 2 minutes, adding only 1 tablespoon flour at a time as needed to prevent sticking. Place in a greased container, turn once to coat the top, and cover with plastic wrap. Let rise at room temperature until doubled in bulk, 1½ to 2 hours.

4. Gently deflate the dough, turn out onto a lightly floured work surface, and divide into 6 equal portions. Using your palms, roll each portion into a 12-inch rope. Using 3 ropes for each loaf, braid the ropes into 2 loaves and tuck under the ends. Place in 2 greased 9-by-5-

inch loaf pans that have been dusted heavily on the bottom and sides with cornmeal or semolina. (Clay pans are nice for this bread.) Cover loosely with plastic wrap and let rise until the dough is even with the rims of the pans, about 45 minutes. Twenty minutes before baking, preheat the oven to 375°.

5. Brush the tops gently with the egg glaze. Bake in the center of the preheated oven until the loaves are light brown and sound hollow when tapped, 35 to 40 minutes. Turn out of the pans onto racks to cool completely before slicing.

FRESH TOMATO JUICE
Any full-flavored tomato variety can be used for making this juice.
YIELD: ABOUT 2 CUPS JUICE

2 to 2½ pounds very ripe tomatoes
Salt and sugar or fresh lemon juice to taste

1. Remove any blemishes from the tomatoes and cut them into chunks. You should have about 4 cups tomato pulp. Place in a nonreactive saucepan and bring to a boil. Simmer, uncovered, until soft and juicy, about 20 minutes.

2. Pass the tomatoes through a food mill or a sieve placed over a bowl to remove all seeds and skin. Let stand 15 minutes, then ladle off the water that separates on the top. Add a small amount of salt and sugar or lemon juice to taste.

Pain de Campagnard

*Here is a superb bread similar to the earthy wheat-rye loaves once made with sharecroppers' grains
at harvest time in the French, Italian, and Hungarian countrysides. It takes three days from start to finish, but the amount
of work is about half an hour total and the rest of the time is devoted to allowing the natural fermentation to work
its magic. This loaf is great with portable meals, such as cheese and fruit, or with big main dish salads, such as a Niçoise, curried
chicken, or cold salmon and pasta shells. Do make the effort to use the organic flours and pure spring water
for the best possible results. Please note that the starters must begin fermenting two days before mixing the dough and baking.*

Yield: 2 oblong loaves

Starter
2 teaspoons active dry yeast
1 cup stone-ground whole-wheat flour
1 cup tepid water (90° to 100°)

Sponge
1½ cups tepid water (90° to 100°)
2 cups unbleached all-purpose or bread flour

Dough
¼ cup wheat berries
Boiling water, to cover
1 teaspoon active dry yeast
⅓ cup medium or pumpernickel rye flour
2 to 2¼ cups unbleached all-purpose or
    bread flour
1 tablespoon salt

Glaze
1 teaspoon cornstarch
⅓ cup water

1. *Day One:* To prepare the starter, place the yeast and whole-wheat flour in a deep bowl or a plastic 2-quart bucket with a lid. Add the tepid water and whisk hard until a smooth batter is formed. Cover and let stand at room temperature for about 24 hours. The starter will bubble and begin to ferment.

2. *Day Two:* To prepare the sponge, alternately add the tepid water and the unbleached flour to the starter in 3 additions. Whisk to combine, changing to a wooden spoon if necessary, and beating until a smooth batter is formed. The sponge will be very sticky. Scrape down the sides of the bowl, cover, and let stand again at room temperature 12 to 24 hours. The sponge will be thick, double in bulk, and have a pleasant sour aroma.

3. *Day Three:* To prepare the dough, in a small bowl, cover the wheat berries with boiling water. Cover and let soak 4 hours at room temperature. When the wheat berries are ready, stir down the sponge with a wooden spoon. Sprinkle with the yeast. Drain the wheat berries and add them to the sponge, along with the rye flour, 1 cup of the unbleached flour, and the salt. Beat hard until combined, about 1 minute. Add the remaining unbleached flour, ½ cup at a time, until a firm, resilient dough is formed.

4. *Turn out the dough* onto a lightly floured work surface and knead until smooth, slightly tacky, and springy, 3 to 5 minutes, adding only 1 tablespoon flour at a time as necessary to prevent sticking. Keep the dough moist, as too much flour will bake into a bread that is too dry. Place the dough in a greased deep container, turn once to coat the top, and cover with plastic wrap. Let rise at room temperature until doubled in bulk, 2 to 2½ hours.

5. *Turn out the dough* onto a lightly floured work surface. Divide the dough into 2 equal portions and pat each into a fat, uneven rectangle. Roll up each rectangle from a short side into a tight cylinder. Pinch together the seams, tuck them under, and taper the ends to form a *batard* shape that is fatter in the middle. Place the loaves on a greased or parchment-lined baking sheet. Cover the dough loosely with floured plastic wrap and let rise at room temperature until doubled in bulk, 1 to 1½ hours. Twenty minutes before baking, preheat the oven to 425°, with a baking stone placed on the lowest rack, if desired. (To produce a crisp crust, about 15 minutes before putting the loaves in the oven, pour hot water into a broiler pan and place the pan on the bottom rack to create steam in the oven for the initial baking period.)

6. *Using a serrated knife,* make 3 diagonal slashes no more than ¼ inch deep in each loaf. To prepare the glaze, in a small bowl, whisk together the cornstarch and water and brush the entire surface of each loaf. Bake in the preheated oven until the loaves are browned, crisp, and sound hollow when tapped, 30 to 35 minutes. The surface of the loaves may be brushed once more with the glaze halfway through baking. Remove from the pan to a rack to cool completely before slicing.

SUMMER TOMATO BRUSCHETTA

For the best flavor, use just-picked vine-ripened tomatoes that have not spent any time in the refrigerator.

YIELD: 6 SERVINGS

6 slices Pain de Campagnard, each 1 inch
    thick (preceding)
2 or 3 garlic cloves
½ cup good-quality virgin olive oil
4 large ripe tomatoes, sliced
Salt and freshly ground black pepper
12 fresh basil leaves, cut into fine shreds

1. *Preheat a broiler* or prepare a charcoal fire in a grill. Toast each bread slice on both sides.

2. *Rub the entire surface* of each toasted slice with the whole garlic clove and place on a serving platter. Drizzle each slice with olive oil and top with overlapping tomato slices. Sprinkle with salt and a few grinds of black pepper and scatter with shreds of basil. Serve immediately.

Sour Poppy Seed Rye

*This bread is exceptional, so if you love the flavor of starter breads, make this immediately.
I prepare the sour starter in the morning, the sponge late in the evening, and mix the dough the following morning. I use Roman
Meal's Cream of Rye flakes (available in natural-foods stores) for extra texture.*

YIELD: 2 OBLONG LOAVES

Sour Starter
¼ teaspoon active dry yeast
1 cup medium or white rye flour
1 cup tepid milk, goat's milk, or buttermilk
   (90° to 100°)

Sponge
1 cup tepid water (90° to 100°)
½ teaspoon active dry yeast
1 cup medium or white rye flour

Dough
1½ teaspoons active dry yeast
Pinch of sugar
¼ cup light molasses
2 tablespoons unsalted butter, melted, or
   vegetable oil
1 egg
1 tablespoon salt
1 teaspoon ground coriander
1 heaping tablespoon caraway seeds
1 heaping tablespoon poppy seeds
½ cup rye flakes (see introduction)
3¼ to 3½ cups unbleached all-purpose or
   bread flour

Rye flakes or coarse-grind yellow cornmeal,
   for sprinkling
1 egg white beaten with 1 tablespoon water,
   for glaze
2 to 3 tablespoons sesame seeds

1. Day One: To prepare the sour starter, in a deep bowl or 4-quart plastic bucket with lid, place the yeast and flour. Add the tepid milk and whisk hard until a smooth batter is formed. Cover and let stand at room temperature 8 to 12 hours. The starter will begin to bubble and pleasantly ferment.

2. Day Two: To prepare the sponge, add the tepid water and the yeast to the sour starter. Whisk to combine. Add the rye flour and beat to form a smooth batter. The sponge will be very wet. Scrape down the sides of the bowl, cover, and let rest again at room temperature 8 to 12 hours.

3. Day Three: To prepare rye dough, stir down the sponge with a wooden spoon and place in a large mixing bowl or in the work bowl of a heavy-duty electric mixer fitted with the paddle attachment. Add the yeast, sugar, molasses, butter or oil, egg, salt, coriander, caraway and poppy seeds, and rye flakes to the sponge and beat hard with a whisk to combine. Add the yeast mixture and 1 cup of the unbleached flour. Beat hard until combined, about 1 minute. Add the unbleached flour, ½ cup at a time, until a soft dough is formed that just clears the sides of the bowl.

4. Turn out the dough onto a lightly floured surface and knead vigorously until it is soft, springy, and no longer sticks to the work surface, about 2 minutes, adding only 1 tablespoon flour at a time as necessary to prevent

sticking. The dough will be smooth yet feel rather dense and remain a little sticky. Place in a greased deep container, turn once to coat the top, and cover with plastic wrap. Let rest at cool room temperature about 2 hours.

5. Turn out the dough onto a lightly floured work surface and divide into 2 equal portions. Form into oblong loaves. Place on a greased or parchment-lined baking sheet heavily sprinkled with rye flakes or cornmeal. Coat the bottom and part of the sides of the loaves by rolling them around the sheet. Cover loosely with plastic wrap and let rise at room temperature until puffy and almost doubled, 45 minutes to 1 hour. Twenty minutes before baking, preheat the oven to 425°, with a baking stone placed on the center or lowest rack, if desired.

6. Using a serrated knife, cut 5 diagonal slashes no more than ½ inch deep down the center of each loaf. Brush the entire surface of each loaf with the egg glaze and sprinkle with the sesame seeds. Place on the center or lowest rack of the preheated oven, and immediately reduce the oven thermostat to 375°. Bake until brown and crusty, 35 to 40 minutes. Remove to racks to cool completely before slicing.

SOUR FOUR-SEED RYE
Add ½ cup each raw pumpkin seeds and sunflower seeds in step 3. Proceed as directed.

Zucchini Squash Country Bread

*Here is an earthy, vegetable-flecked loaf for summer. Zucchini is a truly mutable vegetable,
showing up in casseroles as easily as sweet breads. Although the squash gives moisture, color, and natural savor to
this surprisingly fragrant loaf, please eat the bread the same day it is made. It is great with
teleme cheese or as an accompaniment to cold and hot soups.*

YIELD: 2 CYLINDRICAL LOAVES

1 tablespoon (1 package) active dry yeast
Pinch of sugar
5 to 5½ cups unbleached all-purpose or
   bread flour
1¼ cups warm water (105° to 115°)
4 or 5 medium-sized zucchini squash
   (about 1½ pounds)
1 tablespoon olive oil
1 tablespoon salt
Extra olive oil, for brushing (optional)

1. In a large bowl with a whisk or in the work bowl of a heavy-duty electric mixer fitted with the whisk attachment, sprinkle the yeast, sugar, and 1¼ cups of the unbleached flour over the warm water. Beat well until smooth and creamy, about 1 minute. Cover loosely with plastic wrap and let rise at room temperature until bubbly, about 1 hour. Meanwhile, coarsely grate the zucchini to make 2 packed cups and drain on paper towels at room temperature 30 minutes.

2. Add 1/2 cup of the remaining flour, the 1 tablespoon oil, salt, and grated squash, and beat until smooth, about 1 minute. Add the remaining flour, ½ cup at a time, until a soft, sticky dough is formed that just clears the sides of the bowl, switching to a wooden spoon or the paddle attachment on the mixer as necessary.

3. Turn out the dough onto a lightly floured work surface and knead vigorously until smooth and springy, about 2 minutes, adding only 1 tablespoon flour at a time as necessary to prevent sticking. The dough will be soft and smooth. Place in a greased deep container, turn once to coat the top, and cover with plastic wrap. Let rise until doubled in bulk, 1½ to 2 hours.

4. Turn out the dough onto the work surface and divide into 2 equal portions. Form each portion into a 10-inch cylindrical log with tapered ends, dusting the entire round of dough with a bit of flour, and place seam side down on a greased or parchment-lined baking sheet. Cover loosely with plastic wrap and let rise at room temperature until puffy, about 45 minutes. Meanwhile, preheat the oven to 450° with a baking stone, on the lowest rack, or to 425° without a stone.

5. Using kitchen shears, snip the top of each loaf on the diagonal 3 or 4 times. Brush the top surfaces with some olive oil, if desired. Place the loaves in the center of the preheated oven and reduce the oven thermostat to 425°, if using a baking stone. Bake until the loaves are crusty, brown, and sound hollow when tapped, 40 to 45 minutes. Remove to a rack to cool completely before serving.

Olive Focaccia

My friend Gina de Leon, pastry chef extraordinaire who trained under master baker
Jim Dodge, makes the best focaccia I have ever eaten. It is about three inches high, light, and fluffy,
with a rich aftertaste. Although the exact recipe is a trade secret, she did generously share the techniques
with me. This bread is also good with the olives omitted, topped instead with lots of long-simmered caramelized
onions or spread with a fresh basil pesto to make a focaccia alla genovese. This is a fast, beautiful, and
delicious bread to serve with summer meals or in split sections for savory sandwiches.

YIELD: TEN 6-INCH ROUNDS OR ONE 11-BY-17-INCH RECTANGLE

1 tablespoon (1 package) active dry yeast
4½ cups unbleached all-purpose flour
   (exact measure)
1¼ teaspoons salt
1 cup hot water (120°)
1 cup hot milk (120°)
¼ cup good-quality olive oil
1 cup coarsely chopped, pitted black olives,
   brine or olive oil cured
Olive oil, for oiling bowl
Olive Pesto (page 161)

1. *In a large bowl* with a whisk or in the work bowl of a heavy-duty electric mixer fitted with the paddle attachment, combine the yeast, 2 cups of the flour, and the salt. Add the hot water, hot milk, and ¼ cup oil. Beat until well combined, about 2 minutes. Mix in the olives. Add the remaining flour, ½ cup at a time, until a soft dough is formed that just clears the sides of the bowl, switching to a wooden spoon as necessary if making by hand. The dough will be sticky soft and oily. Scrape down the sides of the bowl, drizzle the sides of the bowl with a bit more olive oil, and cover loosely with plastic wrap. Let rise at room temperature until doubled in volume, about 1 hour.

2. *With the heel of your hand* or a plastic dough scraper, scrape the dough out onto an olive oil–greased, parchment-lined 11-by-17-inch baking sheet, or divide it evenly among eight 6-inch round cake pans at least 1 inch deep. Spread and gently pull the dough, flattening it to fit the entire baking sheet or pans. Smear the top surface evenly with all of the Olive Pesto. Let rest, uncovered, at room temperature 15 minutes. Meanwhile, preheat the oven to 400°, with a baking stone on the center rack, if desired.

3. *Place the sheet* or pans directly on the hot stone, if using, or on the lowest oven rack and bake for 15 minutes. Reduce the oven thermostat to 350° and continue to bake until golden and the bread springs back when pressed gently, an additional 10 minutes for the small rounds or 20 minutes for the large rectangle. Let cool in the pan(s) 5 minutes, then, using a spatula, loosen the sides with a knife and slip the bread(s) out carefully onto a clean dish towel or rack to cool to room temperature. Serve at room temperature.

Petits Pains au Lait

The rond, or "round," shape of this milk roll is a familiar sight in European bakeries.
These rolls have a crisp crust and delicate flavor, making them perfect for accompanying any meal or for making little
sandwiches. Serve with Brie, coarse country pâté, and cornichons for a casual lunch. Please note the rising time
on this dough, a full four to five hours, to develop the flavor. The results are worth the time.
YIELD: 20 SMALL ROLLS

4½ to 5 cups unbleached all-purpose or
　bread flour
½ cup nonfat dry milk powder
1 tablespoon active dry yeast
2 tablespoons sugar
2 teaspoons salt
1½ cups hot water (120°)
1 egg
5 tablespoons unsalted butter, at room
　temperature, cut into pieces
½ cup coarse-grind white cornmeal or farina,
　for dusting

1. *In a large bowl* with a whisk or in the work bowl of a heavy-duty electric mixer fitted with the paddle attachment, combine 2 cups of the flour, the milk powder, yeast, sugar and salt. Add the hot water and egg. Beat hard for 2 minutes. Beat in the butter pieces. Add the remaining flour, ½ cup at a time, until a soft dough is formed that just clears the sides of the bowl, switching to a wooden spoon as necessary if making by hand.

2. *Turn out the dough* onto a lightly floured work surface and knead until smooth and resilient, about 1 minute, adding only 1 tablespoon flour as necessary to prevent sticking. Place in a greased deep container, turn once to coat the top, and cover with plastic wrap. Let rise until fully doubled in bulk, at cool room temperature 4 to 5 hours or in the refrigerator overnight. Gently deflate the dough, re-cover, and let rise until almost doubled in bulk (or tripled if the dough was chilled), about 1½ hours.

3. *Turn out the dough* onto a very lightly floured work surface. Divide the dough into 4 equal portions. Further divide each quarter into 5 equal portions to form 20 small portions. Form each portion into a tight round.

Dust the rolls lightly all over with flour. Place the rolls on 1 or 2 greased or parchment-lined baking sheets dusted with the cornmeal or farina. The rolls should be just touching one another in rows of 4, with about 2 inches between the rows. Cover loosely with plastic wrap and let rest at room temperature for about 30 minutes. Meanwhile, preheat the oven to 450° with a baking stone on the lowest rack, or to 400° without a stone.

4. *Using a serrated knife,* quickly make a slash down the middle of each roll. Place 1 baking sheet directly on the baking stone, if used, or directly on the oven rack. If the oven is set at 450°, immediately reduce the thermostat to 400° and bake the rolls until golden brown, 12 to 15 minutes. Remove from the oven and bake the second sheet. Immediately pile the baked rolls into a basket to serve or remove to a rack to cool.

HOT TOMATO GARLIC ROLLS

These rolls are adapted from a favorite recipe by San Francisco chef Ric O'Connell and are nothing short of sensational with roasted or barbecued meats or with salads. I use the flavorful imported tomato paste sold in a tube, which will keep indefinitely in the refrigerator. Try the rolls in place of plain garlic bread at your next gathering.

YIELD: 20 PIECES

10 Petits Pains au Lait (preceding)
½ cup (1 stick) unsalted butter, at room temperature, cut into pieces
¼ cup good-quality olive oil
¼ cup good-quality tomato paste
3 or 4 cloves garlic, pressed or minced
About 1½ cups freshly grated Parmesan, Asiago, or dry Jack cheese

1. Preheat a broiler. Cut the milk rolls in half lengthwise and place on an aluminum foil–lined baking sheet. In a small bowl with a fork or an electric mixer, beat together the butter, oil, tomato paste, and garlic until smooth. Spread each roll half with some of the butter mixture and then sprinkle each half with about 1 tablespoon of the cheese.

2. Broil 6 inches from the heat until toasted. Serve immediately.

Grilled Pan Bagna with Mayonnaise Rouge

Pan bagna ("bathed bread") is a popular French café sandwich from Nice and Cannes that is often
sold by outdoor vendors in the summer. Use your oblong loaves of homemade bread or a good store-bought sourdough.
The sandwich is best grilled in one of the large, oval hinged metal grills with a wooden handle used for grilling whole fish,
but any hinged grill will do. Serve the smoky picnic sandwich with cracked black olives, white wine,
and a bowl of mayonnaise rouge for extra slathering.

YIELD: 4 SERVINGS

4 or 5 large red or yellow bell peppers
1 oblong-shaped Pain de Campagnard (page 78) or Tuscan Peasant Bread (page 19), 8 Petits Pains au Lait (page 84), or 1 Semolina Sesame Seed Twist (page 57), or other country bread, halved horizontally

Shallot Vinaigrette
2 shallots, minced
1 teaspoon Dijon mustard
1 tablespoon balsamic vinegar
1 tablespoon red wine vinegar
½ cup good-quality olive oil
1 bunch arugula, tough stems removed
3 large tomatoes, thickly sliced
12 ounces fresh mozzarella cheese, thinly sliced
8 ounces smoked turkey, thinly sliced

Mayonnaise Rouge
1 cup good-quality mayonnaise
Reserved ¼ cup chopped roasted red or yellow bell pepper
1 tablespoon Italian tomato paste or sun-dried tomato paste

1. To prepare the peppers: Spear them on a long-handled fork and hold them over a gas flame, set them on a charcoal grill, or place them on a baking sheet under a preheated broiler. Roast, turning as necessary, until the skin is blackened and blistered on all sides. Transfer immediately to a paper bag, close tightly, and let stand until cool, about 20 minutes. Using your fingers or a small knife, peel off the skin. Remove the stems, seeds, and veins. Lay the peppers flat and cut them into long, wide strips. Place on a platter and let stand at room temperature, or cover and refrigerate overnight before serving.

2. Lay the split bread or rolls, cut side up, on a work surface. To make the shallot vinaigrette, in a small bowl, whisk together the shallots, mustard, and vinegars with a whisk. Gradually whisk in the olive oil. Brush all of the vinaigrette on the cut sides. It will soak into the bread as it sits.

3. Chop enough of the roasted pepper to yield ¼ cup and set aside for making the mayonnaise. Layer all of the arugula leaves, tomato slices, mozzarella, turkey, and roasted peppers on the bottom half of the bread loaf or divide equally among the bottom halves of

the rolls. Replace the top(s) and place on a platter or in a shallow pan. Press together firmly. Wrap tightly in plastic wrap and weight with a heavy object. Refrigerate 30 minutes or up to 4 hours.

4. To prepare the mayonnaise rouge: In a blender or in a food processor fitted with the metal blade, combine the mayonnaise, reserved chopped pepper, and tomato paste. Alternatively, combine the ingredients in a deep bowl and use a hand-held blender. Purée until just smooth. Store in a covered container in the refrigerator until serving time.

5. Prepare a charcoal fire in a grill. Unwrap the loaf or rolls and place in a hand-held hinged metal grill. Place on the rack 4 to 5 inches above the hot coals and grill, turning once, until the cheese begins to melt, about 8 minutes total. If made with a loaf, immediately cut into fat sections; leave the rolls whole. Serve hot.

Autumn & Harvest

Autumn marks the end of hot summer weather and the start of the harvest season. There are warm days and cool nights and colorful falling leaves decorate yards and clutter avenues. Sugar maple foliage turns auburn, liquidambars are fiery crimson spires, and flowering dogwood leaves carpet the ground as the initial cold snaps hit. Weathervanes point the direction of the first big winds, and the air is filled with the expectancy of the first chills and snows. Indian summer is a time of plenty, signaling the return of richer, denser foods after summer's heat. ❧ The Native American moon calendar is Mudjeleewis, or *Spirit Keeper of the West,* the time when the earth's power of growth slows to prepare for the time of rest that precedes the season of renewal. The fall equinox is September 23, when day and night are once again equally balanced and the days begin to grow shorter. ❧ Golden grains—oats, millet, buckwheat, field corn, quinoa, and spring-planted wheats—from the Dakotas to New York are abundant. They are ready to be reaped (cut and bound into sheaves), threshed (grain shaken from the stalk head), and winnowed (the grain separated from the chaff and straw bits), and then freshly ground by hand or by machine, an important process practiced for thousands of years. Canoe-gathered lake- and paddy-grown wild rices are collected throughout September. The lake-grown aquatic grass ripens to bursting purple beads that are hand-harvested with wooden flails and then parched over open fires before being hulled. The potato harvest is in full swing, as the swollen, fleshy tuberous stems are brought up into the light. Persimmon trees are decorated with bright globes of fruit (living up to their botanical genus that translates to "fire of Zeus"), ready to be harvested by Thanksgiving. Wild mushrooms are at their peak and the European truffle harvest brings out earthy gourmands to dig in the moist soil around old oak trees. ❧ Green and black olives are packed into crocks for preserving, while winter squashes of all shapes and colors adorn kitchens, waiting to be steamed or baked. The first cranberries appear from the bogs of the Northwest, Canada, and Maine. Sunflowers nod their heavy seedheads, ready for harvesting. Local Louisiana oranges and pecans hit the market, along with basketfuls of almonds, walnuts, hazelnuts, chestnuts, and undyed pecans in their ecru-to-russet-toned brown shells. ❧ The end-of-the-summer fruits—apples, pears, quinces—hold a concentration of flavor. Everyone has a favorite baking apple, from lime-green Granny Smiths and pippins and crisp Rome Beauties and Cortlands to honey-sweet McIntoshes, and they are known as the most comforting and satisfying of fruits. There is a continual harvest of one kind of apple or another throughout the summer until early December, with the last Winesaps bringing the season to a close. ❧ Vintners anxiously scan the skies, hoping that no rain will interfere with the vigorous harvesting of their grapes. Crushes are a celebration, as well as plenty of work, with some of the intensely sweet fresh-pressed juices scooped out of the barrels for a refreshing drink on the spot before the rest is spirited away to ferment. The residue from the crush, known as the must, can be wrapped in cheesecloth and suspended in a flour-and-water batter to procreate wild yeasts for baking, in place of a traditional starter. Fruity-flavored raisins, often still on the vine, are now ready to sweeten homemade breads and scones. Common commercial varieties range from dark (which are sun-dried Thompson seedless grapes) to golden (made from the same grape, but oven-dried, giving them a tart-sweet flavor). Look for the extra-large, deeply fruity dark Muscat raisins (dried from the Muscat of Alexandria grape) at this time as well. The old climbers that border my vegetable garden and cover the surrounding fence give off enough fruit to make into delicate translucent grape jellies for spreading on toast during the coming months. ⦗ Rosh Hashanah, the Jewish New Year, is celebrated for two days each September. It is customary during this time to eat foods sweetened with honey to symbolize the wish of sweet life in the coming year. It is also a good idea to bake my Sweet Vanilla Challah (page 154), for a Challah loaf symbolizes the hope of good luck year-round. Dip wedges of fresh fall apple and slices of challah into honey to secure the future. ⦗ The Irish Michaelmas, or Feast of Saint Michael the Archangel, is September 29, with fresh potato pancakes and potato breads, known as boxty (named for the tin box that was used for grating), the traditional elements. Struan Miceil, a mixed-grain loaf, was customarily baked by the eldest daughter in a Scottish home and served to honor this guardian saint of the harvest. These dense cottage-style loaves were often made from maslin, known as méteil in France, a field crop of wheat mixed with rye common throughout the British Isles and northern Europe. ⦗ September 30 is the San Gerónimo Feast Day at the Taos and San Juan pueblos in New Mexico, one of a myriad of saint's days introduced by the Spanish to the American Southwest. Cribs of multicolored corn cobs are proof of a good harvest, and ristras of drying red chiles are hung from outdoor house beams. Visitors will find the old adobe hornos that dot each New Mexican village fired up with juniper, cedar, or piñon wood to roast chicos (steamed dried corn kernels) and for baking dozens of oversized round wheat loaves that are now symbolic of daily life in an Indian pueblo. Sometimes a cornmeal-laced bread, such as Zuni Indian Sun Bread (page 98), is shaped into a radiating crescent with split comb edges (a shape common in Central and South American baking), to symbolize the sun's corona as it peeks over the dawn horizon. ❦ Germany, Switzerland, Alsace, and Austria mark the harvest with Oktoberfest, a celebration inspired by the massive pastoral wedding party held for Prince Ludwig of Bavaria. Wherever there are Germanic communities in America, such as Amana, Iowa, Oktoberfest has become an annual affair, a celebration that revolves around food, hay rides, brass bands, freshly pressed apple cider, and trademark stone steins of October beer. Look for a display of wonderful, hearty breads, such as Krauterbrot (herb bread), Rosinenstuten (raisin bread), Walnußbrot (walnut bread) and Mohnbrötchen (white flour poppy seed rolls), that remind one of the gabled reed-thatched farmhouses of the rural countryside. ❦ Hallowmas, or the Irish Halloween, marks the halfway point between the summer and winter solstices. Leaves are changing color and falling, water is drying up, and the land is dying. It is a solemn time, with festivals celebrated at burial grounds. The Welsh bara brith, a fruit and nut loaf from medieval times, is always served in every household at this time of year, accompanied by fresh apples and freshly churned buttermilk. This recipe appears as Irish Freckle Bread (page 47) in the spring section of this collection. ❦ Día de Los Muertos, which falls on November 1, is a day of remembrance in Mexico. It marries Indian and Hispanic traditions and is thick with a rich blend of all-night candlelight vigils, lots of flowers, and music. Pan de muerto is the orange-flavored sweet bread, often tear-shaped or decorated with the sugar-crusted image of a skull and crossbones, that adorns makeshift altars in the graveyards. Some regions even shape the breads into monos, small human or animal shapes, in the belief that the living are conduits of nourishment to the other world. ❦ All Souls' Day, on November 2, is celebrated with traditional braided breads to honor departed ancestors. They are eaten at graveside picnics with wine and hot chocolate or distributed to the poor. The Italian Fair of the Dead, I Morti, is a widely attended harvest market on this holiday that dates back to the Middle Ages. Bruschetta or fett'unta, thick toasted or grilled slices of peasant bread soaked in olive oil, and roasted chestnuts are generously served to the strolling participants. ❦ Twenty-three years before the Pilgrims held their feast, the very first American Thanksgiving fest was celebrated on the banks of the Río Grande. The gathering included five hundred Spanish colonists, who were en route to northern New Mexico under the leadership of Don Juan de Oñate, and a group of Pueblo Indians. But the American holiday we practice today is modeled after the old English Harvest Home communal feast, when villages worked together to bring in the loads of grain from the fields. It commemorates the first harvest by New England settlers, who were aided by local Narraganset Indians. The breads served at the first Thanksgiving harvest festival of 1621 were simple skillet breads or ashcakes, cooked over an open fire and probably made from corn that was mixed with persimmon pulp or crushed berries.

White Oatmeal-Potato Bread

A noble loaf, this crusty, deep-colored bread has a nubby, sweet, moist texture.
It is an easy bread to master and one of the first highly successful breads I ever made. I have
baked it often as a gift for a friend, as well as for myself. For an excellent flavor, use imported Irish oatmeal,
available in a bright green box in the cereal section of your supermarket. For those who dare, substitute
a jigger or two of single-malt scotch in place of an equal amount of the milk, Highland style.
Slice and serve spread with homemade grape jelly (page 162).

YIELD: TWO 9-BY-5-INCH OR ROUND LOAVES

1 russet potato (about 6 ounces), unpeeled and cut into large chunks

2 tablespoons unsalted butter, at room temperature

1 tablespoon (1 package) active dry yeast

1 tablespoon sugar

1½ cups warm milk (105° to 115°)

1 tablespoon salt

1½ cups regular rolled oats

5½ to 6 cups unbleached all-purpose or bread flour

Extra rolled oats, for coating the bottoms of the loaves

1. In a medium saucepan, combine the potato chunks with water to cover. Bring to a boil, reduce the heat to low, and cook until tender, about 20 minutes. Drain, reserving ½ cup of the liquid. Let the potato water cool to 105° to 115°. Meanwhile, peel the potato and pass it and the butter through a food mill placed over a bowl or purée it in a food processor fitted with the metal blade just until smooth. You will have ¾ to 1 cup purée.

2. In a small bowl, sprinkle the yeast and a pinch of the sugar over the potato water. Stir to dissolve. Let stand until foamy, about 10 minutes.

3. In a large mixing bowl with a whisk or in the work bowl of a heavy-duty electric mixer fitted with the paddle attachment, combine the puréed potato, yeast mixture, the remaining sugar, the warm milk, salt, rolled oats, and 2 cups of the flour. Beat hard to combine, about 1 minute. Add the remaining flour, ½ cup at a time, beating with a wooden spoon if making by hand, until a shaggy dough is formed that just clears the sides of the bowl.

4. Turn out the dough onto a lightly floured surface and knead until just smooth and springy, about 3 minutes, adding only 1 tablespoon flour at a time as necessary to prevent sticking. Take care not to add too much flour, as the oats will absorb extra moisture during rising and the dough will end up being too dry. Place in a greased deep container, turn once to coat the top, and cover with plastic wrap. Let rise at room temperature until doubled in bulk, about 1½ hours.

5. Turn out the dough onto a lightly floured work surface and divide it into 2 equal portions. Form into rectangular or round loaves. Roll the bottom surfaces of each loaf in rolled oats to coat. Place in two greased 9-by-5-inch clay or metal loaf pans or the round loaves on a greased or parchment-lined baking sheet. Cover lightly with plastic wrap and let rise at room temperature until doubled in bulk, about 40 minutes. Twenty minutes before baking, preheat the oven to 425°, with a baking stone, if desired.

6. Bake on the center rack of the preheated oven for 10 minutes. Reduce the oven thermostat to 350° and continue baking until the loaves are browned and pull away from the sides of the pans, 35 to 40 minutes longer. Remove from the pans to racks to cool completely before slicing.

Italian Whole-Wheat Walnut-Raisin Bread

I think this is one of the best breads in the Western world. It is distinctively stamped with the fragrance of raisins and walnuts. Use a fruity Italian extra-virgin olive oil for this pane alle noci e uva, *as the special quality it gives the bread is very desirable. Serve with Grilled Cheese in Fragrant Leaves (page 162) as a harvest-time appetizer.*

YIELD: 3 ROUND OR 2 BAGUETTE LOAVES

2 tablespoons (2 packages) active dry yeast

Pinch of light brown sugar or
   1 teaspoon honey

2½ cups warm water (105° to 115°)

½ cup extra-virgin olive oil

¼ cup honey

1 tablespoon salt

4 cups fine-grind whole-wheat flour, preferably
   stone-ground

1½ to 1¾ cups unbleached all-purpose flour

2 cups (10 ounces) dark raisins, plumped
   in hot water 1 hour and drained on
   paper towels

3 cups (12 ounces) broken or chopped walnuts

2 tablespoons whole-wheat flour,
   for sprinkling

2 tablespoons unprocessed wheat bran,
   for sprinkling

1. *In a small bowl,* sprinkle the yeast and sugar over ½ cup of the warm water. Stir to dissolve. Let stand until foamy, about 10 minutes.

2. *In a large mixing bowl* with a whisk or in the work bowl of a heavy-duty electric mixer fitted with the paddle attachment, whisk together the remaining 2 cups warm water, the olive oil, honey, salt, and 2 cups of the whole-wheat flour. Add the yeast mixture. Beat vigorously until smooth, about 1 minute. Add the remaining whole-wheat flour, ½ cup at a time. Then add the unbleached flour, ¼ cup at a time, until a soft dough is formed that just clears the sides of the bowl, switching to a wooden spoon as necessary if making by hand.

3. *Turn out the dough* onto a very lightly floured work surface and knead until soft and springy yet resilient to the touch, adding only 1 tablespoon flour at a time as necessary to prevent sticking. The dough should retain a smooth, soft quality, with some tackiness under the surface, yet still hold its shape. Do not add too much flour, or the loaf will be too dry and hard to work. Place in a greased deep container, turn once to coat the top, and cover with plastic wrap. Let rise at room temperature until doubled in bulk, 2 to 2½ hours.

4. *Turn out the dough* onto the work surface without punching it down. Pat it into a large oval and sprinkle evenly with half each of the drained raisins and the walnuts. Press the nuts and fruit into the dough and roll it up. Pat it into an oval once again and sprinkle evenly with the remaining raisins and nuts. Press in and roll the dough up again. Divide the dough into 3 equal portions or in half. Shape into 3 tight round loaves or into 2 baguettes each about 14 inches long, gently pulling the surface taut from the bottom on both. In a small bowl, combine the 2 tablespoons each whole-wheat flour and wheat bran and sprinkle on a greased or parchment-lined baking sheet. Place the loaves on the prepared pan. Cover loosely with plastic wrap and let rise at room temperature until doubled in bulk, 45 minutes to 1 hour. Twenty minutes before baking, preheat the oven at 400°, with a baking stone, if desired.

5. *Using a serrated knife,* slash the round or baguette loaves quickly with 2 parallel lines and one line intersecting no deeper than ¼ inch. Place the baking sheet directly on the stone or on an oven rack and bake until the loaves are brown, crusty, and sound hollow when tapped on the bottom, 35 to 40 minutes for the round loaves and 25 to 30 minutes for the baguettes. Remove to a rack to cool completely before slicing.

Three-Onion Rye

When cottage cheese is an ingredient in a yeast bread, you are tipped off to the hairline
crust and extra-moist texture of the finished loaf. Take care when warming the curd cheese, as it will
separate and change in consistency if it becomes too hot. The gently simmered bouquet of onions adds a savory
sweetness to the bread and fills the kitchen with a delightful scent during baking. Three-Onion Rye makes great
sandwiches, or the dough is wonderful formed and baked into pretzel shapes for serving with soups.

YIELD: 3 ROUND LOAVES OR 16 LARGE SOFT PRETZELS

¼ cup olive oil
½ yellow onion, diced
1 small white onion, diced
1 large shallot, minced
1 tablespoon (1 package) active dry yeast
Pinch of sugar or 1 teaspoon honey
1½ cups warm water (105° to 115°)
1 cup small-curd cottage cheese,
    warmed slightly
2 eggs
1 heaping tablespoon caraway seeds
1¼ teaspoons salt
2 cups medium rye flour
4½ to 5 cups unbleached all-purpose or
    bread flour
Yellow cornmeal, for sprinkling
1 egg beaten with 1 tablespoon water, for glaze
Coarse kosher salt, for sprinkling (optional)

1. In a medium skillet, warm the oil. Add the yellow and white onions and the shallot and sauté over medium heat until soft, about 10 minutes. Meanwhile, in a small bowl, sprinkle the yeast and sugar or honey over ½ cup of the warm water. Stir to dissolve. Let stand until foamy, about 10 minutes. Remove the skillet from the heat and let the onion mixture cool slightly.

2. In a large bowl with a whisk or in the work bowl of a heavy-duty electric mixer fitted with the paddle attachment, combine the remaining 1 cup warm water, the warm cottage cheese, the 2 eggs, caraway seeds, salt, and rye flour. Add the yeast mixture and beat until combined, about 1 minute. Stir in the onions and their oil. Add the unbleached flour, ½ cup at a time, until a soft dough is formed that just clears the sides of the bowl, switching to a wooden spoon as necessary if making by hand.

3. Turn out the dough onto a lightly floured work surface and knead until smooth and elastic, about 3 minutes, adding only 1 tablespoon flour at a time as necessary to prevent sticking. Push back any onions that fall out during the kneading. Place in a greased deep container, turn once to coat the top, and cover with plastic wrap. Let rise at room temperature until doubled in bulk, 1 to 1½ hours.

4. Turn out the dough onto the work surface. To make loaves, divide into 3 equal portions. Form each portion into a tight round and place on a cornmeal-sprinkled greased or parchment-lined baking sheet. To form pretzels, pat the dough into a thick rectangle. Cut into 16 long strips of equal size. Using the palms of your hands, roll each strip to form a 20-inch-long rope. Holding one end in each hand, cross the ends about 4 inches from the tips. Twist the loose ends together twice. Fold the twisted end toward you, over, and then down into the center of the loop and attach it to the far side of the loop. Dampen the end of the dough with a bit of water before pressing together to form the pretzel shape. Carefully lift and place the pretzels about 2 inches apart on 2 prepared baking sheets. Cover loosely with plastic wrap and let rise at room temperature until level with the rims of the pans, about 45 minutes for the loaves and 20 minutes for the pretzels. Twenty minutes before baking, preheat the oven to 350°.

5. Gently brush the surfaces with the egg glaze and sprinkle with the coarse salt, if desired (a must for the pretzels). Bake in the center of the preheated oven until golden brown, 40 to 45 minutes for the loaves, 20 to 25 minutes for the pretzels. Remove from the pans to racks to cool. Let the loaves cool completely before slicing.

The Hermit's Bread with Oats, Polenta, and Brown Rice

I love nubby whole-grain loaves with a modicum of sweetener added to feed the yeast.
Coarse-textured polenta blends perfectly with the brown rice and rolled oats. This is what an excellent
homemade bread looks and tastes like and you don't need to live in seclusion to make and enjoy it.
Use this loaf for sandwiches and toast, as well as for croutons.

YIELD: TWO 8-BY-4-INCH LOAVES

1½ tablespoons (1½ packages) active
   dry yeast
1 tablespoon light molasses or honey
1 cup warm water (105° to 115°)
1¼ cups warm buttermilk (105° to 115°)
¼ cup corn or sunflower seed oil
1 tablespoon salt
¾ cup cooled, cooked short-grain brown rice
½ cup polenta (coarse-grind yellow cornmeal)
½ cup rolled oats
½ cup whole-wheat flour
⅓ cup unprocessed wheat bran
4⅓ to 4⅔ cups unbleached all-purpose or
   bread flour

1. In a small bowl, sprinkle the yeast and molasses or honey over the warm water. Stir to dissolve. Let stand until foamy, about 10 minutes.

2. In a large bowl with a whisk or in the work bowl of a heavy-duty electric mixer fitted with the paddle attachment, combine the buttermilk, oil, salt, rice, polenta, oats, whole-wheat flour, wheat bran, and 1 cup of the unbleached flour. Beat hard until combined. Add the yeast mixture and beat for 1 minute. Add the remaining unbleached flour, ½ cup at a time, until a soft dough is formed that just clears the sides of the bowl, switching to a wooden spoon as necessary if making by hand.

3. Turn out the dough onto a lightly floured work surface and knead until smooth and elastic, about 3 minutes, adding only 1 tablespoon flour at a time as necessary to prevent sticking. The dough will retain a nubby, tacky quality. Place in a greased deep container, turn once to coat the top, and cover with plastic wrap. Let rise at room temperature until doubled in bulk, about 1½ hours.

4. Turn out the dough onto the work surface and divide into 4 equal portions. Using your palms, roll each portion into a 12-inch-long rope. Twist 2 ropes of dough around each other to form a 2-strand braid. Repeat with the remaining 2 ropes to form the second loaf. Place in 2 greased 8-by-4-inch loaf pans. Cover loosely with plastic wrap and let rise at room temperature until level with the rims of the pans, about 45 minutes. Twenty minutes before baking, preheat the oven to 375°.

5. Bake in the center of the preheated oven until crusty and golden, 40 to 45 minutes. Turn out of the pans onto racks to cool completely before slicing.

Zuni Indian Sun Bread

*The dehydrated cornmeal specifically used for tortillas is known as masa harina
and has a distinctive limey taste. You can buy it in a well-stocked grocery store or Hispanic
market or order it by mail. This bread is formed into a sunburst crescent, a haunting representation of the
sun rising on the horizon (a shape commonly made by bakers in the Southwest pueblos along
the Rio Grande). Enjoy this rustic bread with a pot of green chile stew. I also like it toasted for breakfast
with eggs poached in salsa, or spread with cream cheese and jalapeño jelly.*

YIELD: 2 CRESCENTS OR 9-BY-5-INCH LOAVES

1 tablespoon (1 package) active dry yeast
Pinch of sugar, or 1 teaspoon light molasses
¾ cup warm water (105° to 115°)
1½ cups warm buttermilk (105° to 115°)
⅓ cup light molasses
¼ cup corn or sunflower seed oil
2 eggs
1 tablespoon salt
½ cup raw sunflower seeds
1 cup *masa harina* (see headnote)
1½ cups whole-wheat flour, preferably stone-ground and fine-grind
About 3½ cups unbleached all-purpose or bread flour
Masa harina, for sprinkling

1. In a small bowl, sprinkle the yeast and sugar or 1 teaspoon molasses over the warm water. Stir to dissolve. Let stand until foamy, about 10 minutes.

2. In a large bowl with a whisk or the work bowl of a heavy-duty electric mixer fitted with the paddle attachment, combine the buttermilk, the ⅓ cup molasses, oil, eggs, salt, sunflower seeds, 1 cup *masa harina,* and ½ cup of the whole-wheat flour. Beat hard until combined, about 1 minute. Add the yeast mixture and the remaining 1 cup whole-wheat flour, beating for another minute. Add the unbleached flour, ½ cup at a time, until a soft dough is formed that just clears the sides of the bowl, switching to a wooden spoon as necessary if making by hand.

3. Turn out the dough onto a lightly floured work surface and knead until smooth and elastic, about 2 minutes, adding only 1 tablespoon flour at a time as necessary to prevent sticking. The dough will retain a nubby, tacky quality, yet be quite soft. Place in a greased deep container, turn once to coat the top, and cover with plastic wrap. Let rise at room temperature until doubled in bulk, 1½ to 2 hours.

4. Turn out the dough onto a work surface heavily sprinkled with *masa harina.* Divide

into 2 equal portions. Form each portion into a tight ball with just a few kneads (this is very important for the proper shape of the finished loaf) and roll or pat out into a round about 9 inches in diameter and about 1 inch thick. Using a sharp knife, make 2-inch-long cuts about 4 inches apart all around the edge of each round. Fold the round in half, so that the top overlaps the bottom by 1 inch. Dust the surface of each loaf with *masa harina.* Carefully transfer both loaves to a greased or parchment-lined baking sheet at least 3 inches apart and arrange the corners so that the cut portions along the edges fan apart slightly. Alternatively, form each portion into a rectangular loaf and place in greased 9-by-5-inch loaf pans. Cover loosely with plastic wrap and let rise at room temperature until doubled in bulk, about 40 minutes. Dust the surface with more *masa harina,* if necessary to cover. Twenty minutes before baking, preheat the oven to 375°, with a baking stone, if desired.

5. Bake in the center of the preheated oven until crusty and golden, 35 to 40 minutes. Remove the loaves to racks to cool completely before slicing.

Potato Cinnamon Rolls with Irish Cream Glaze

The following recipe resides at the apex of the cinnamon roll world.
The use of a potato and an egg results in a fluffy dough that is complemented by the addition of a
liqueur-spiked glaze. If you cannot eat these rolls the same day they are made, freeze them
once they are cool, to preserve their light texture and fresh appeal.

YIELD: 18 ROLLS

1 medium-sized russet potato (about 6 ounces) peeled and cut into large chunks

1 tablespoon (1 package) active dry yeast

½ cup granulated or light brown sugar

¼ cup warm water (105° to 115°)

2 tablespoons vegetable oil

1 egg

1 teaspoon salt

5 to 5½ cups unbleached all-purpose or bread flour

4 tablespoons (½ stick) unsalted butter, melted

1¼ cups light brown sugar

1½ tablespoons ground cinnamon

1 cup dark raisins or dried currants, plumped in hot water 10 minutes and drained on paper towels (optional)

1 cup (4 ounces) walnuts or pecans, toasted and coarsely ground (optional)

Irish Cream Glaze

1½ cups powdered sugar, sifted

4 to 5 tablespoons Irish Cream liqueur or milk

1. In a medium saucepan, combine the potato chunks with water to cover. Bring to a boil, reduce the heat to a simmer, and cook uncovered, until tender, about 20 minutes. Drain, reserving 1 cup of the liquid. Let the potato water cool to 105° to 115°. Meanwhile, pass the potato with the butter through a food mill placed over a bowl or purée it in a food processor fitted with the metal blade just until smooth. You will have ¾ to 1 cup purée.

2. In a small bowl, sprinkle the yeast and a pinch of the granulated or brown sugar over the warm water. Stir to dissolve. Let stand until foamy, about 10 minutes.

3. In a large mixing bowl with a whisk or in the work bowl of a heavy-duty electric mixer fitted with the paddle attachment, combine the puréed potato, warm potato water, yeast mixture, the remaining granulated or brown sugar, oil, egg, salt, and 2 cups of the flour. Beat hard to combine, about 1 minute. Add the remaining flour, ½ cup at a time, beating with a wooden spoon if making by hand, until a shaggy dough is formed that just clears the sides of the bowl.

4. Turn out the dough onto a lightly floured surface and knead until smooth and springy, 1 to 2 minutes, adding only 1 tablespoon flour at a time as necessary to prevent sticking. Take care not to add too much flour, as the dough should be very satiny. Place in a greased deep

container, turn once to coat the top, and cover with plastic wrap. Let rise in a warm place until doubled in bulk, 1 to 1½ hours. Gently deflate the dough and let rise a second time until doubled in bulk, 50 minutes to 1 hour.

5. Gently deflate the dough, turn it out onto a lightly floured work surface, and divide into 2 equal portions. Roll out each portion into a 10-by-14-inch rectangle at least ¼ inch thick. Brush the surface of each rectangle with the melted butter. Sprinkle the surface of each rectangle evenly with half of the brown sugar and cinnamon, leaving a 1-inch border around the edges. Sprinkle with the raisins or currants and ground nuts, if using. Starting from a long side, roll up, jelly-roll fashion. Pinch the seams together and, using a serrated knife or dental floss, cut each roll crosswise into 9 equal portions each 1 to 1½ inches thick. Place each portion cut side up on a parchment-lined baking sheet at least 2 inches apart. Press gently to flatten each swirl slightly. Or place in 18 greased 3-inch muffin-pan cups for a topknot shape. Cover loosely with plastic wrap and let rise at room temperature just until puffy, about 20 minutes. (If you like, let rise 40 minutes at this point, refrigerate and transfer the rolls directly from the refrigerator to a pre-heated oven.) Twenty minutes before baking, preheat the oven to 350°.

6. Bake in the center of the preheated oven until golden brown, 25 to 30 minutes. Using a metal spatula, remove to a rack. Immediately prepare the Irish Cream glaze by combining the powdered sugar and liqueur in a small mixing bowl and whisking until smooth. Adjust the consistency of the glaze by adding more liqueur, a few drops at a time, to make a thin mixture capable of being poured. Dip your fingers or a large spoon into the glaze and drizzle it over the rolls by running your hand or the spoon back and forth over the tops. Alternatively, apply the glaze to the rolls with a brush. Let stand until just warm before eating, or let cool completely and freeze in individual freezer bags up to 3 months.

Fresh Mushroom Croustade

Individual mushroom croustades are old-fashioned treats for grand occasions. They are good for a light lunch with a vinaigrette-dressed salad of mixed greens or an omelet brunch with fruit and wine. Do not be tempted to cook the mushrooms too long, as they must retain their texture and taste. A good-quality Madeira, either a Portuguese or California label, imparts a deep accent to the mushrooms. Serve with a fork and serrated knife for easiest eating.

YIELD: 6 SERVINGS

6 Petits Pains au Lait (page 84) or Cajun French Quarter Rolls (page 27), fresh or day old
½ to ⅔ cup good-quality olive oil
2 tablespoons unsalted butter
4 shallots, minced
3 pounds fresh mushrooms such as domestic white, shiitake, oyster, chanterelle, or morel, in any combination, thickly sliced or quartered
3 tablespoons all-purpose or whole-wheat pastry flour
1 cup chicken broth (canned or homemade)
¼ cup Madeira wine
½ cup heavy cream or *crème fraîche*
Salt and freshly ground pepper to taste
¼ cup chopped fresh Italian (flat-leaf) parsley or chervil

1. Preheat the oven to 375°. Cut off the top of each roll to form a small lid and hollow out the rolls to form shells ½ to 1 inch thick. Reserve the removed bread and lids. Make a few slashes around the rim of each shell, if necessary, to open up the top. Brush the insides and outsides of each roll with some of the olive oil. Place on a parchment-lined baking sheet and bake in the preheated oven until crisped, 10 to 15 minutes. Set aside and keep warm until serving. (The croustades may be baked up to 6 hours in advance and rewarmed before serving.)

2. Meanwhile, in a large skillet, warm ¼ cup of the olive oil and the butter. Add the shallots and mushrooms and sauté over medium-high heat until the mushrooms have given off their liquid. Continue to stew them until they are cooked through. The timing will depend on the type of mushrooms you are using. With a slotted spoon, remove the mushrooms and set aside.

3. Stir the flour into the mushroom liquid and cook over medium heat, stirring constantly, 1 minute. Whisk in the chicken broth and wine and bring to a boil. Stirring constantly with a whisk, simmer until thickened, about 2 minutes. Add the cream or *crème fraîche* and salt and pepper and stir until evenly blended. Return the mushrooms to the pan and keep warm.

4. In a food processor fitted with the metal blade, combine the reserved bread and the parsley or chervil and process to make coarse crumbs. In a skillet over medium heat, heat 2 to 3 tablespoons of the olive oil. Add the herbed crumbs and sauté, stirring constantly, until crisp. Remove from the heat and set aside.

5. To serve, place each warmed croustade on an individual serving plate. Spoon the hot creamed mushrooms into the cavities, filling to overflowing. Sprinkle with the herbed crumbs, balance the lids on top, and serve immediately.

Cottage Granary Loaf

*Granary loaves are usually made with premixed blends of wheat, rye, and malted grain concocted
by millers throughout England, Wales, and up to the Isle of Skye. Its sweetness is derived from the malted grain
and its considerable texture is a product of a combination of cracked grains. My version brings together cracked
and flaked cereals (I use Quaker brand Multi-Grain Oatmeal) for a granary-style flour.*

YIELD: 2 COTTAGE LOAVES

2 tablespoons (2 packages) active dry yeast
Pinch of barley malt powder or brown sugar
1¼ cups warm water (105° to 115°)
⅓ cup raw seven-grain cracked cereal
1½ cups multigrain cereal flakes (a
  combination of rolled rye, barley, oats,
  and wheat)
2 tablespoons malt powder or
  light brown sugar
4⅓ to 4⅔ cups unbleached all-purpose
  or bread flour
1¼ cups warm milk (105° to 115°)
¼ cup vegetable oil
1 tablespoon salt
Extra multigrain cereal flakes, for sprinkling
1 tablespoon vegetable oil, for brushing

1. In a small bowl, combine the yeast, pinch of malt powder or brown sugar, and ½ cup of the warm water. Stir to dissolve. Let stand until foamy, about 10 minutes.

2. Prepare the granary flour by combining the seven-grain cereal, multigrain rolled cereal flakes, malt powder or brown sugar, and 1 cup of the unbleached flour in a food processor fitted with the metal blade. Process only 5 to 10 seconds to make a coarse flour. There will still be small pieces of cracked grains throughout.

3. In a large bowl with a whisk or in the work bowl of a heavy-duty electric mixer fitted with the paddle attachment, combine the remaining ¾ cup warm water, the warm milk, oil, granary flour mixture, and the yeast mixture. Add the salt and 1 cup more of the flour. Whisk hard until smooth, about 1 minute. Let stand, uncovered, 30 minutes. Add the remaining unbleached flour, ½ cup at a time, until a soft dough is formed that just clears the sides of the bowl, switching to a wooden spoon as necessary if making by hand.

3. Turn out the dough onto a lightly floured work surface and knead until light-colored, smooth, and springy, about 2 minutes, adding only 1 tablespoon flour at a time as needed to prevent sticking. Because of the whole grains, this dough will retain a slightly tacky quality. Place in a deep greased container, turn once to coat the top, and cover with plastic wrap. Let rise at room temperature until doubled in bulk, 1½ to 2 hours.

4. Turn out the dough onto a lightly floured work surface and divide into 2 equal portions. Cut each portion into 2 uneven pieces. Form the 2 larger pieces into tight round loaves. Place on a greased or parchment-lined baking sheet sprinkled with more cereal flakes. Using your fingers, pull the top of each round to form an indentation. Roll the 2 smaller pieces into teardrop-shaped ovals and place in the indentations on the larger rounds, centering them. Using a floured finger, poke into the middle of each loaf right through the middle to the bottom (known in English baking as "bashing"). This is important to join the two sections to form one loaf. Cover loosely with plastic wrap and let rise at room temperature until doubled in bulk, about 45 minutes. Twenty minutes before baking, preheat the oven to 375°, with a baking stone, if desired.

5. Gently brush the tops of the loaves with the 1 tablespoon oil. Refine the indentation through the center of each loaf. Bake in the lower third of the preheated oven until the loaves are golden brown and the bottoms sound hollow when tapped, 35 to 40 minutes. It is okay if the topknots lean to one side and become very dark brown. Remove to racks to cool completely before slicing.

Pumpkin Pumpernickel

I have a passion for the dense, moist dark ryes known as pumpernickel.
Look for rye pumpernickel flour, ground whole rye with lots of bran flecks, in natural-foods stores.
It is an important ingredient in this bread. The heavy, sticky dough is best mixed with a heavy-duty electric
mixer, as the beating must be vigorous. Serve thinly sliced with butter or with assorted smoked meats
and liverwurst with pistachios spread with a thin layer of grainy mustard.

YIELD: THREE 8-BY-4-INCH LOAVES

1 heaping tablespoon caraway seeds
1 small white boiling onion, finely chopped
¼ cup apple cider vinegar
2¼ cups water
4 tablespoons (½ stick) unsalted butter, cut
    into pieces
¼ cup unprocessed wheat bran or oat bran
½ cup light or dark buckwheat flour
¾ cup polenta (coarse-grind yellow cornmeal)
1½ cups graham or whole-wheat flour
1½ cups rye pumpernickel flour
1 tablespoon instant espresso powder
¼ cup unsweetened cocoa powder
1 tablespoon salt
2 tablespoons (2 packages) active dry yeast
2 cups Fresh Pumpkin Purée (following), or
    one 16-ounce can solid-pack pumpkin
3¾ to 4¼ cups unbleached all-purpose or
    bread flour

1. In a small saucepan, combine the caraway seeds, chopped onion, vinegar, and water. Bring to a boil, reduce the heat to medium, and simmer 2 minutes. Add the butter and stir to melt. Cool to 120° to 130°. The onion pieces will be softened.

2. In a large bowl, stir together the bran, buckwheat flour, polenta, graham or whole-wheat flour, rye pumpernickel flour, espresso powder, cocoa, and salt. Set aside.

3. In the work bowl of a heavy-duty electric mixer fitted with the paddle attachment, combine 2 cups of the flour mixture and the yeast. Add the hot onion-caraway water and beat until smooth, 1 minute. Add the pumpkin purée and 2 more cups of the flour mixture. Beat 1 minute longer. Add the remaining flour mixture and the unbleached flour, ½ cup at a time, until a sticky, soft dough is formed that just clears the sides of the bowl and begins to work its way up the paddle.

4. Turn out the dough onto a lightly floured work surface and scrape any dough off the paddle. Knead vigorously until springy and dense, about 3 minutes, adding as little extra flour as possible. This will be a tacky dough under a smooth exterior. It is important not to add too much flour or the finished bread will

be too dry. Place in a deep greased container, turn once to coat the top, and cover with plastic wrap. Let rise at room temperature until doubled in bulk, about 1½ hours. Punch down and let rise again until doubled in bulk, an additional 1½ hours.

5. Turn out the dough onto a lightly floured work surface and divide into 3 equal portions. Pat each portion into a rectangle and roll up tightly, jelly-roll fashion, to create rectangular loaves. Place seam side down in three 8-by-4-inch greased loaf pans. (I like using clay pans for this bread.) The dough will fill the pans one-third to one-half full. Cover loosely with plastic wrap and let rise at room temperature until level with the rims of the pans, 30 to 45 minutes. Twenty minutes before baking, preheat the oven to 375°, with a baking stone, if desired.

6. Place the pans on the center rack of the preheated oven or directly on the baking stone and bake for 35 to 40 minutes. The loaves will be lightly browned, sound hollow when tapped on the bottom, and spring back when pressed on the surface with your finger. Remove from the pans to racks to cool completely before slicing.

FRESH PUMPKIN PURÉE

Other winter squashes, such as the Hubbard or butternut, can be used for making the purée.
YIELD: ABOUT 1 POUND RAW PUMPKIN YIELDS ABOUT 1 CUP PURÉE

1 Sugar Pie pumpkin

1. Preheat the oven to 350°. Cut off the top of the pumpkin, then cut the pumpkin in half. Scoop out the seeds and fibers. Cut into large cubes, leaving the skin intact. Place, flesh down, in a deep baking dish filled with water to a depth of 1 inch. Cover and bake in the preheated oven until tender, 1 to 1½ hours.

Remove from the oven and let cool to room temperature.

2. Peel off and discard the skin. In a blender, a food mill, or a food processor fitted with the metal blade, purée the pulp until smooth. Cover and refrigerate up to 5 days or freeze up to 9 months.

Swiss Egg Braid

Every Saturday for the last half century in Thun, a town outside Bern, Switzerland,
the mother of my friend Rosmarie has baked loaves of Zupfe (which translates to "braid" in Swiss German).
They eat two large loaves on Sundays, take some skiing, and always bring a loaf when visiting friends. An egg-yolk
glaze gives the baked loaf a beautiful shiny-brown finish. The four-strand braid, a shape also known as Jacob's
ladder, makes a unique loaf that is thick at one end and tapered at the other.

YIELD: TWO 4-STRAND BRAIDED LOAVES

1 tablespoon (1 package) active dry yeast,
    or ½ ounce fresh cake yeast
Pinch of sugar
½ cup warm water (105° to 115°)
2 cups warm milk (105° to 115°)
1 egg
½ cup (1 stick) unsalted butter, at room
    temperature, cut into small pieces
2½ teaspoons salt
5½ to 6 cups unbleached all-purpose flour
1 egg yolk beaten with 1 teaspoon water,
    for glaze

1. In a small bowl, sprinkle the yeast and sugar over the warm water. Stir to dissolve. Let stand until foamy, about 10 minutes.

2. In a large bowl with a whisk or in the work bowl of a heavy-duty electric mixer fitted with the paddle attachment, combine the warm milk, 1 egg, butter, salt, 2 cups of the flour, and the yeast mixture. Beat hard to combine, about 1 minute. Add the remaining flour, ½ cup at a time, until a shaggy dough is formed that just clears the sides of the bowl, switching to a wooden spoon as necessary if making by hand.

3. Turn out the dough onto a lightly floured surface and knead until smooth and satiny, about 3 minutes, adding only 1 tablespoon flour at a time as necessary to prevent sticking. Add enough flour so that the dough holds its shape yet is not too dry. Place in a greased deep container, turn once to coat the top, and cover with plastic wrap. Let rise at room temperature until doubled in bulk, 1½ to 2 hours.

4. Turn out the dough onto a lightly floured work surface and divide it into 2 equal portions. Divide each portion in half and, using your palms, form each half into a 14-inch-long rope. Lay the 2 rope strands together so that they form a cross. There will be a bump in the middle where the top rope covers the bottom rope. Bring the two opposite ends of the bottom strand up and over to cross the top strand, exchanging their exact positions by placing each end on the opposite side and laying side by side. One set of strands will alternate back and forth, laying over the top of the braided dough. Working right to left, repeat crossing the two ends of the bottom strand of dough over the top section until all the dough is used up (if you are left-handed, you will be forming the braid in the opposite direction), forming a tapered braid. Pinch the tapered end together and tuck under. Repeat with the remaining pair of dough ropes to form a second loaf. Place on a greased or parchment-lined baking sheet. Cover lightly with plastic wrap and let rise at room temperature until doubled in bulk, 45 minutes to 1 hour.

5. Gently brush the egg glaze over the surface of the loaves. Place in the cold oven on the center rack and turn the oven thermostat to 425°. Bake 15 minutes. Immediately turn the oven thermostat down to 325° and bake until the loaves are browned and sound hollow when tapped, an additional 50 minutes to 1 hour. Remove from the pans to racks to cool completely before slicing.

Limpa with Wild Rice

Judy Larsen's limpa, or Swedish rye bread, is one of the first whole-grain recipes I mastered. It is a sweet rye bread, unequaled for baking during the winter months. The definition of the center hole is reminiscent of rye loaves made at the harvest and strung on poles in the rafters for eating later during the winter. Serve with soups, pork roasts stuffed with prunes, or a whole chicken sprinkled with chili powder and stuffed with fresh lemon and onion halves before roasting.

YIELD: 3 ROUND LOAVES

1½ tablespoons (1½ packages) active
    dry yeast
Pinch of light brown sugar
1½ cups warm water (105° to 115°)
1 cup warm milk (105° to 115°)
¼ cup sunflower seed or other vegetable oil
¼ cup light molasses
¼ cup light brown sugar
1½ cups cooled, cooked wild rice (following)
Grated zest of 1 large lemon
1 tablespoon aniseeds, crushed
1 tablespoon salt
3 tablespoons buckwheat flour
2½ cups light or medium rye flour
5 to 5⅓ cups unbleached all-purpose or
    bread flour

1. In a small bowl, sprinkle the yeast and pinch of brown sugar over the warm water. Stir to dissolve. Let stand until foamy, about 10 minutes.

2. In a large bowl with a whisk or in the work bowl of a heavy-duty electric mixer fitted with the paddle attachment, combine the milk, oil, molasses, ¼ cup brown sugar, wild rice, lemon zest, aniseeds, salt, buckwheat flour, and rye flour. Add the yeast mixture. Beat hard until smooth, 1 minute. Add the unbleached flour, ½ cup at a time, until a soft dough is formed that just clears the sides of the bowl, switching to a wooden spoon as necessary if making by hand. Because of the whole grains, the dough will retain a very moist consistency.

3. Turn out the dough onto a well-floured work surface and knead (I use a plastic dough scraper to start, as it is very sticky) until dense yet quite soft and still springy, about 2 minutes, adding only 1 tablespoon flour at a time as necessary to prevent sticking. Because of the whole-grain flour, the dough will retain a tacky, sticky quality. Do not add too much flour, or the dough will harden and the bread will be dry. Place in a greased deep container, turn once to coat the top, and cover with plastic wrap. Let rise at room temperature until doubled in bulk, 2 to 2½ hours. Do not worry if rising takes a bit longer.

4. Turn out the dough onto a lightly floured work surface and divide into 3 equal portions. Form each portion into a round loaf and place staggered on a greased or parchment-lined baking sheet. Dip the handle of a wooden spoon into flour and then gently poke the handle through the center of each loaf. For a traditional "hole bread" shape, pat each round into a flat 9-inch round and, using a 2½-inch biscuit cutter, cut out a center hole. Cover loosely with plastic wrap. Let rise at room temperature until doubled in bulk, about 1 hour. Twenty minutes before baking, preheat the oven to 375°, with a baking stone, if desired.

5. Carefully repoke the center of each loaf to accentuate the indentation. Bake in the center of the preheated oven until the loaves are browned and sound hollow when tapped, 35 to 40 minutes. Remove from the pans to a rack to cool completely before slicing.

To Cook Wild Rice

Use a paddy-cultivated rice (also known as "tame rice") or a hand-harvested rice for bread baking. The rice helps keep the bread moist for days.

YIELD: ABOUT 1 1/2 CUPS

1½ cups water
¾ cup wild rice

1. In a medium saucepan, bring the water a rolling boil over high heat. Add the wild rice. Bring back to a rolling boil. Cover tightly and reduce the heat to the lowest setting. Cook until the rice is tender and all liquid has been absorbed, 55 minutes for paddy-cultivated rice and 30 minutes for hand-harvested rice. If any liquid remains, use it as some of the measured liquid in the recipe.

2. Set aside to cool before adding to the dough or cover and refrigerate up to 3 days.

Fresh Apple-Walnut Braid

Apples were probably the first fruit to be cultivated by man. There are thousands of different apple varieties, each with a distinct color, texture, and flavor. The dried Zante currants that dot the interior of this loaf are unrelated to currant berries, and are instead tiny sun-dried grapes. Please note that the amount of flour called for in this recipe will vary slightly depending on what type of apple you use. This nut-and-spice fruit bread makes such good toast when it is a day old that you will want to tuck away a loaf to save just for that. It is also very good eaten plain with a wedge of Cabot Creamery's Private Stock black wax Cheddar cheese.

YIELD: TWO 9-BY-5-INCH LOAVES

1 tablespoon (1 package) active dry yeast

2 tablespoons light brown sugar

1 cup warm water (105° to 115°)

1 cup warm milk (105° to 115°)

6 to 6½ cups unbleached all-purpose or bread flour

2 medium-large tart cooking apples, peeled, cored, and coarsely chopped (2 to 3 cups)

½ cup (2 ounces) dried currants

½ cup (2 ounces) walnuts, coarsely chopped

2 tablespoons walnut oil

2 eggs

2 teaspoons ground cinnamon

½ teaspoon ground mace

½ teaspoon ground allspice

1 tablespoon salt

1. In a large bowl with a whisk or in the work bowl of a heavy-duty electric mixer fitted with the paddle attachment, combine the yeast, brown sugar, warm water, warm milk, and 2 cups of the flour. Beat until smooth, about 1 minute. Cover the bowl loosely with plastic wrap and let stand at room temperature until bubbly, about 1 hour.

2. Add the apples, currants, walnuts, oil, eggs, cinnamon, mace, allspice, salt, and 1 cup more of the flour. Beat until creamy, about 2 minutes. Add the remaining flour, ½ cup at a time, until a soft dough is formed that just clears the sides of the bowl, switching to a wooden spoon as necessary if making by hand.

3. Turn out the dough onto a lightly floured work surface and knead until smooth and springy yet firm, about 3 minutes, adding only 1 tablespoon flour at a time as necessary to prevent sticking. Push back any fruit or nuts that fall out during the kneading. Place in a greased deep container, turn once to coat the top, and cover with plastic wrap. Let rise at room temperature until doubled in bulk, 1½ to 2 hours.

4. Turn out the dough onto a lightly floured work surface and divide into 6 equal portions. Roll each portion into a fat strip and lay 3 strips side by side. Braid the 3 strips and taper the ends. Pinch the ends together and tuck them under. Repeat to make a second loaf. Place the loaves in 2 greased 9-by-5-inch loaf pans. Cover loosely with plastic wrap and let rise at room temperature until 1 inch above the rims of the pans, about 45 minutes. Twenty minutes before baking, preheat the oven to 350°.

5. Bake in the center of the preheated oven until the loaves are browned and sound hollow when tapped, 45 to 50 minutes. Remove from the pans immediately to racks to cool completely before slicing.

Pumpkin Spice Swirl

Recognized as one of the basic foods of colonial America, pumpkins can be put away in a cool, dark space until needed for winter sustenance, or sliced and dried for even longer storage. Bread made with it is particularly delicious toasted for breakfast. This recipe may also be used to make a dozen beautiful cinnamon rolls, if desired.

YIELD: TWO 9-BY-5-INCH LOAVES

1 tablespoon (1 package) active dry yeast

Pinch of granulated sugar or granulated maple sugar

¼ cup warm water (105° to 115°)

1 cup warm buttermilk (105° to 115°)

1 cup pumpkin purée, homemade (page 105) or canned

3 tablespoons granulated sugar or granulated maple sugar

3 tablespoons corn oil

1 egg

Grated zest of 2 oranges

1 tablespoon salt

6¼ to 6½ cups unbleached all-purpose or bread flour

Sweet Spice Streusel

¼ cup granulated sugar

¼ cup light brown sugar

Grated zest of 1 orange

1 teaspoon ground cinnamon

Pinch *each* of ground ginger, nutmeg, and cloves

⅓ cup unbleached all-purpose flour

4 tablespoons (½ stick) unsalted butter, cold, cut into pieces

Spiced Cinnamon Sugar

1¼ cups light brown sugar

1 tablespoon ground cinnamon

1½ teaspoons ground ginger

1½ teaspoons freshly grated nutmeg

1 teaspoon ground cloves

2 tablespoons unsalted butter, melted, for brushing

1. In a small bowl, sprinkle the yeast and the pinch of sugar over the warm water. Stir to dissolve. Let stand until foamy, about 10 minutes.

2. In a large bowl with a whisk or in the work bowl of a heavy-duty electric mixer fitted with the paddle attachment, combine the warm buttermilk, pumpkin purée, the 3 tablespoons sugar, oil, egg, orange zest, salt, and 2 cups of the unbleached flour. Beat until smooth, about 1 minute. Add the yeast mixture and 1 cup more of the flour. Beat 1 minute longer. Add the remaining flour, ½ cup at a time, until a soft dough is formed that just clears the sides of the bowl, switching to a wooden spoon as necessary if making by hand.

3. Turn out the dough onto a lightly floured work surface and knead until smooth and springy, about 3 minutes, adding only 1 tablespoon flour at a time as necessary to prevent sticking. Place in a greased deep container, turn once to coat the top, and cover with plastic wrap. Let rise at room temperature until doubled in bulk, 1 to 1½ hours.

4. Meanwhile, prepare the sweet spice streusel. In a small bowl, combine the sugars, orange zest, cinnamon, ginger, nutmeg, cloves, and flour. Using your fingers or a pastry blender, cut in the butter pieces until coarse crumbs are formed. Alternatively, use a food processor to combine the ingredients. Set aside.

5. Turn out the dough onto the work surface and divide into 2 equal portions. Roll or pat each portion into a thick rectangle about 8 by 12 inches. To make the spiced cinnamon sugar, in a small bowl, combine the brown sugar and spices. Brush the surface of each rectangle lightly with melted butter and sprinkle with half of the cinnamon sugar, leaving a 1-inch border around the edges. Starting from a narrow end, roll up jelly-roll fashion to form a fat loaf shape. Pinch all the seams together to seal completely. Place each loaf, seam side down, in a greased 9-by-5-inch loaf pan. Cover loosely with plastic wrap and let rise at room temperature until 1 inch above the rims of the pans, about 1¼ hours. Twenty minutes before baking, preheat the oven to 350°.

6. *Sprinkle the top* of each loaf heavily with half of the sweet spice streusel. Bake in the center of the preheated oven until the loaves are golden brown, sound hollow when tapped, and a cake tester inserted into the center of a loaf comes out clean, 40 to 45 minutes. Remove from the pans to a rack to cool completely before slicing.

Pumpkin Cornmeal Bread

*A beautiful fall bread to serve with your hearty soups and stews, this loaf was a favorite
of New England poet Emily Dickinson. The dough also makes wonderful dinner rolls for your harvest
celebration meals. Use a fresh Sugar Pie pumpkin or Blue Hubbard squash for the purée for
both the bread and the butter, or canned purée as for easy alternative. If using your own frozen
purée, defrost the day before baking and drain well before adding to the batter.*

YIELD: 2 OR 3 ROUND LOAVES OR 24 DINNER ROLLS

1½ tablespoons (1½ packages) active
   dry yeast
Pinch of sugar
1 cup warm water (105° to 115°)
1 cup warm buttermilk (105° to 115°)
5 tablespoons unsalted butter, melted, or
   corn oil
⅓ cup light molasses
½ cup pumpkin purée (homemade, page 105,
   or canned)
1 tablespoon salt
1 cup fine- or medium-grind yellow cornmeal
1 cup medium rye flour
4¼ to 4¾ cups unbleached all-purpose or
   bread flour

1. *In a small bowl*, sprinkle the yeast and sugar over the warm water. Stir to dissolve. Let stand until foamy, about 10 minutes.

2. *In a large bowl* with a whisk or in the work bowl of a heavy-duty electric mixer fitted with the paddle attachment, combine the warm buttermilk, melted butter or oil, molasses, pumpkin purée, salt, cornmeal, and rye flour. Beat until smooth, about 1 minute. Add the yeast mixture and beat 1 minute longer. Add the unbleached flour, ½ cup at a time, until a soft dough is formed that just clears the sides of the bowl, switching to a wooden spoon as necessary if making by hand.

3. *Turn out the dough* onto a lightly floured work surface and knead until springy yet slightly tacky and smooth, about 3 minutes, adding only 1 tablespoon flour at a time as needed to prevent sticking. Place in a greased bowl, turn once to coat the top, and cover with plastic wrap. Let rise at room temperature until doubled in bulk, 1½ to 2 hours.

4. *Turn out the dough* onto the work surface, and, if making loaves, divide into 2 or 3 equal portions. Form into 2 or 3 tight rounds. Place on a greased or parchment-lined baking sheet. Cover loosely with plastic wrap and

let rise at room temperature until doubled in bulk, about 45 minutes. To make dinner rolls, divide the dough in half and then divide each half into 12 equal portions. Using your palms, roll each portion into an 8-inch-long rope about ½ inch in diameter. Starting at one end, wind the strip of dough around itself to form a spiral. Tuck the end firmly under. Place the rolls on a greased or parchment-lined baking sheet about 2 inches apart to allow for expansion. Cover loosely with plastic wrap and let rise until doubled in bulk for about 20 minutes at room temperature or 2 hours to overnight in the refrigerator. Twenty minutes before baking, preheat the oven to 375°, with a baking stone, if desired.

5. *Bake in the center* of the preheated oven until the loaves are golden brown and sound hollow when tapped, 40 to 45 minutes. Bake the rolls until golden brown, 15 to 18 minutes. Immediately remove from the baking sheets to a rack to cool completely.

Sweet Potato Cloverleafs

As soon as the windfall of fresh sweet potatoes and yams hits my produce market,
I always have a few on hand. I especially like Ruby or Jewell yams for their bright color, which will
determine the tone of your dough. Serve these feather-weight rolls alongside roast turkey or
mustard-glazed baked ham for a special-occasion dinner.

YIELD: 12 CLOVERLEAF ROLLS

1 tablespoon (1 package) active dry yeast

Pinch of light brown sugar, or 1 teaspoon pure maple syrup

½ cup warm water (105° to 115°)

1 cup cooked puréed or mashed sweet potato or yam

Grated zest of 1 orange

1½ teaspoons salt

¼ teaspoon freshly grated nutmeg

3 eggs

4 tablespoons (½ stick) unsalted butter, melted

1 cup whole-wheat pastry flour

2¼ to 2½ cups unbleached all-purpose or bread flour

Melted unsalted butter, for brushing (optional)

1. In a small bowl, sprinkle the yeast and sugar or maple syrup over the warm water. Stir to dissolve. Let stand until foamy, about 10 minutes.

2. In a large bowl with a whisk or in the work bowl of a heavy-duty electric mixer fitted with the paddle attachment, combine the sweet potato or yam, orange zest, salt, nutmeg, eggs, 4 tablespoons butter, and whole-wheat flour. Add the yeast mixture and 2 cups of the unbleached flour. Beat until smooth and creamy, about 2 minutes. Gradually add the remaining unbleached flour, ½ cup at a time, until a soft dough is formed that just clears the sides of the bowl, switching to a wooden spoon as necessary if making by hand.

3. Turn out the dough onto a lightly floured work surface and knead until satiny and elastic, about 2 minutes, adding only 1 tablespoon flour at a time as necessary to prevent sticking. This should be a very smooth dough. Place in a greased deep container, turn once to coat the top, and cover with plastic wrap. Let rise at room temperature until doubled in bulk, about 1 hour.

4. Turn out the dough onto a lightly floured work surface and divide into 4 equal portions. Divide each portion into 3 equal portions. Divide each of these portions into 3 portions. Form these portions into small balls about the size of a walnut (about 1 inch in diameter). You should have 42 balls in all. Arrange 3 balls of dough in each of 14 lightly greased standard muffin cups. Cover loosely with plastic wrap and let rise at room temperature until doubled in bulk, about 30 minutes. Alternatively, brush the tops with melted butter and cover loosely with 2 layers of plastic wrap with some room for expansion, taking care to wrap tightly around the edges. Immediately refrigerate for 2 to 24 hours. When ready to bake remove from the refrigerator and let stand for 20 minutes. Meanwhile, preheat the oven to 375°.

5. Bake in the preheated oven until golden brown, 18 to 25 minutes. Remove from the muffin cups immediately to cool on racks or pile in a basket to serve warm.

Orange Bread with Cranberries, Dates, and Pecans

This is a festive loaf that smacks of the holidays and is a welcome special-occasion breakfast treat.
Use commercial Deglet Noor dates, or be bold and hunt out fresh Medjools, Zahidis, or Halawys from California's Coachella
Valley. This dough also bakes up perfectly in mini loaf pans (4 1/2 by 2 1/2 inches), to yield 10 to 12 individual loaves.
The loaves, large or mini, can be frozen up to a month or two. Do not glaze them before freezing.

YIELD: TWO 9-BY-5-INCH LOAVES

1 tablespoon (1 package) active dry yeast

Pinch of sugar

¼ cup warm water (105° to 115°)

¾ cup warm milk (105° to 115°)

¾ cup orange juice

⅓ cup sugar

2½ teaspoons salt

6 tablespoons (¾ stick) unsalted butter, melted

1 egg

Grated zest of 2 oranges

4¾ to 5 cups unbleached all-purpose or
    bread flour

1½ cups cranberries

1 cup (4 ounces) chopped pecans

1 cup chopped, pitted dates

½ cup dried cranberries, plumped for
    30 minutes in 3 tablespoons
    cranberry liqueur

Orange Syrup

½ cup orange juice (may be part orange
    liqueur, if desired)

½ cup sugar

1. *In a small bowl*, sprinkle the yeast and the pinch of sugar over the warm water. Stir to dissolve. Let stand until foamy, about 10 minutes.

2. *In a large bowl* with a whisk or in the work bowl of a heavy-duty electric mixer fitted with the paddle attachment, combine the warm milk, orange juice, sugar, salt, butter, egg, orange zest, and 2 cups of the flour. Beat until smooth, about 1 minute. Add the yeast mixture and 1 cup more of the flour. Beat 1 minute longer. Add the remaining flour, ½ cup at a time, until a soft dough is formed that just clears the sides of the bowl, switching to a wooden spoon as necessary if making by hand.

3. *Turn out the dough* onto a lightly floured work surface and knead until smooth and springy, about 3 minutes, adding only 1 tablespoon flour at a time as necessary to prevent sticking. Place in a greased deep container, turn once to coat the top, and cover with plastic wrap. Let rise at room temperature until doubled in bulk, about 1½ hours. Combine the fresh cranberries, pecans, dates, and dried cranberries and liqueur in a bowl and set aside.

4. *Turn out the dough* onto the work surface and roll out or pat into a thick rectangle. Sprinkle with the fruit-nut mixture. Fold the edges over and knead to distribute evenly.

Divide into 2 equal portions. Divide each portion in half and, using your palms, form each into a fat rope about 10 inches long. Wrap 2 ropes around each other to form a simple twist. Repeat with the remaining 2 ropes to form a second loaf. Place each loaf in a greased 9-by-5-inch loaf pan and tuck under the ends. Cover loosely with plastic wrap and let rise at room temperature until 1 inch above the rims of the pans, 45 minutes to 1 hour. Twenty minutes before baking, preheat the oven to 350°.

5. *Bake in the center* of the preheated oven until the loaves are golden brown, sound hollow when tapped, and a cake tester inserted into the center of a loaf comes out clean, 40 to 45 minutes.

6. *Ten minutes before* the breads are ready to be removed from the oven, make the Orange Syrup. Combine the orange juice and the sugar in a small microwaveproof bowl or a small saucepan. Heat just until the sugar dissolves, stirring occasionally.

7. *When the loaves are ready*, remove them from their pans to a rack placed over a plate to catch the drips. Spoon the hot syrup over the hot loaves, letting it drip down the sides. Pour any glaze that pools on the plate back over the loaves. Cool completely before serving.

Hazelnut Bread with Maple Glaze

I like to make this loaf with fresh Oregon hazelnuts, also known as filberts,
named for the English Saint Philibert, whose saint day on August 22 corresponds with the filbert
harvest. This perfumed nut filling is typical of Polish, Austrian, and German baking and is a good basic
recipe that can be made with other types of nuts. Serve in thin slices from Halloween on
through the holidays with coffee, eggnog, or hot cider.

YIELD: 1 LARGE OR 2 MEDIUM TWISTS

4 teaspoons active dry yeast
Pinch of light brown sugar
1/3 cup warm water (105° to 115°)
1 cup warm milk (105° to 115°)
4 tablespoons (1/2 stick) unsalted butter, melted
1/4 cup light brown sugar
2 eggs
Grated zest of 1 lemon
1 teaspoon salt
3 3/4 to 4 cups unbleached all-purpose flour

Hazelnut Paste
2 1/2 cup hazelnuts
1/2 cup light brown sugar
1/3 cup water
3 tablespoons unsalted butter, at
    room temperature
2 teaspoons pure vanilla extract
2 tablespoons golden rum
1 egg white

Maple Glaze
1/2 cup sifted powdered sugar
1 tablespoon hot water
2 tablespoons maple syrup

1. In a small bowl, sprinkle the yeast and the pinch of brown sugar over the warm water. Stir to dissolve. Let stand until foamy, about 10 minutes.

2. In a large bowl with a whisk or in the work bowl of a heavy-duty electric mixer fitted with the paddle attachment, combine the warm milk, butter, 1/4 cup brown sugar, eggs, lemon zest, salt, and 2 cups of the unbleached flour. Beat until smooth, about 1 minute. Add the yeast mixture and 1 cup more of the flour. Beat 1 minute longer. Add the remaining flour, 1/2 cup at a time, until a soft dough is formed that just clears the sides of the bowl, switching to a wooden spoon as necessary if making by hand.

3. Turn out the dough onto a lightly floured work surface and knead until smooth and springy, about 3 minutes, adding only 1 tablespoon flour at a time as necessary to prevent sticking. Place in a greased deep container, turn once to coat the top, and cover with plastic wrap. Let rise at room temperature until doubled in bulk, 1 1/2 to 2 hours.

4. While the dough is rising, prepare the hazelnut paste. Preheat the oven to 350°. Place the nuts in a single layer on a baking sheet and toast in the preheated oven until the skins blister and the nuts are lightly colored, 8 to 10 minutes. Immediately wrap the nuts in a clean

dish towel and let stand 1 minute. Rub vigorously in the towel to remove the skins. Let cool to warm. Place the nuts in a food processor and process until finely ground or grind by hand in a nut grinder. Combine the brown sugar, water, and butter in a small saucepan. Heat, stirring, just until the sugar is dissolved and the butter is melted. Add the ground nuts and vanilla. Mix with a wooden spoon or in the food processor until a paste is formed. Cool to room temperature and stir in the rum and egg white. Refrigerate until ready to use.

5. Turn out the dough onto the work surface and roll out or pat into a thick 14-by-18-inch rectangle. Spread evenly with all of the hazelnut paste, leaving a 1/2-inch border around the edges. Starting from a long edge, roll up jelly-roll fashion. Pinch together all the seams to seal. Place seam side down on a greased or parchment-lined baking sheet. Using a sharp knife, cut in half lengthwise, leaving a 2-inch section uncut at one end. Holding the solid end, twist both halves so that the cut sides face upward in many sections, and then wrap them around each other to form one large twist. Pinch the ends and tuck under. Shape the loaf so that it is high and compact and about 18 inches in length. Connect the two ends to form a wreath. The dough may also be divided into 2 equal portions, rolled out, filled, and shaped into 2 medium loaves. Cover loosely with plastic wrap and let rise at room temperature until doubled in bulk, about 50 minutes. Twenty minutes before baking, preheat the oven to 350°, with a baking stone, if desired.

6. *Bake in the lower third* of the preheated oven until the bread(s) is deep brown and sound hollow when tapped, 35 to 45 minutes.

Using a spatula, remove from the baking sheet to a rack placed over a sheet of parchment or waxed paper.

7. *To make the maple glaze,* in a small bowl, combine the powdered sugar, hot water and 2 tablespoons of the maple syrup. Whisk until smooth. If necessary, adjust the

consistency of the glaze to make it pourable by adding more maple syrup, a few drops at a time. Using your fingers or a large spoon, drizzle the glaze over the warm bread(s) in a back-and-forth pattern. Let stand until cool and the glaze is set before slicing.

Pan de Muerto

Pan de muerto, or "bread of the dead," is an orange- and anise-spiked brioche-like egg bread made especially for All Souls' Day, a Mexican national holiday symbolizing the love and respect the Mexicans show for their family members. Bread has been an important element at their graveside ceremonies for centuries, and my Mexican friends emphasize that this is a very happy loaf, despite the name.

YIELD: 2 LARGE ROUND LOAVES

Sponge
1¼ tablespoons (1 package plus 1 teaspoon) active dry yeast
1 tablespoon sugar
½ cup warm water (105° to 115°)
1 cup unbleached all-purpose or bread flour
2 tablespoons aniseeds
⅓ cup water

Dough
5 eggs
2 tablespoons Curaçao or other orange liqueur
½ cup (1 stick) unsalted butter, melted and cooled
Grated zest of 2 large oranges
½ cup sugar
2 teaspoons salt
3¼ to 3½ cups unbleached all-purpose or bread flour

Sweet Powdered Sugar Glaze
1 cup sifted powdered sugar
2 to 3 tablespoons milk or Curaçao or other orange liqueur
½ teaspoon pure vanilla extract, if using milk

1. *To prepare the sponge:* In a large bowl with a whisk or in the work bowl of a heavy-duty electric mixer fitted with the paddle attachment, combine the yeast, sugar, water, and the flour. Beat until smooth, about 1 minute. Scrape down the sides and cover with plastic wrap. Let stand at room temperature until bubbly, about 1 hour. Meanwhile, in a small saucepan, combine the aniseeds and ⅓ cup water. Boil until the liquid is reduced to 3 tablespoons, about 3 minutes. Strain and discard the aniseeds. Set the water aside.

2. *To prepare the dough:* Stir down the sponge and add the aniseed water, eggs, orange liqueur, butter, orange zest, sugar, salt, and 1 cup of the flour. Beat hard until creamy, about 1 minute. Add the remaining flour, ¼ cup at a time, until a soft dough is formed that just clears the sides of the bowl, switching to a wooden spoon as necessary if making by hand.

3. *Turn out the dough* onto a lightly floured work surface and knead until soft, smooth, and springy, about 4 minutes, adding only 1 tablespoon flour at a time as necessary to prevent sticking. Place in a greased deep container, turn once to coat the top, and cover with plastic wrap. Let rise at room temperature until doubled in bulk, 1½ to 2 hours.

4. *Turn out the dough* onto a lightly floured work surface and divide into 2 equal portions. Form into 2 tight round loaves and place on a greased or parchment-lined baking sheet. Cover loosely with plastic wrap and let rise at room temperature until puffy but not quite doubled in bulk, about 30 minutes. These loaves will expand considerably in the oven. Meanwhile, preheat the oven to 375°.

5. *Bake in the center* of the preheated oven until the loaves are golden brown and sound hollow when tapped, 35 to 40 minutes. Remove from the pan and place on a rack over a piece of waxed paper to catch the drips while glazing.

6. *To prepare the glaze:* In a small bowl, combine the powdered sugar, milk or liqueur, and the vanilla, if using milk. Whisk to form a glaze that is smooth and thick, but pourable. Adjust the consistency of the glaze by adding more liquid a few drops at a time. Pour the glaze over the still-hot loaves, letting it drip down the sides. Let cool completely before slicing.

To Decorate Pan de Muerto in the Traditional Manner

In Step 4, divide the dough into 3 portions, with 2 larger portions equal in size to form the loaves and a small piece for the decorations. Refrigerate the small piece. Form the remaining 2 portions into round loaves and place on a baking sheet as directed. (These portions may also be formed into thick crucifixes.) Press on both loaves to form flattish rounds no more than 1 inch thick.

Remove the reserved dough from the refrigerator and place on the work surface. Divide the dough in half, then divide each half into 4 equal pieces. Working with 4 of the pieces, make the "bones" by rolling 2 pieces of dough into fat cylinders, then rolling with your hands to lengthen in the middle. To make the "skull," form 1 piece into a ball. To form the "tears," break the remaining piece into small pieces and roll each of them into a small ball, pinching the ends. Place the "skull" on 1 of the loaves, cross the "bones" around it, and sprinkle the "tears" in the empty spaces. Press firmly to adhere the decorations to the loaf, then glaze with a mixture of 1 egg beaten with 1 teaspoon milk or water. Repeat with the remaining 4 pieces and the remaining loaf. Let the loaves rise as in step 4.

Dried-Chile Brioche

*The shiny mahogany-colored dried Anaheim chile is a staple in my kitchen and is a
gently aromatic dried pepper, with a fragrance likened to spicy raisins. It is about six inches long and
two inches wide and is the chile commonly strung into ristras (ropes) in the Southwest. The batter is made in an
electric mixer for easiest handling, risen, and chilled overnight before forming, so plan accordingly.*

YIELD: 16 SMALL BRIOCHES

4½ cups unbleached all-purpose flour
   (exact measure)

3 tablespoons fine-grind blue or
   yellow cornmeal

1 package (1 tablespoon) active dry yeast

1 tablespoon sugar

2 teaspoons salt

¼ cup hot water (120°)

⅓ cup Dried-Chile Paste (following), heated
   to 100° to 120°

5 eggs, at room temperature

1 cup (2 sticks) unsalted butter, at room
   temperature, cut into small pieces

2 tablespoons fine-grind blue or yellow
   cornmeal, for sprinkling

2 tablespoons milk or cream, for brushing

1. In the bowl of a heavy-duty mixer fitted with a paddle attachment, combine 1 cup of the flour, the 3 tablespoons cornmeal, yeast, sugar, and salt. Add the hot water and chile paste. Beat at medium speed until smooth, about 2 minutes.

2. Add the eggs, one at a time, beating well after each addition. Gradually add 2 cups more of the flour. When well blended, add the butter, a few pieces at a time. Beat just until completely incorporated. Reduce the speed to low and gradually add the remaining 1½ cups flour, ¼ cup at a time. Beat until thoroughly blended and creamy in consistency. The dough will be very soft and have a batterlike consistency.

3. Using a large spatula or dough scraper, scrape the dough into a greased bowl. Cover tightly with plastic wrap and let rise at cool room temperature until doubled in bulk, about 3 hours. Gently deflate the dough with a spatula to release excess air, cover tightly, and refrigerate for 12 hours or overnight. (The dough may be frozen at this point up to 2 weeks. When ready to use, place in the refrigerator to thaw for 1 day.)

4. Using a dough scraper, turn out the chilled dough onto a lightly floured work surface. Divide it into 4 equal portions. Working quickly, use your palms to roll each portion into a rope about 12 inches long and 1 inch in diameter. Divide each rope into four 3-inch pieces. Shape each piece into a ball with your palms. You will have 16 balls. Do not worry if the rolls vary slightly in size. Place them in well-buttered 3½-inch fluted molds or standard muffin cups that have been sprinkled with the 2 tablespoons cornmeal. (It is convenient to place the individual molds on a baking sheet for easier handling.) Let rise at *cool* room temperature until doubled in bulk, about 45 minutes. Do not worry if the rising takes longer. Take note that the butter will separate from the dough if it is risen in the traditional "warm place" called for in most bread recipes. Twenty minutes before baking, preheat the oven to 400°.

5. Gently brush each brioche with some milk or cream and, using kitchen shears, snip 3 cuts on top of each brioche to form little peaks. Bake in the center of the preheated oven until golden brown, 10 to 15 minutes. Remove from the molds to a rack to cool slightly before eating. The brioches are best served warm or reheated.

Dried-Chile Paste

Anaheim chiles go under several names, includ-ing California, New Mexico, and Rio Grande chiles. They can be found in the ethnic section of most supermarkets.

YIELD: ABOUT 1/2 CUP

4 whole dried Anaheim chiles
Boiling water, to cover

1. *Preheat the oven* to 450°. Remove the stems from the chiles, then slit the chiles and scrape out the seeds. Place the chiles on a baking sheet and roast in the preheated oven until they are puffed, fragrant, and slightly dried out, 1 to 2 minutes. Place the roasted chiles in a bowl and add boiling water to cover. Soak 2 hours.

2. *Drain the chiles* and purée in a food processor fitted with the metal blade or in a blender. Push the purée through a fine-mesh sieve to separate the skin from the flesh; discard the skin. Store in a covered container in the refrigerator up to 5 days or freeze up to 3 months.

Cornmeal and Pine Nut Dinner Twists

Here is a sweet dinner roll that is beautiful to look at and fun to shape.
If possible, for an extra flavor treat, use fresh stone-ground yellow cornmeal (also known as
johnnycake meal) from a small grist mill such as Gray's (508-636-6075) or Kenyon (401-783-4054)
in New England, or blue cornmeal from Casados Farm in New Mexico (505-852-2433).
Serve with a tangy New England classic, Crowley cheese, or the Mozzarella Company's ancho
chile cheese, available at your local specialty cheese shop.

YIELD: 20 ROLLS

1 cup pine nuts
4½ to 5 cups unbleached all-purpose flour
1¼ cups fine- or medium-grind yellow, blue, or
   white cornmeal, preferably stone-ground
1 tablespoon salt
1½ tablespoons (1½ packages) active
   dry yeast
2 cups hot water (120°)
4 tablespoons (½ stick) unsalted butter, melted
⅓ cup honey
Melted unsalted butter, for brushing

1. *Preheat the oven* to 350°. Place the pine nuts on a baking sheet and toast in the preheated oven until lightly golden, 8 to 10 minutes. Set aside to cool.

2. *In a large bowl* with a whisk or in the work bowl of a heavy-duty electric mixer fitted with the paddle attachment, combine 1 cup of the flour, the cornmeal, salt, and yeast. Add the hot water, the 4 tablespoons butter, and the honey and beat hard until creamy, about 2 minutes. Add the toasted pine nuts and the remaining unbleached flour, ½ cup at a time, until a soft dough is formed that just clears the sides of the bowl, switching to a wooden spoon as necessary if making by hand.

3. *Turn out the dough* onto a lightly floured work surface and knead until soft, springy, and slightly sticky to the touch, 2 to 3 minutes, adding only 1 tablespoon flour at a time as necessary to prevent sticking. The dough should have a rough, tacky quality. Place in a greased deep container, turn once to coat the top, and cover with plastic wrap. Let rise at room temperature until doubled in bulk, 1 to 1½ hours.

4. *Turn out the dough* onto the work surface and divide into 4 equal portions. Divide each portion into 5 equal pieces; you will have 20 pieces in all. Form each portion into a ball and, using your palms, roll it into a 10-inch-long rope. Tie the rope in a loose knot, leaving the two long ends hanging. Tuck the top end under the knot and the bottom end up and over the knot, tucking them into the center of the roll to form bowknots. Place 2 inches apart on a greased or parchment-lined baking sheet. Brush the tops with melted butter and cover loosely with plastic wrap. Let rise at room temperature until doubled in bulk, about 45 minutes. Twenty minutes before baking, preheat the oven to 375°.

5. *Bake in the center* of the preheated oven until browned, 15 to 18 minutes. Remove to a rack to cool 15 minutes, then serve warm. Or let cool completely and reheat before serving.

Wild Rice Country Rolls

Exotic-tasting wild rice transforms these crusty peasant rolls into chewy, nourishing delights.
A few snips of your kitchen shears form them into charming flower-shaped rounds. Serve these rolls throughout
the holidays with roasts, cheeses, and stews. Or set them out for breakfast or tea with Cherry Chèvre (page 163), an enticing
butter-and-cheese spread adapted from a recipe of California goat cheese maven Laura Chenel. These rolls
are so good, be prepared for each guest to eat more than one or two.

YIELD: 20 DINNER ROLLS OR 4 ROUND LOAVES

1½ tablespoons (1½ packages) active
    dry yeast
2 tablespoons maple syrup or granulated
    maple sugar
2¼ cups warm water (105° to 115°)
1½ cups cooled, cooked wild rice (page 108)
1 tablespoon salt
2½ cups whole-wheat flour
2 to 2½ cups unbleached all-purpose or
    bread flour
Yellow cornmeal, for sprinkling

1. In a small bowl, sprinkle the yeast and 1 teaspoon of the maple syrup or a pinch of the sugar over ½ cup of the warm water. Stir to dissolve. Let stand until foamy, about 10 minutes.

2. In a large bowl with a whisk or in the work bowl of a heavy-duty electric mixer fitted with the paddle attachment, combine the remaining 1¾ cup warm water, the remaining maple syrup or sugar, the wild rice, salt, and whole-wheat flour. Beat until smooth, about 1 minute. Add the yeast mixture and 1 cup of the unbleached flour. Beat 30 seconds longer. Add the remaining unbleached flour, ¼ cup at a time, until a soft dough is formed that just clears the sides of the bowl, switching to a wooden spoon as necessary if making by hand.

3. Turn out the dough onto a lightly floured work surface and knead until springy and smooth, 1 to 2 minutes, adding only 1 tablespoon flour at a time as necessary to prevent sticking. The dough will be slightly dense and retain a moist quality under the smooth surface. Do not add too much flour or the bread will be dry. Sprinkle the top with a bit of flour. Place in a greased deep container and cover with plastic wrap. Let rise at room temperature until doubled in bulk, 1 to 1½ hours.

4. Turn out the dough onto the work surface and divide into 4 equal portions. Divide each portion into 5 equal portions; you will have 20 pieces in all. Shape into round balls, tucking the ends under to smooth the tops. Press to flatten slightly. Place seam side down and 1 inch apart on 2 greased or parchment-lined baking sheets sprinkled with cornmeal. Alternatively, to make round loaves, form the 4 portions into 4 tight rounds and place on the prepared baking sheets. Cover loosely with plastic wrap and let rise until almost doubled in bulk, 30 to 40 minutes. Twenty minutes before baking, preheat the oven to 400°, using a baking stone, if desired.

5. Using floured kitchen shears, snip each roll in 5 places around the outside, cutting from the edge completely through almost to the center. The dough will stay connected at the center, much like a flower or the hub of a wheel. This is most efficiently done by turning the roll with one hand while snipping with the other. Dust the tops of the rolls with flour. Bake on the lower and upper racks of the preheated oven, switching their positions halfway through the baking, until lightly brown around the edges, 18 to 22 minutes. The round loaves will bake in about 35 minutes. Let cool 10 minutes, then serve warm.

Winter Darkness

In winter, the days are short and darkness comes early. Referred to as the most powerful time of year by ancient peoples, the winter solstice contains recurring cycles of myth, folklore, and symbolism still intimately connected to the harmony of nature, even as it lies dormant. Festive breads were often a strong focal point for winter religious practices. Hearty breads rich in grains are served warm to help nourish and sustain us in the cold environment. ℂ There is great energy underground, and feasts feature slow-cooked root vegetables—beets, carrots, parsnips, turnips, potatoes, yams, and onions. In milder climates, such as the Mediterranean, Mexico, Arizona, and Florida, citrus orchards are flourishing and markets are flooded with tangerines, oranges, tangelos, limes, lemons, grapefruit, and mandarins. ℂ In December and January, the California olive country is flush with the ripening of the Manzanillo, Mission, and Sevillano varieties. The black stone-fruits produce an oil that is mellow and golden in contrast to the distinctive jade-green hue and more fruity flavor of oil drawn from green September olives. Originally planted by the Spanish Franciscans during the California mission period, California olives are pressed into oils that provide strong competition for the ancient-lineage olive oils of Spain, Greece, France, and Italy. ℂ The four Sundays before Christmas mark the Christian period of Advent and the baker's art blossoms at this darkest, yet most festive time of year. The passionate baker goes into high gear for the holidays with fluted babkas, sugar-encrusted loaves, bejeweled yeast buns, and nostalgia's beloved child, the liqueur-soaked, fruit-packed loaf. The way these breads look is just as important as how they taste. For me, most commercial candied fruits have fallen out of flavor, and I now prefer spice-scented doughs to be full of glistening natural dried fruits and nuts. The combination of dried currants, apples, raisins, cherries, and prunes is a colorful mosaic of texture and flavor in my Dried Fruit and Nut Baguettes (page 132), loaves that are perfect with wine and cheese. ⁋ Guadalupe Day, December 12, is the Mexican festival honoring the country's patron saint, the Virgin of Guadalupe. Dressed in colorful peasant finery, somber religious processionals carrying flower-bedecked shrines and candles move through the streets of towns throughout Mexico. My Mexican Sweet Bread (page 156), laced with glossy, honey-glazed dried fruits, is a distinctive holiday loaf. ⁋ The Feast of Saint Lucia is an exciting prelude to Christmas for the Swedish. It opens the holiday season on December 13, the longest night of the year by the old calendars. The word Lucia comes from the Latin lux, which means "light." On this day, young girls, dressed as the early Christian miracle worker in long white robes with a red sash and a crown of green lingonberry sprigs topped with lighted candles, serve other members of their households coffee and lussekattor (Lucia buns scented with saffron). The gently golden, double S—shaped little sweet breads are probably one of the most widely recognized in the vast repertoire of home-baked Svensk bröds, appearing here as my Saffron-Currant Buns (page 138). ⁋ The winter solstice falls just a few cold, dark days before Christmas Eve, once observed as Adam and Eve Day. Scandinavian bakers are busy preparing a beautiful array of holiday rye breads, many of them flavored with orange and barley malt extract, and their wonderful assortment of coffee breads seasoned with cardamom, almonds, or saffron. On Christmas morning, each family member is presented with the julhög, a stack of breads specially baked for the occasion, a tradition left over from times of scarcity. The table is set with big red apples, saffron buns with raisins, white bread with sugar and almond toppings, and a bittersweet molasses rye bread, such as limpa. ⁋ Norwegian dinners include stacks of homemade lefse, a yeast flat bread, alongside a beautiful stave-constructed wooden tub filled with fresh butter. Lefse is rolled out with a grooved rolling pin, then baked on a hearth plate placed directly over the coals. Whatever is extra is stacked in storehouses and carried as needed in traditional birch baskets. Julkuse are made from cardamom-scented sweet dough in the shape of farm animals, a practice left over from pre-Christian times when animals were sacrificed to appease the gods. To give your Scandinavian breads a more rustic dimension bake them on clean oat straw, which imparts a smoky fragrance. Soak a dozen stalks and trim to fit on a parchment-lined baking sheet to form a single layer. Place the shaped dough on top of the straw, taking care not to have any overhang. Clean oat straw is available during the holiday season from handicraft stores. ⁋ German Christmas specialties are worth the wait all year, and each town has its Christmas Market, or Weihnachtsmarkt, where handmade ornaments, painted nutcrackers, multicolored marzipan confections, loaves of stollen rich with rum-soaked fruits, hand-dipped candles, and evergreen wreaths from local artisans are sold. The air is scented with fresh gingerbread and roasting chestnuts. The twelve days of Christmas between December 25 and January 6 are sacred to Frau Holle, the Old Hag of winter who reigned over the regeneration of nature in Austrian, German, and Swiss folktales. All grains were hand-ground at this time. Her feast day is celebrated on the winter solstice, and a bread known as Hollenzopf, or "Frau Hollen's braid," is baked. ⁋ On Christmas Eve in Provence the table is laid with a centerpiece of Provence's famous wheat. Thirteen desserts are made to symbolize Christ, his apostles, and the journey of the Magi. Pompe à l'huile, a rustic fougasse of orange flower water and olive oil slashed in several places to form an open lattice, is always one of the desserts. It is broken by hand to ensure good luck in the New Year. Les mendiants—almonds, hazelnuts, raisins, and dried figs—are the mandatory baking ingredients for the rest of the desserts, and they also appear in a number of European winter breads, suggesting the colors of the robes worn by the humble Carmelite, Augustinian, Dominican, and Franciscan monks. ❦ The tall, domed Italian panettone is a continental masterpiece that originated in Milan. Pan dolce, made by the Ligurians, is hauntingly similar to panettone, except that it is made in round free-form loaves. Buccellato, a ring bread flavored with anise and sweet wine; pane al cioccolato, a chocolate yeast bread; pandoro di Verona, the traditional golden bread of Verona that is baked in a spectacular star tin mold; and ciambella mandorlata (page 131), a sublime almond ring cake, are just a few more dazzling handiworks of the Italian baker. Look for the marca di pane, the imprint of a baker's hand or family crest or initials, upon homemade loaves. A trademark New Year's Eve loaf is pan pepato, or pampepato, a medieval sweet bread from Ferrara in the province of Emilia-Romagna. It was originally baked into the shape of a priest's cap (which later became the toque blanche trademark cap of the chef), and contains a mouth-watering blend of cocoa, honey, almonds, sweet spices, and pepper. ❦ At Christmas, the Greeks serve Christópsomo, decorating with a Byzantine cross of anise dough and unshelled walnuts for good fortune. The cross is a universal visual representation of communication between heaven and earth, and is a common decoration for Greek breads. Versions include combinations of raisins, dried figs, and dried apricots with pine nuts, walnuts, sesame seeds, or almonds. Flavorings are predominantly fresh orange, with undertones of ground bay, cloves, or cinnamon. ❆ January 1 is Saint Basil's Day in Greece, and it is celebrated with the baking of vasilopitta, to honor the Orthodox Patriarch and his fellow monks, Saint John and Saint Gregory. It is traditionally baked in a round pan called a tapsi and topped with sesame seeds. A foil-wrapped coin or trinket (or more commonly nowadays, a whole pecan) is embedded in the bread for a lucky diner to discover, a custom in memory of the saint's timely rescue from Roman looters long ago. The bread is broken apart just after midnight, with the first piece reserved for the saint, the second for the poor, and the third for an elder. ❆ On January 6, Twelfth Night, the last party of the Christmas season is known variously as King's Day, Día de Los Santos, or Feast of the Epiphany. The Portuguese bake a loaf known as festa do Natal or bolo-rei, rich in eggs, butter, candied fruits, and shaped into a ring to symbolize the crowns worn by the Magi on this day. A raw fava bean is embedded in the unbaked bread and the person who finds it must either buy or make the next year's loaf or host a party for Candlemas four weeks later. The same wreath-shaped loaf and hidden token shows up in Germany and Switzerland as Dreikönigsbrot, in Hispanic baking as rosca de reyes, and in French baking as gateau de roi, which contains a fabulous precious jewel. The French loaf was created by a sixteenth-century monk for a Louvre palace feast. It was made from a savarin dough and baked in an octagonal mold, resulting in a loaf markedly similar to the Roman Janus flat breads of earlier centuries. ❆ Valentine's Day on February 14 finds bakers reshaping their wreaths into hearts and tucking in red fillings, such as sour cherry preserves. Throughout the centuries, Valentine's Day has become more romantic, with gift giving—often a poetic bread or sweet confection—a ritual.

Ciambella Mandorlata

*A ciambella is a "ring cake," and throughout Italy the baked braided wreath
is a symbol of the holiday season. In France, the ring shape, known as a couronne, is affectionately
called la baisure, or the "kissing crust." Cultivated since prehistoric times, the almond is an irresistible addition
to breads in the form of both the kernel and the perfumed extract. Serve this handsome loaf
with jam and Italian roast coffee.*

YIELD: 1 LARGE LOAF

1 tablespoon (1 package) active dry yeast
½ cup sugar
1 tablespoon fresh grated lemon zest
1½ teaspoons salt
4½ to 5 cups unbleached all-purpose flour
1 cup milk
½ cup water
5 tablespoons unsalted butter or good-quality
    olive oil
1 tablespoon pure almond extract
3 eggs

Almond Crust
¼ cup sugar cubes or coarse raw sugar
½ cup raw almonds
Pinch of ground cinnamon
1 egg beaten with 1 teaspoon water, for glaze

1. In a large mixing bowl with a whisk or in the work bowl of a heavy-duty electric mixer fitted with the paddle attachment, combine the yeast, sugar, lemon zest, salt, and 2 cups of the flour. In a small saucepan, combine the milk, water, and butter or oil and heat until just hot. Stir to melt the butter, if used. Let cool to 120°.

2. Add the warm milk mixture, almond extract, and eggs to the dry mixture and beat hard until creamy, 1 minute. Add the remaining flour, ½ cup at a time, until a soft dough is formed that just clears the sides of the bowl, switching to a wooden spoon as necessary if making by hand.

3. Turn out the dough onto a lightly floured work surface and knead until smooth, springy, and soft, about 2 minutes, adding only 1 tablespoon flour at a time as necessary to prevent sticking. Transfer to a greased deep container, turn once to coat the top, and cover with plastic wrap. Let rise in a warm place until doubled in bulk, 1½ to 2 hours. Deflate the dough and let rise again until doubled in bulk, 1 to 1¼ hours.

4. While the dough is rising, make the almond crust. In a food processor fitted with the metal blade, combine the sugar cubes,

almonds, and cinnamon. Process until the sugar and almonds are finely chopped. (If using coarse sugar, it can still be processed with the almonds.) Do not overprocess. Set aside.

5. Turn out the dough onto the work surface and divide it into 3 equal portions. To shape the braided wreath, using your palms, roll each portion into a rope about 30 inches long. Lay the ropes side by side and braid together firmly. Place in a loose ring on a greased or parchment-lined baking sheet or 15-inch pizza pan. Press the ends together, sealing with a few drops of water, if necessary. Loosely cover with plastic wrap and let rise until almost doubled in bulk, no more than 40 minutes. Twenty minutes before baking, preheat the oven to 350°.

6. Brush the entire surface of the wreath with the egg glaze. Sprinkle with the almond crust mixture. Bake the bread in the center of the preheated oven until it is browned and sounds hollow when tapped, 40 to 45 minutes. Using a spatula, remove to a rack to cool completely before serving in small slices.

Dried Fruit and Nut Baguettes

The holiday peasant bread, known as bièrewecke in France, is a dense
packing of dried fruits held together by a simple unsweetened yeast dough. If you like your fruits more
spirited, spike the raisins and cherries by macerating them in a few tablespoons of pear or
raspberry eau-de-vie for an hour before mixing them into the dough.

YIELD: 3 BAGUETTES

1 tablespoon (1 package) active dry yeast

1 teaspoon sugar or honey

2¼ cups warm water (105° to 115°)

1½ cups (6 ounces) walnuts or pecans

2 cups whole-wheat flour

½ cup dry buttermilk powder

2 tablespoons sugar or honey

1 tablespoon salt

1 egg

3½ to 3¾ cups unbleached all-purpose or
   bread flour

¾ cup (2½ ounces) dried apples, finely
   chopped

¾ cup (5 ounces) moist pitted prunes, chopped

½ cup golden raisins

½ cup pitted dried cherries

⅓ cup dried currants

Unbleached flour, for dusting

1. In a small bowl, sprinkle the yeast and the 1 teaspoon sugar or honey over ½ cup of the warm water. Stir to dissolve. Let stand until foamy, about 10 minutes. In a food processor fitted with the metal blade, combine ¾ cup of the nuts and 1 cup of the whole-wheat flour. Process until a nut flour is formed, about 10 seconds.

2. In a mixing bowl with a whisk or in the work bowl of a heavy-duty electric mixer fitted with the paddle attachment, combine the remaining 1 cup whole-wheat flour and 1¾ cups warm water, the nut flour, dry butter-milk powder, salt, the 2 tablespoons sugar or honey, egg, and 1 cup of the unbleached flour. Beat hard for 1 minute. Add the yeast mixture and beat again for 1 minute. Add the remaining unbleached flour, ½ cup at a time, until a soft dough is formed that just clears the sides of the bowl, switching to a wooden spoon as necessary if making by hand.

3. Turn out the dough onto a lightly floured work surface and knead until soft, smooth, and elastic, 1 to 2 minutes, adding only 1 tablespoon flour at a time as necessary to prevent sticking. Too much flour will toughen the dough; it should feel sticky. Place in an oiled deep container, turn once to coat the top, and cover with plastic wrap. Let rise at room temperature until doubled in bulk, 1½ to 2 hours. Gently deflate and let rise again until doubled in bulk, about 1 hour.

4. Combine the apples or pears, prunes, raisins, cherries and the remaining ¾ cup nuts in a bowl and toss to mix evenly. Turn out the dough onto the work surface and pat into a large oval. Sprinkle with half of the fruits, pressing them into the dough. Fold the dough in half and sprinkle with the rest of the fruit mixture. Fold again and knead gently to dis-tribute the fruits and nuts evenly. Press back any fruits that fall out during the kneading. Cover the dough with a clean towel and let rest on the work table 15 minutes.

5. Divide the dough into 3 equal portions. Pat each portion into a rectangle and, starting from a long side, roll up into a 14-inch-long cylinder to form a baguette, pinching the seams together to seal. Place seam side down on 2 greased or parchment-lined baking sheets or in 3 baguette molds. Dust the surfaces heavily with a layer of flour. Cover loosely with plastic wrap and let rise at room temper-ature until doubled in bulk, about 1 hour. Twenty minutes before baking, preheat the oven to 400°, with a baking stone, if desired.

6. Using a serrated knife, slash the surface of each loaf a few times on the diagonal no more than ¼ inch deep. Bake in the center of the preheated oven until the breads are well browned and sound hollow when tapped, 35 to 40 minutes. Remove to a rack to cool com-pletely before slicing.

Roasted-Chestnut Bread

Chestnuts are a sweet, starchy, yet low fat fall nut with a crunch and tough outer shell;
they must be cooked before using in recipes. Chestnut flour, ground from dried chestnuts, is nutty in flavor,
silky in texture, and must be stored in the refrigerator for freshness, as it is highly perishable.
High-quality imported chestnut flour is available through Chestnut Hill Orchards, 3300 Bee Cave Road,
Austin, Texas, 78746 (800-745-3279/512-477-3020). Use a nectar-flavored honey from France,
such as mild lavender, or a good local honey.

YIELD: 2 ROUND LOAVES

15 raw chestnuts (about 8 ounces)
1 tablespoon (1 package) active dry yeast
¼ teaspoon fresh ground nutmeg
2 teaspoons salt
½ cup chestnut flour
4½ to 5 cups unbleached all-purpose or
    bread flour
¾ cup milk
¾ cup water
¼ cup mild honey
½ cup (1 stick) unsalted butter, at room
    temperature
3 eggs
Plain or vanilla powdered sugar, for dusting
    (optional)

1. Preheat the oven to 400°. To prepare the chestnuts for baking, using a short-bladed or chestnut knife, carve an X onto the flat side of each nut to prevent it from bursting. Place in a single layer on a baking sheet and roast in the preheated oven for 15 to 20 minutes. Alternatively, they may be cooked in the microwave for about 5 minutes at full power. The nuts should be mealy in the center when pierced with the tip of a knife. Remove immediately from the baking sheet to a thick, clean cloth. When barely cool enough to handle, crack the nuts with your hands and then use the same knife to peel off the outer shell and then the thin inner skin. (At this point you may cover the whole nuts tightly and refrigerate until needed.) Coarsely chop the nuts and set aside. (Commercial fresh-frozen steam-peeled chestnuts may be substituted.)

2. In a large mixing bowl with a whisk or in the work bowl of a heavy-duty electric mixer fitted with the paddle attachment, combine the yeast, nutmeg, salt, chestnut flour, and 2 cups of the unbleached flour. In a small saucepan, combine the milk, water, honey, and butter and heat until just hot. Stir to melt the butter. Let cool to 120°.

3. Add the hot milk mixture to the dry ingredients and beat hard until creamy, about 1 minute. Beat in the eggs and chopped chestnuts. Add the remaining unbleached flour,

½ cup at a time, until a soft dough is formed that just clears the sides of the bowl, switching to a wooden spoon as necessary if making by hand.

4. Turn out the dough onto a lightly floured work surface and knead until smooth, springy, and soft, about 3 minutes, adding only 1 tablespoon flour at a time as necessary to prevent sticking. Push back any nuts that fall out during kneading. Transfer the dough to a greased deep container, turn once to coat the top, and cover with plastic wrap. Let rise at room temperature until doubled in bulk, 1½ to 2 hours.

5. Turn out the dough onto the work surface and divide into 2 equal portions. Form each into a tight round ball and place at least 3 inches apart on a greased or parchment-lined baking sheet. Using a serrated knife, cut an X ½ inch deep into the top of each loaf. Cover loosely with plastic wrap and let rise again at room temperature until doubled in bulk, about 45 minutes. Twenty minutes before baking, preheat the oven to 350°.

6. Bake in the center of the preheated oven until the loaves are browned and sound hollow when tapped, 35 to 40 minutes. Remove from the baking sheets immediately to racks to cool completely before slicing. Dust the loaves with powdered sugar before serving, if desired.

Pernod Panettone

Said to have been fashioned by a humble baker's apprentice to impress a prospective marriage partner, panettone is a specialty of Milan. Serve the bread on Christmas Eve, Venetian style, with the tall loaf scooped out, filled with vanilla ice cream, and served with a hot bittersweet chocolate sauce and cups of camomilla tea. Day-old panettone makes a sublime main ingredient in your favorite bread pudding recipe.

YIELD: 2 MEDIUM ROUND OR I TALL LOAF

½ cup golden raisins
½ cup snipped dried apricots
½ cup Pernod liqueur
1 tablespoon (1 package) active dry yeast
Pinch of sugar
¼ cup warm water (105° to 115°)
1 cup warm milk (105° to 115°)
½ cup (1 stick) unsalted butter, melted
⅓ cup sugar
1 teaspoon salt
2 eggs
2 tablespoons Pernod liqueur
About 4 cups unbleached all-purpose flour
¼ cup pine nuts
¼ cup slivered blanched almonds
3 tablespoons sugar, for glaze

1. *In a small bowl*, combine the dried fruits and the ½ cup Pernod. Let stand for 1 hour.

2. *In another small bowl*, sprinkle the yeast and the pinch of sugar over the warm water. Stir to dissolve. Let stand until foamy, about 10 minutes.

3. *In a large bowl* with a whisk or in the work bowl of a heavy-duty electric mixer fitted with the paddle attachment, combine the warm milk, butter, the ⅓ cup sugar, and salt. Add the eggs, the 2 tablespoons Pernod, and 1 cup of the flour, and beat until smooth and creamy, about 1 minute. Add the yeast mixture and 1 cup more of the flour. Beat 1 minute longer. Drain the fruits, reserving the liqueur for the glaze. Add the fruits, pine nuts, and almonds; add the remaining flour, ½ cup at a time, until a soft dough is formed that just clears the sides of the bowl, with the solids evenly distributed. Switch to a wooden spoon as necessary if making by hand.

4. *Turn out the dough* onto a lightly floured work surface and knead until smooth and springy, about 3 minutes, adding only 1 table-spoon flour at a time as necessary to prevent sticking. Push back any fruits that fall out of the dough during kneading. The dough should remain soft. Place the dough in a greased deep container, turn once to coat the top, and cover with plastic wrap. Let rise at room temperature until doubled in bulk, about 2 hours.

5. *Turn out the dough* onto the work surface and divide into 2 equal portions for round loaves, or leave in one piece for a tall loaf. Form each of the 2 portions into a tight round ball and place at least 3 inches apart on a greased or parchment-lined baking sheet. Using a serrated knife, cut an X ½ inch deep into the top of each loaf. To make a cylindrical loaf, place the whole amount of dough in a greased *panettone* mold or 2-pound coffee can. Cover loosely with plastic wrap and let rise again at room temperature until doubled in bulk, about 45 minutes. Twenty minutes before baking, preheat the oven to 375°.

6. *Bake in the low center* of the preheated oven until the bread(s) is browned and sounds hollow when tapped, 40 to 45 minutes. Remove from the baking sheet or mold to a rack.

7. *While the bread(s) is still warm*, prepare the glaze. Combine the reserved liqueur and add enough water to equal ¼ cup. (If all the liqueur has been absorbed by the fruits, combine 2 tablespoons water with 2 tablespoons Pernod.) Place in a small saucepan and add the 3 tablespoons sugar; heat, stirring just until the sugar dissolves. Brush the warm bread(s) twice all over and let stand to dry completely before serving.

Carrot and Poppy Seed Twists

This loaf has a warm, haunting aroma that is akin to a delicate nocturnal floral fragrance.
Handle it gently while it is still warm, however, as it is quite tender. It freezes perfectly and is great toasted.

YIELD: 2 LARGE TWISTS

2 tablespoons (2 packages) active dry yeast
1 teaspoon light brown sugar
1 cup warm water (105° to 115°)
¾ cup mashed or puréed cooked carrot
    (about 2 medium carrots), or one 6-ounce
    jar junior baby food carrots
2 eggs
½ cup light brown sugar
⅓ cup dry buttermilk powder
2 teaspoons salt
1 cup whole-wheat pastry flour
4⅓ to 4⅔ cups unbleached all-purpose or
    bread flour
½ cup (1 stick) unsalted butter, at room
    temperature, cut into pieces

Cinnamon–Poppy Seed Paste
One 12-ounce can poppy seed filling
1 egg yolk
2 tablespoons golden rum
1 teaspoon ground cinnamon
About ⅓ cup crushed twice-baked cookie
    crumbs, such as zweiback, *biscotti,* or
    Swedish rusks
⅔ cup chopped almonds
⅔ cup golden raisins

Plain or vanilla powdered sugar, for dusting

1. In a small bowl, sprinkle the yeast and the 1 teaspoon brown sugar over the warm water. Stir to dissolve. Let stand until foamy, about 10 minutes.

2. In a large bowl using a whisk or in the work bowl of a heavy-duty electric mixer fitted with the paddle attachment, combine the carrot, eggs, the ½ cup brown sugar, buttermilk powder, salt, and whole-wheat pastry flour. Beat hard until creamy, about 1 minute. Add the yeast mixture and ½ cup of the unbleached flour. Beat for 1 minute longer. Add the butter pieces and beat until incorporated. Add the remaining unbleached flour, ½ cup at a time, until a soft dough is formed that just clears the sides of the bowl, switching to a wooden spoon as necessary if making by hand.

3. Turn out the dough onto a lightly floured work surface and knead until smooth and elastic, 1 to 2 minutes, adding only 1 tablespoon flour at a time as necessary to prevent sticking. Do not add too much flour or dough will be stiff and hard to work. Place in a greased deep container, turn once to coat the top, and cover with plastic wrap. Let rise at room temperature until doubled in bulk, 2 to 2½ hours. Do not worry if the dough takes longer to rise.

4. While the dough is rising, make the cinnamon–poppy seed paste. In a small bowl, beat together the poppy seed filling and egg yolk. Stir in the rum, cinnamon, and enough cookie crumbs to make a thick paste. Cover and refrigerate until needed.

5. Turn out the dough onto the work surface and divide into 4 equal portions. Pat each portion into a 6-by-14-inch rectangle and spread each one with one-fourth of the cinnamon–poppy seed paste, leaving a small border around the edges. Sprinkle 2 of the rectangles with the almonds and the other 2 rectangles with the raisins. Starting from a long edge, roll up each rectangle jelly-roll fashion to make 4 long rolls. Pinch the seams together to seal in the filling, taking care not to rip the dough. Place 2 rolls side by side and twist each around the other in a spiral fashion to form the loaf. Pinch the ends to seal and tuck under. Repeat with the second twist. Place each twist seam side down on a greased or parchment-lined baking sheet and compress each to form a compact 9-inch loaf. Cover loosely with plastic wrap and let rise at room temperature until doubled in bulk, about 1½ hours. Twenty minutes before baking, preheat the oven to 350°, with a baking stone, if desired.

6. Bake in the center of the preheated oven until the twists are well browned and a cake tester inserted into the center comes out clean, 30 to 35 minutes. Let stand for 10 minutes before removing with a spatula to a rack to cool completely. Dust with powdered sugar before slicing.

Bohemian Sweet Rolls

Luckily for us, Czech bakers have passed along a jewel of yeast pastry tradition, the kolachki. *These puffy, round feather-light buns, which conceal a dried fruit or cheese filling, are, along with gingerbread figures, favorite holiday tree ornaments. Be warned, though: one bite and you'll be hooked. My favorite filling is made with sour dried cherries, but any of the other fillings, such as apricot, cranberry, prune, peach, or ricotta cheese, is also wonderful. This is a classic.*

YIELD: 24 ROLLS

1 tablespoon (1 package) active dry yeast
3 tablespoons sugar
½ cup warm water (105° to 115°)
1½ cups milk (105° to 115°)
Grated zest of 1 lemon
2 eggs
1½ teaspoons salt
6 to 6½ cups unbleached all-purpose flour
½ cup (1 stick) unsalted butter, at room
   temperature, cut into pieces

Dried-Fruit Filling
8 ounces dried fruit, such as pitted dried
   cherries, apricots, peaches, cranberries,
   or prunes
2 tablespoons fruit brandy
⅓ cup sugar
Grated zest and juice of 1 lemon
2 tablespoons unsalted butter

Fresh Cheese Filling
1½ cups (12 ounces) ricotta cheese or
   fromage blanc
½ cup sugar
1 egg
1 teaspoon pure vanilla extract
Grated zest of 1 lemon

1. In a small bowl, sprinkle the yeast and a pinch of the sugar over the warm water. Stir to dissolve. Let stand until foamy, about 10 minutes.

2. In a large bowl with a whisk or in the work bowl of a heavy-duty electric mixer fitted with the paddle attachment, combine the remaining sugar, the warm milk, lemon zest, eggs, salt, and 2 cups of the flour. Beat hard for 1 minute. Add the yeast mixture and ½ cup more of the flour. Beat again for 1 minute. Add the butter pieces and beat until incorporated. Add the remaining flour, ½ cup at a time, until a soft dough is formed that just clears the sides of the bowl, switching to a wooden spoon as necessary if making by hand.

3. Turn out the dough onto a lightly floured work surface and knead until smooth and elastic, 1 to 2 minutes, adding only 1 tablespoon flour at a time as necessary to prevent sticking. Do not add too much flour or the bread will be dry. Place in a greased deep container, turn once to coat the top, and cover with plastic wrap. Let rise at room temperature until doubled in bulk, 1 to 1½ hours.

4. While the dough is rising, prepare the fruit or cheese filling. To make the fruit filling, in a small saucepan, combine the dried fruit of choice with a corresponding fruit brandy and water to cover. Bring to a boil, cover, and reduce the heat to low. Simmer until tender, about 20 minutes. Drain, reserving ¼ cup of the liquid. Combine the warm fruit, reserved liquid, sugar, lemon zest and juice, and butter in a food processor fitted with the metal blade and process just until smooth. For the cheese filling, combine all the ingredients in a food processor and purée just until smooth. Set aside or cover and refrigerate until needed.

5. Turn out the dough onto the work surface. Gently deflate the dough and divide into 2 equal portions. Divide each portion into 12 equal portions. Form each portion into a round ball. Flatten each ball into a disk about 3 inches in diameter. Arrange about 2 inches apart on two greased or parchment-lined baking sheets. Cover loosely with plastic wrap and let rise at room temperature until puffy, about 30 minutes. (The pastries may also rise overnight in the refrigerator.) Twenty minutes before baking, preheat the oven to 350°.

6. With your thumb or the back of a large spoon, press an indentation into the center of each roll to form a hollow. Spoon a heaping tablespoon of filling into each hollow. Bake one pan at a time in the center of the preheated oven until the rolls are golden brown, 20 to 25 minutes. Remove to a rack to cool. Serve warm or at room temperature.

Saffron-Currant Buns

*Here is my recipe for saffron-tinted Swedish Lucia buns. Although the most familiar shape is
a single or double serpentine twist, the buns are also formed into some of the most wonderful shapes in
bread baking. There is the Christmas wheel (back-to-back double crescent), the vicar's hair (a U-shaped mass to
represent layered curls), the curved V-shaped goat head with coils forming his horns, and the shepherd's star
(which looks like a Ferris wheel), all with dried currants dotting the multitude of furls.*

YIELD: 20 BUNS

½ cup whole-wheat pastry flour

⅓ cup almonds

1½ tablespoons (1½ packages) active
dry yeast

Pinch of sugar

½ cup warm water (105° to 115°)

¾ cup warm milk (105° to 115°)

⅛ teaspoon saffron threads, finely crumbled

½ cup sugar

2 eggs

1 teaspoon ground or freshly crushed
cardamom

1 teaspoon pure almond extract

2 teaspoons salt

4¾ to 5¼ cups unbleached all-purpose or
bread flour

½ cup (1 stick) unsalted butter, at room
temperature, cut into pieces

2 tablespoons dried currants

3 tablespoons unsalted butter, melted

1 egg beaten with 1 tablespoon water, for glaze

1. In a food processor fitted with the metal blade, combine the whole-wheat flour and the almonds and process until a coarse flour is formed. Set aside. In a small bowl, sprinkle the yeast and the pinch of sugar over the warm water. Stir to dissolve. Let stand until foamy, about 10 minutes. In another bowl, combine the warm milk with the saffron threads. Let steep 10 minutes.

2. In a large bowl with a whisk or in the work bowl of a heavy-duty electric mixer fitted with the paddle attachment, combine the ½ cup sugar, saffron milk, almond flour, 2 eggs, cardamom, almond extract, salt, and 1 cup of the unbleached flour. Beat hard until creamy, about 1 minute. Add the yeast mixture and ½ cup more flour. Beat 1 minute longer. Add the butter pieces and beat until incorporated. Add the remaining flour, ½ cup at a time, until a soft dough is formed that just clears the sides of the bowl, switching to a wooden spoon as necessary if making by hand.

3. Turn out the dough onto a lightly floured work surface and knead until smooth and elastic, 1 to 2 minutes, adding only 1 table-spoon flour at a time as necessary to prevent sticking. Do not add too much flour or the rolls will be tough. Place in a deep greased container, turn once to coat the top, and cover with plastic wrap. Let rise at room temperature until doubled in bulk, 1 to 1½ hours.

4. Turn out the dough onto a lightly floured work surface. Divide the dough into 2 equal portions. Then divide each portion into 10 equal portions. Using your palms, roll each portion into a 12-inch rope. To shape the Lucia cat, use a knife to cut each rope in half and then overlap the 2 pieces in the center to form an X. Coil to curl each end in the same direction. Press a currant in the center of each tight curl. Alternatively, to shape the vicar's hair, lay the ropes side by side, join them together into a U, and then coil the ends to make the vicar's beard. Or lay the ropes side by side and coil the ends away from each other, to form the Christmas wheel. Larger buns can be made by crossing 3 strands at the center and forming the coils in the same direction to make the shepherd's star. Arrange about 2 inches apart on a greased or parchment-lined baking sheet. Brush the surface of each roll lightly with some melted butter. Cover loosely with plastic wrap and let rise at room temperature until puffy, about 30 minutes. Twenty minutes before baking, preheat the oven to 350°.

5. Brush each bun with some egg glaze and push in any currants that have popped up. Bake in the center of the preheated oven until the rolls are golden brown, 18 to 20 minutes. Remove to a rack to cool. Serve warm or at room temperature.

White Fog Bread with Quinoa and Honey

The Newfoundland and Labrador coasts are populated with legions of hospitable home bakers, all making some version of white "fog" bread. The loaf has three distinct sections, which pull apart easily. One piece of the trisectional loaf is perfect for a fisherman to pack in his lunch pail. This is a very moist and chewy loaf.

YIELD: THREE 8-BY-4-INCH LOAVES

1 tablespoon (1 package) active dry yeast
Pinch of sugar or 1 teaspoon of honey
1 cup warm water (105° to 115°)
1 cup warm buttermilk (105° to 115°)
¼ cup honey
¼ cup cold-pressed sesame oil (*not* toasted sesame oil)
2½ teaspoons salt
1¾ cups cooled, cooked firmly packed quinoa (following)
5½ to 6 cups unbleached all-purpose or bread flour

1. In a small bowl, sprinkle the yeast and sugar or honey over the warm water. Stir to dissolve. Let stand until foamy, about 10 minutes.

2. In a large bowl with a whisk or in the work bowl of a heavy-duty electric mixer fitted with the paddle attachment, combine the buttermilk, the ¼ cup honey, oil, and salt. Add the quinoa and beat until smooth. Add the yeast mixture and 2 cups of the flour. Beat hard until smooth, about 2 minutes. Add the remaining flour, ½ cup at a time, until a soft, shaggy dough is formed that just clears the sides of the bowl, switching to a wooden spoon as necessary if mixing by hand.

3. Turn out the dough onto a lightly floured work surface and knead until firm, yet quite springy, about 3 minutes, adding only 1 tablespoon flour at a time as necessary to prevent sticking. The dough will retain a slightly sticky quality due to the whole grains. Place in a greased deep container, turn once to coat the top, and cover with plastic wrap. Let rise at warm room temperature until doubled in bulk, 1½ to 2 hours.

4. Turn out the dough onto a lightly floured work surface and divide into 3 equal portions. Then further divide each portion into 3 equal portions. You will have 9 equal portions in all. Flatten each portion into a small rectangle and roll up from a long side to form fat squares of dough. Repeat with 2 more portions, fitting

the three separate pieces side by side to fill the bottom of a greased 8-by-4-inch loaf pan. Flatten the remaining portions to form the other 2 pull-apart loaves. Cover loosely with plastic wrap and let rise at warm room temperature until doubled in bulk and about 1 inch above the rims of the pans, 1 to 1½ hours. Twenty minutes before baking, preheat the oven to 350°.

5. Bake in the center of the preheated oven until the loaves are brown and sound hollow when tapped, 40 to 45 minutes. Remove from the pans to a rack to cool completely before pulling apart to serve.

TO COOK QUINOA

Quinoa is mild-flavored, high in protein, and has a soft, yet slightly crunchy consistency.
YIELD: 3 TO 3 1/2 CUPS

2 cups water
1 cup quinoa, well rinsed

1. In a small saucepan over high heat, bring the water to a rolling boil. Add the quinoa and reduce the heat to the lowest setting. Cover and cook until the water is absorbed and the quinoa is tender, about 15 minutes.

2. Let stand off the heat 10 minutes before eating, or set aside to cool and/or chill until ready to use.

Blueberry Bread with Cardamom

This is a not-too-sweet, cardamom-laced fruit bread based on the Swedish julbröd or
Danish julekake loaves that are made in every household during the holidays. It is an egg bread that
is rich yet chewy, and the dried blueberries that lace it remind me of the wild cloudberries that grow close to the
Arctic Circle. Peel cardamom pods and crush the seeds in a mortar with a pestle for the most pronounced spice
flavor and aroma. Serve for New Year's Day with hot spiced apple juice and wedges of Cheddar cheese.

YIELD: TWO 8-BY-4-INCH LOAVES

¼ cup wheat berries

2 cups water

¾ cup (4 ounces) dried blueberries

¼ cup orange liqueur, such as Grand Marnier
  or Mandarin Napoleon

1 tablespoon (1 package) active dry yeast

Pinch of light brown sugar

½ cup warm water (105° to 115°)

½ cup warm milk (105° to 115°)

2 eggs

½ cup light brown sugar

4 tablespoons (½ stick) unsalted butter, melted

¼ cup vegetable oil

2 teaspoons ground cardamom (or crushed
  seeds from about 20 cardamom pods)

2 teaspoons salt

About 4 cups unbleached all-purpose or
  bread flour

1 egg white beaten with 1 teaspoon of water,
  for glaze

⅓ cup slivered or sliced almonds

2 tablespoons sugar mixed with 1/8 teaspoon
  ground cardamom, for topping

1. *In a medium saucepan*, combine the wheat berries and 2 cups water. Bring to a boil. Remove from the heat and let the berries soak for 1 hour. Return to a boil, immediately reduce the heat, cover, and simmer until tender, about 30 minutes. Add more water as needed to keep the berries covered. Drain and set aside to cool. You should have about ¾ cup. Meanwhile, in a small bowl, combine the dried blueberries and the orange liqueur. Macerate about 1 hour.

2. *In a large bowl* with a whisk or in the work bowl of a heavy-duty electric mixer fitted with the paddle attachment, sprinkle the yeast and the pinch of brown sugar over the warm water. Stir to dissolve. Let stand until foamy, about 10 minutes.

3. *Stir in the cooled wheat berries*, warm milk, eggs, the ½ cup brown sugar, butter, oil, cardamom, salt, and 1 cup of the flour. Beat hard until smooth, about 1 minute. Stir in the macerated blueberries and liqueur and the remaining flour, ½ cup at a time, until a soft dough is formed that just clears the sides of the bowl, switching to a wooden spoon as necessary if making by hand.

4. *Turn out the dough* onto a lightly floured work surface and knead until smooth and springy, about 3 minutes, adding only 1 tablespoon flour at a time as necessary to prevent sticking. The dough will have a nubby, tacky quality due to the whole grains. Place in a greased deep container, turn once to coat the top, and cover with plastic wrap. Let rise at room temperature until doubled in bulk, 1½ to 2 hours.

5. *Turn out the dough* onto the work surface and divide into 2 equal portions. Form into rectangular loaves and place in two 8-by-4-inch greased loaf pans. Cover loosely with plastic wrap and let rise at room temperature until the dough is about 1 inch above the rims of the pan, about 40 minutes. Twenty minutes before baking, preheat the oven to 350°.

6. *Using a serrated knife*, cut the tops decoratively, first lengthwise down the center, and then with 4 or 5 diagonal slits on either side of the central slash. The cuts should be no more than ¼ inch deep. Brush the tops with the egg white glaze and sprinkle each with the almonds and sugar mixture. Bake in the preheated oven until the loaves are browned and sound hollow when tapped, 40 to 45 minutes. Remove from the pans immediately to racks to cool completely before slicing.

Whole-Wheat Bread with Yogurt Starter

Known as le lait de la vie éternele *in France,* yourti *in Greece,* dahi *in India,*
and kisselo mleko *in Bulgaria, yogurt can be made from the milk of goats, sheep, or cows.*
The consistency of whole-grain flours can vary dramatically, so each time you make this loaf do not worry
if it feels slightly different. Serve with homemade Apricot-Piña Marmalade (page 163).

Yɪᴇʟᴅ: 2 ᴏʙʟᴏɴɢ ʟᴏᴀᴠᴇs

Yogurt Starter
1 teaspoon active dry yeast
¾ cup plain lowfat yogurt
1½ cups tepid bottled spring water (100°)
2 cups whole-wheat flour

Dough
2 teaspoons active dry yeast
2½ cups unbleached all-purpose or bread flour
1½ cups hot water (120°)
¼ cup light or dark brown sugar
⅓ cup olive oil
1 tablespoon salt
3½ to 3¾ cups whole-wheat flour

2 tablespoons yellow cornmeal, for sprinkling

1. To make the yogurt starter, in a plastic, ceramic or glass container (I use a 1-quart glass jar), whisk together the yeast, yogurt, lukewarm water, and whole-wheat flour until smooth. Scrape down the sides of the container with a spatula and cover with several thicknesses of 100-percent cotton cheesecloth. Do not cover with a tight-fitting lid, as the gases need to evaporate. Let stand at cool room temperature (75° to 85°) for 2 days (about 48 hours), stirring twice a day (the starter may be used any time after 12 hours, depending on the degree of tanginess you desire). The starter will rise and fall, form bubbles, and have a gentle grain-sweet fermented smell that recalls beer. Clear pools of liquid will form on the surface of the starter. If the liquid is blackish green, discard the starter and make a new batch. The starter may be refrigerated for another 24 hours, if needed, and brought to room temperature before using. You will have about 2 cups.

2. To prepare the dough: In a large bowl with a whisk or in the work bowl of a heavy-duty electric mixer fitted with the paddle attachment, combine the yeast and unbleached flour. Add the hot water, sugar, oil, and salt. Beat hard until smooth, about 1 minute. Add the yogurt starter and beat 1 minute longer. Add the whole-wheat flour, ½ cup at a time, until a soft, rather sticky dough is formed that just clears the sides of the bowl, switching to a wooden spoon as necessary if making by hand.

3. Turn out the dough onto a lightly floured work surface and knead until smooth and springy, yet slightly moist and with a definite sticky quality, about 3 minutes, adding only 1 tablespoon unbleached flour at a time as necessary to prevent the dough from sticking to the work surface. Do not add too much flour, as the dough must retain that definite stickiness, which will smooth out during the rising process. The dough will also have a slightly abrasive quality due to the whole grains. Place in a greased deep container, turn once to coat the top, and cover with plastic wrap. Let rise in a warm place until doubled in bulk, 1½ to 2 hours.

4. Turn out the dough onto the work surface and divide it into 2 equal portions. Shape into oblong loaves about 12 inches long and 4 inches wide and place at least 4 inches apart on a greased or parchment-lined baking sheet that has been sprinkled with cornmeal. Cover loosely with plastic wrap and let rise at room temperature until not quite doubled in bulk, about 45 minutes. (Alternatively, cover tightly and refrigerate 12 hours to overnight.) Twenty minutes before baking, preheat the oven to 375°, with a baking stone, if desired.

5. *Using a serrated knife,* make 4 or 5 diagonal slashes no more than ¼ inch deep in the top of each loaf. Bake in the center of the preheated oven until the loaves are deep brown and sound hollow when tapped, 35 to 40 minutes. Place a piece of aluminum foil over the tops to control excessive browning, if necessary, and take care not to overbake. Remove to racks to cool completely before slicing.

PRUNE WHOLE-WHEAT BREAD WITH
YOGURT STARTER
In step 2, add 2½ cups chopped, pitted prunes with the starter. Proceed as directed.

Four-Seed Buttermilk Bread

Any combination of nuts and seeds tends to turn a daily wheat bread into a superior loaf.
Beginning bakers will swoon over this easy and delicious bread. Use it for sandwiches and toast.

YIELD: 2 ROUND OR 9-BY-5-INCH LOAVES

1 tablespoon (1 package) active dry yeast
Pinch of light brown sugar, or 1 teaspoon
   of honey
¾ cup warm water (105° to 115°)
½ cup bulgur (cracked wheat)
1 cup raw sunflower seeds
1 cup raw pumpkin seeds
¼ cup sesame seeds
¼ cup whole millet
1½ cups warm buttermilk (105° to 115°)
¼ cup sunflower seed oil
½ cup honey
½ cup unprocessed wheat bran
1 tablespoon salt
5½ to 6 cups unbleached all-purpose or
   bread flour

1. In a small bowl, sprinkle the yeast and the pinch of sugar or teaspoon of honey over ¼ cup of the warm water. Stir to dissolve. Let stand until foamy, about 10 minutes. In another small bowl, cover the bulgur wheat with the remaining ½ cup warm water and let stand about 10 minutes to soften.

2. In a large, heavy skillet, toast the sunflower, pumpkin, and sesame seeds over medium-high heat until just golden brown, shaking the pan to avoid burning. Remove immediately to a large mixing bowl or to the work bowl of a heavy-duty electric mixer fitted with the paddle attachment and add the millet. Let cool slightly.

3. Add the buttermilk, yeast mixture, bulgur and soaking water, oil, honey, bran, salt, and 2 cups of the flour to the toasted seeds. Whisk or beat hard with the paddle attachment for about 1 minute. Add the remaining unbleached flour, ½ cup at a time, until a soft dough is formed that just clears the sides of the bowl, switching to a wooden spoon as necessary if making by hand.

4. Turn out the dough onto a lightly floured work surface and knead until light-colored, smooth, and springy, about 3 minutes, adding only 1 tablespoon flour at a time as needed to prevent sticking. Place in a deep greased container, turn once to coat the top, and cover with plastic wrap. Let rise at room temperature until doubled in bulk, 1½ to 2 hours.

5. Turn out the dough onto the work surface and divide into 2 equal portions. Form into 2 tight rounds or into rectangular loaves. Place the rounds on a greased or parchment-lined baking sheet or the rectangles in 2 greased 9-by-5-inch loaf pans (clay pans are wonderful for this bread). Cover loosely with plastic wrap and let rise until doubled in bulk or just above the rims of the loaf pans, about 45 minutes. Twenty minutes before baking, preheat the oven to 375°, with a baking stone, if desired.

6. Using a serrated knife, cut an X on the round loaves and a long slash down the length of the rectangular loaves no more than ¼ inch deep. Bake in the lower third of the preheated oven until the loaves are golden brown and sound hollow when tapped, 40 to 45 minutes. Remove immediately to racks to cool completely before slicing.

Buckwheat and Honey Oatmeal Bread

If you follow my work, you have probably noticed my love of oatmeal breads. Here, the buckwheat and rolled oats are highly complementary. Both are old-timers, used extensively in baking for centuries. Use regular rolled oats or quick-cooking cereal, as they both absorb liquid quickly and make the substantial texture that are characteristic of oatmeal breads. Use a locally gathered honey for the best flavor. Serve with plain or hot-pepper Jack cheese from the Sonoma Cheese Factory.

YIELD: THREE 8-BY-4-INCH LOAVES

2 tablespoons (2 packages) active dry yeast
1 teaspoon honey
1⅓ cups warm water (105° to 115°)
1 cup warm milk (105° to 115°)
½ cup honey
¼ cup vegetable oil or melted unsalted butter
2 eggs
1 tablespoon salt
1 cup buckwheat flour
2 cups rolled oats
4½ to 5 cups unbleached all-purpose or
     bread flour
Extra rolled oats, for sprinkling

1. *In a small bowl*, sprinkle the yeast and the 1 teaspoon honey over ⅓ cup of the warm water. Stir to dissolve. Let stand until foamy, about 10 minutes.

2. *In a large bowl* with a whisk or in the work bowl of a heavy-duty electric mixer fitted with the paddle attachment, combine the remaining 1 cup warm water, the warm milk, the ½ cup honey, oil or butter, eggs, salt, buckwheat flour, and the 2 cups oats. Add the yeast mixture and beat hard until creamy, 2 minutes. Add the remaining unbleached flour, ½ cup at a time, until a soft dough is formed that just clears the sides of the bowl, switching to a wooden spoon as necessary if making by hand.

3. *Turn out the dough* onto a well-floured work surface and knead until firm yet still quite soft and springy, about 3 minutes, adding only 1 tablespoon flour at a time as necessary to prevent sticking. The dough will retain a nubby, tacky quality because of the whole-grain flour. Do not add too much flour, or the dough will be hard and the bread will be dry. Place in a greased deep container, turn once to coat the top, and cover with plastic wrap. Let rise in a warm place until doubled in bulk, 1½ to 2 hours.

4. *Turn out the dough* onto the work surface. Divide into 3 equal portions and form into rectangular loaves. Place the loaves in 3 greased clay or metal 8-by-4-inch loaf pans that have been sprinkled on the bottom and sides with rolled oats. Cover loosely with plastic wrap and let rise at room temperature until doubled in bulk, about 1 hour. Twenty minutes before baking, preheat the oven to 350°.

5. *Bake in the center* of the preheted oven until the loaves are golden brown and sound hollow when tapped, 40 to 45 minutes. Remove from the pans to racks to cool completely before slicing.

Italian Amaretto Sweet Bread

Serve this briochelike sweet bread for New Year's Eve, as is the custom in Venice.
Laced with citrus and almond liqueur, it has a cap of crunchy sugar and nuts. I like it served in long wedges late
in the evening with small cups of Italian roast café filtre and fresh grapes, or toasted under the
broiler with ice-cold tangerine juice for brunch the next day.

YIELD: TWO 7-INCH ROUND LOAVES

1 tablespoon (1 package) active dry yeast
Pinch of sugar
¼ cup warm water (105° to 115°)
1 cup warm milk (105° to 115°)
½ cup (1 stick) unsalted butter, melted
⅓ cup sugar
1 teaspoon salt
2 eggs
3 tablespoons amaretto liqueur
2 teaspoons pure vanilla extract
Grated zest of 1 large orange
Grated zest of 1 large lemon
About 4 cups unbleached all-purpose flour

Almond Paste Topping
½ cup good-quality almond paste,
    at room temperature
3 tablespoons granulated sugar
2 egg whites
⅓ cup sliced almonds
3 tablespoons sifted powdered sugar

1. In a small bowl, sprinkle the yeast and the pinch of sugar over the warm water. Stir to dissolve. Let stand until foamy, about 10 minutes.

2. In a large bowl with a whisk or in the work bowl of a heavy-duty electric mixer fitted with the paddle attachment, combine the warm milk, butter, the ⅓ cup sugar, and salt. Add the eggs, liqueur, vanilla, orange and lemon zests, and 1 cup of the flour. Beat until smooth and creamy, about 1 minute. Add the yeast mixture and 1 cup more of the flour. Beat 1 minute longer. Add the remaining flour, ½ cup at a time, until a soft dough is formed that just clears the sides of the bowl and the embellishments are evenly distributed, switching to a wooden spoon as necessary if making by hand.

3. Turn out the dough onto a lightly floured work surface and knead until smooth and springy, about 3 minutes, adding only 1 tablespoon flour at a time as necessary to prevent sticking. The dough should remain soft. Place the dough in a greased deep container, turn once to coat the top, and cover with plastic wrap. Let rise at room temperature until doubled in bulk, about 2 hours.

4. Turn out the dough onto a lightly floured work surface and divide into 2 equal portions. Form each portion into a tight round ball and place in 2 greased and parchment-lined 7-inch

charlotte molds or 8-inch springform pans with the sides extended with 4-inch-high aluminum foil collars. Cover loosely with plastic wrap and let rise again at room temperature until doubled in bulk, about 45 minutes.

5. Meanwhile, make the almond paste topping. In the work bowl of an electric mixer, beat together the almond paste, granulated sugar, and egg whites until creamy and of a spreadable consistency. Set aside. (If made ahead and refrigerated, bring back to a spreadable consistency before using.) Twenty minutes before baking, preheat the oven to 350° and gently spread the surface of each of the risen loaves with half of the topping, taking care not to deflate the dough.

6. Sprinkle the top of each loaf with half of the almonds. Dust with powdered sugar. Bake in the center of the preheated oven until the loaves are browned and sound hollow when gently tapped, 40 to 45 minutes. Remove from the oven and let stand 10 minutes in the pans. If using springform pans, release the sides and remove the breads to racks. If using charlotte molds, loosen the loaves from the pan sides with a small knife, if necessary, then gently invert onto racks. Let the breads cool completely before slicing.

Mediterranean White Bread with Fennel

This is a stunning loaf of white bread with a tender, moist crumb and the appealing addition
of fennel seeds liberally dispersed throughout. Fennel seeds and chopped fresh fennel sprigs are a well-loved addition
to European breads and have been cultivated since antiquity along the Mediterranean. The ancient Athenians
favored fine wheat breads studded with them, and the modern Scandinavians bake a number of rye and white breads that
include them. The seeds impart a distinctive aniselike flavor that makes this bread wonderful for toasting or
sandwich making. Serve with cold beer, thinly sliced cold meats,
and a sharp mustard for memorable picnic fare.

YIELD: TWO 8-BY-4-INCH LOAVES

1 tablespoon (1 package) active dry yeast
½ teaspoon sugar
1¾ cup warm water (105° to 115°)
2 tablespoons sugar
2 tablespoons unsalted butter, melted
2½ teaspoons salt
1 heaping tablespoon fennel seeds
4½ to 5 cups unbleached all-purpose or
   bread flour
Extra unbleached all-purpose or bread flour,
   for sprinkling

1. In a small bowl, sprinkle the yeast and the ½ teaspoon sugar over ½ cup of the warm water. Stir to dissolve. Let stand until foamy, about 10 minutes.

2. In a large bowl using a whisk or in the work bowl of a heavy-duty electric mixer fitted with the paddle attachment, combine the remaining 1¼ cups warm water, the 2 tablespoons sugar, melted butter, and yeast mixture. Add the salt, fennel seeds, and 2 cups of the flour. Beat hard until creamy, about 1 minute. Add the remaining flour, ½ cup at a time, until a soft, shaggy dough is formed that just clears the sides of the bowl, switching to a wooden spoon as necessary if mixing by hand.

3. Turn out the dough onto a lightly floured work surface and knead until firm yet quite springy, about 3 minutes, adding only 1 table-spoon flour at a time as necessary to prevent sticking. Place in a greased deep container, turn once to coat the top, and cover with plastic wrap. Let rise at warm room temperature until doubled in bulk, 1½ to 2 hours.

4. Turn out the dough onto the work surface and divide into 4 equal portions. Using your palms, roll each portion into a 12-inch-long log. Twist 2 sections of dough around each other to form a 2-strand braid. Repeat with the remaining 2 portions to form the second loaf. Place in 2 greased 8-by-4-inch loaf pans. Dust the tops with a sprinkling of flour and spread gently with your fingers. Cover loosely with plastic wrap and let rise at warm room temperature until doubled in bulk and about 1 inch above the rims of the pans, about 45 minutes. Twenty minutes before baking, preheat the oven to 375°.

5. Bake in the center of the preheated oven until the loaves are golden brown and sound hollow when tapped, 40 to 45 minutes. Remove from the pans to racks to cool completely before slicing.

Oatmeal-Graham Bread

*This is certainly one of the most popular daily breads I make. The graham flour, a coarse
grind of whole wheat, is nutty-sweet and a wonderful surprise to the uninitiated. The novelist D. H. Lawrence
reputedly declared it one of his favorite flours for bread making. Serve in thick slices
with soups on a blustery day and for toast the next morning.*

YIELD: 3 ROUND OR TWO 8-BY-4-INCH LOAVES

2 cups boiling water
1 cup rolled oats
½ cup honey or maple syrup
4 tablespoons (½ stick) unsalted butter, at
    room temperature
1½ tablespoons (1½ packages) active
    dry yeast
Pinch of sugar
¼ cup warm water (105° to 115°)
2 teaspoons salt
1½ cups graham flour or other coarse-grind
    whole-wheat flour
2½ to 3 cups unbleached all-purpose or
    bread flour
Extra rolled oats, for sprinkling
1 egg yolk, beaten
2 tablespoons sesame seeds

1. In a large bowl or in the work bowl of a heavy-duty electric mixer fitted with the paddle attachment, pour the boiling water over the rolled oats. Add the honey or maple syrup and butter and whisk or beat into the oatmeal. Let stand 30 minutes to soften and cool to room temperature.

2. In a small bowl, sprinkle the yeast and sugar over the warm water. Stir to dissolve. Let stand until foamy, about 10 minutes.

3. Add the yeast mixture to the oatmeal mixture. Add the salt, graham or whole-wheat flour, and 1 cup of the unbleached flour. Beat hard until smooth, about 1 minute. Add the remaining unbleached flour, ½ cup at a time, until a soft, sticky dough is formed that just clears the sides of the bowl, switching to a wooden spoon as necessary if making by hand.

4. Turn out the dough onto a lightly floured work surface and knead until soft and springy, about 3 minutes, adding only 1 tablespoon unbleached flour at a time as necessary to prevent sticking. The dough will have a nubby, slightly tacky feel. Place in a greased deep container, turn once to coat the top, and cover with plastic wrap. Let rise at room temperature until doubled in bulk, 1½ to 2 hours.

5. Turn out the dough onto the work surface. Divide into 3 equal portions for round loaves or 2 equal portions for rectangular loaves. Shape the loaves and place the round loaves on a greased or parchment-lined baking sheet and the rectangular loaves in 2 greased 8-by-4-inch clay or metal loaf pans that have been sprinkled with extra rolled oats. Cover loosely with plastic wrap and let rise at room temperature until doubled in bulk, 45 minutes to 1 hour. Twenty minutes before baking, preheat the oven to 375°.

6. Gently brush the surface of the loaves with the egg yolk and sprinkle with the sesame seeds. Bake in the center of the preheated oven until the loaves are golden brown and sound hollow when tapped, 35 to 40 minutes. Remove from the pans to cool on racks before slicing.

Italian Olive Oil Bread

This is my pane casalinga, *a good, sweet whole-wheat loaf in the Italian low-fat tradition.*
In Italy, simple daily loaves made with a sponge starter come in a stunning display of rustic flour-dusted
guises from the simple round pagnotta *to a* ruota *(wheel),* treccia *(braid),* quattrocorni *(four horns), and* corrolla
(crown). I like it plain spread with some fresh domestic chèvre or cut into dunkable
chunks for a creamy apre-ski Emmentaler Fondue.

YIELD: 2 MEDIUM ROUND LOAVES

Sponge
1¼ teaspoons active dry yeast
1 cup tepid water (about 100°)
1 cup tepid milk (about 100°)
3 cups fine-grind whole-wheat flour, preferably
  stone-ground

Dough
1 teaspoon active dry yeast
1 tablespoon salt
¼ cup olive oil
¼ cup unprocessed wheat bran, raw wheat
  germ, or Cream of Rye flakes
2¼ to 2½ cups unbleached all-purpose
  or bread flour
Unbleached all-purpose or bread flour,
  for dusting

Coarse-grind yellow cornmeal or farina,
  for sprinkling

1. To prepare the sponge: In a large bowl, sprinkle the yeast over the tepid water and milk. Stir to dissolve. Add the flour and beat with a whisk until smooth. The starter will be thick and sticky. Cover loosely with a few layers of cheesecloth and let stand at cool room temperature 8 to 12 hours. It will be bubbly and pleasantly fermented. (This sponge can be stored up to 1 week in the refrigerator before using, if necessary.)

2. To prepare the dough: Add the yeast, salt, oil, bran, wheat germ or rye flakes, and ½ cup of the unbleached flour to the sponge. Beat hard with a wooden spoon for 2 minutes, or for 1 minute in a heavy-duty electric mixer fitted with the paddle attachment. Add the remaining flour, ½ cup at a time, switching to a wooden spoon as necessary if making by hand. The dough will be rather sticky, yet pull away from the sides of the bowl.

3. Turn out the dough onto a lightly floured surface and knead vigorously until very elastic yet still moist and tacky, about 3 minutes. This is important for a good, light texture. Slam the dough hard against the work surface to develop the gluten. Set aside, uncovered, 5 to 10 minutes to relax. Knead again, and the sticky dough will smooth out without any extra flour. Place in a greased deep container

(plastic is good), cover with plastic wrap, and let rise at room temperature until tripled in bulk, for 3 hours to overnight.

4. Turn out the dough onto a lightly floured work surface and divide into 2 equal portions. Knead lightly into rounds and flatten slightly. Dust lightly all over with flour and place, smooth side up, on a greased or parchment-lined baking sheet that has been sprinkled with the cornmeal or farina. Let rise, uncovered, at room temperature until soft and springy, about 1 hour. Twenty minutes before baking, preheat the oven to 425°, with a baking stone, if desired.

5. Using a serrated knife, slash 4 strokes no more than ¼ inch deep in the top of each loaf to form a diamond design. Place the baking sheet in the hot oven, directly on the baking stone, if desired. Bake 15 minutes. Reduce the oven thermostat to 375° and continue to bake until golden brown and crusty, 25 to 30 minutes longer. Remove to racks to cool completely before slicing.

Mozzarella en Carozza

A cross between grilled cheese and French toast, these sandwiches are a rustic delight. Excellent as an hors d'oeuvre or snack, mozzarella "in a carriage" is as famous in Italy as pizza is here and is wonderful made with Italian Olive Oil Bread (preceding). Bel Paese or Cheddar cheese may be substituted for the mozzarella.

YIELD: 4 SERVINGS

1 small loaf day-old Italian Olive Oil Bread, preferably shaped into an oblong rather than round loaf

12 ounces fresh mozzarella

½ cup well-drained oil-packed sun-dried tomatoes

2 eggs

2 tablespoons milk

½ to ¾ cup good-quality olive oil, or as needed

1. Cut the bread and cheese into thin slices. You will need 16 slices of bread and 8 slices of cheese. Trim the cheese to fit the bread so it does not overhang the edges. Make about 8 small sandwiches, each with 2 slices of bread, 1 slice of cheese, and a piece of sun-dried tomato. In a shallow bowl, beat together the eggs and milk until foamy. Dip both sides of the sandwich into the mixture, pressing the edges together firmly so that the cheese is enclosed.

2. In a large skillet or sauté pan, pour in enough olive oil to just cover the surface with a film. Heat to medium-high. Add the sandwiches and sauté, turning once, until golden on both sides, about 4 minutes' total cooking time. Drain on paper towels and serve immediately while hot.

Golden Raisin Kugelhopf

*This Kugelhopf is in the style of a Hungarian kelt kuglóf. It has a delicate texture and a
golden raisin filling, and welcomes a touch of butter, as it is not too rich or too sweet. It is a traditional yeast
cake for celebrating your saint's name day, a European custom in lieu of your birthday.*

YIELD: ONE 9-INCH COFFEE CAKE

1½ tablespoons active dry yeast
½ teaspoon sugar
1 cup warm milk (105° to 115°)
3¼ cups unbleached all-purpose flour
   (exact measure)
⅓ cup sugar
1 teaspoon salt
1½ teaspoons pure vanilla extract
2 eggs
¾ cup (1½ sticks) unsalted butter, at room
   temperature, cut into small pieces

Golden Raisin Filling
1½ cups golden raisins
⅓ cup Cognac or brandy
⅓ cup sugar
1 tablespoon ground cinnamon, or
   3 tablespoons unsweetened cocoa powder
Grated zest of 1 large orange

Brown Sugar Streusel
½ cup light brown sugar
Pinch of ground cinnamon
⅓ cup unbleached all-purpose flour
4 tablespoons (½ stick) unsalted butter, cold,
   cut into pieces

1. In the work bowl of a heavy-duty electric mixer fitted with the paddle attachment, sprinkle the yeast and the ½ teaspoon of sugar over the warm milk. Stir to dissolve. Let stand until foamy, about 10 minutes.

2. Add the flour, the ⅓ cup sugar, salt, vanilla, and eggs all at once. Beat on low speed until creamy, about 1 minute. Add the butter in 3 additions, incorporating each addition into the batter before the next addition. The batter will be very soft and sticky. Scrape into a greased container with room for the batter to expand, cover tightly with plastic wrap, and refrigerate at least 4 hours or as long as overnight. To make the golden raisin filling, in a small bowl, combine the raisins and Cognac or brandy and macerate the same amount of time at room temperature.

3. Scrape out the chilled dough onto a lightly floured work surface and divide into 2 equal portions. Using a rolling pin, gently roll out each portion into a 16-by-18-inch rectangle. To finish the filling, in a small bowl, combine the sugar, cinnamon or cocoa, and orange zest. Sprinkle each rectangle with half of the mixture, leaving a 1-inch border at both short ends. Distribute the macerated raisins evenly over the rectangle and press into the dough with the rolling pin. Starting from a long side, roll up each rectangle jelly-roll fashion and pinch the ends together to seal. Lay one roll, seam side up, in a greased 9-inch tube pan. Place the other dough roll directly on top,

with the seam side down but not directly on top of the seam of the bottom roll. The pan will be no more than two-thirds full. Cover loosely with plastic wrap and let rise at room temperature until even with the rim of the pan, about 1½ hours.

4. While the dough is rising, prepare the brown sugar streusel. In a bowl, stir together the brown sugar, cinnamon, and flour until blended. Using your fingers, a pastry blender, or a fork, cut in the butter until the mixture has the consistency of coarse crumbs. (A food processor may also be used for mixing the streusel.) Set aside. Twenty minutes before baking, preheat the oven to 350°.

5. Sprinkle the top of the *Kugelhof* with the streusel. If the tube pan seems overly full, place it on a thin baking sheet to catch drips. Bake in the center of the preheated oven until golden brown and a cake tester inserted into the center comes out clean, 55 to 65 minutes. Overbaking will dry out the cake. As a fail-safe step, insert an instant-read thermometer into the center of the cake at the end of the required baking time. The temperature should read about 190°. Let stand 5 minutes in the pan, then carefully turn out onto a rack, streusel top up. If the sides are paler than you desire, return the unmolded cake to the oven on a baking sheet to bake 5 minutes more. Cool at least 4 hours before slicing. Store, wrapped in plastic, at room temperature.

Whole-Wheat Sweet Bread with Dates and Oat Streusel

Dates were a staple in the hot, dry climates of early desert nomads.
Softened in fruit juice, the dates become very moist, and when puréed, form a luscious paste
filling, which can be made one day ahead and refrigerated until needed.

YIELD: 2 LARGE LOAVES ABOUT 15 INCHES LONG

Dough

1½ tablespoons (1½ packages) active
   dry yeast
Pinch of date sugar or light brown sugar
Pinch of ground ginger
¼ cup warm water (105° to 115°)
1 cup warm milk (105° to 115°)
6 tablespoons unsalted butter, melted
⅓ cup date sugar or light brown sugar
2 teaspoons salt
2 eggs
2 cups whole-wheat flour
2½ to 2¾ cups unbleached all-purpose or
   bread flour

Date Butter Filling

Two 8-ounce packages pitted dates (4 cups)
1½ cups unsweetened pineapple juice
1 small banana, peeled and cut up
⅓ cup drained unsweetened crushed pineapple
4 tablespoons (½ stick) unsalted butter,
   at room temperature

Oat Streusel

⅓ cup date sugar or light brown sugar
½ teaspoon ground cinnamon
¼ cup rolled oats
3 tablespoons unbleached all-purpose flour
6 tablespoons unsalted butter, cold, cut into
   8 pieces

1. To prepare the dough: In a small bowl, sprinkle the yeast, pinch of sugar, and ginger over the warm water. Stir to dissolve. Let stand until foamy, about 10 minutes.

2. In a large bowl with a whisk or in the work bowl of a heavy-duty electric mixer fitted with the paddle attachment, combine the warm milk, melted butter, the ⅓ cup sugar, salt, eggs, and whole-wheat flour. Beat until creamy, about 1 minute. Add the yeast mixture and 1 cup of the unbleached flour. Beat 1 minute longer. Add remaining flour, ¼ cup at a time, until a soft dough is formed that just clears the sides of the bowl.

3. Turn out the dough onto a lightly floured work surface and knead until smooth, firm, and elastic, about 3 minutes, adding only 1 tablespoon flour at a time as necessary to prevent sticking. Do not add too much flour. The dough should hold its shape but be soft and pliable. Place in a greased deep container, turn once to coat the top, and cover with plastic wrap. Let rise at room temperature until doubled in bulk, 1 to 1½ hours.

4. While the dough is rising, make the date butter filling. In a medium saucepan, combine the dates and pineapple juice. Bring to a boil. Lower the heat to medium and simmer 10 minutes. Remove from the heat and set aside to cool. The dates will absorb all the juice. Transfer the dates to a food processor and add the banana, pineapple, and butter.

Process until just puréed. Set aside or cover and chill until needed.

5. Turn out the dough onto a lightly floured work surface and divide into 2 equal portions. Roll out each portion into a 9-by-15-inch rectangle. Transfer to a greased or parchment-lined baking sheet and even the edges. Spread half the date filling down the center third of each rectangle. Using a sharp knife, cut strips at 2-inch intervals on the diagonal on both sides of the filling, cutting almost through to the filling. Starting at the top, fold the strips alternately from each side at a slight angle to make a crisscross braid. Tuck under any excess dough at the end. Repeat to make the second loaf. Cover loosely with plastic wrap and let rise at room temperature until doubled in bulk, about 1 hour. Twenty minutes before baking, preheat the oven to 350°.

6. While the oven is heating, make the oat streusel. In a small bowl, combine the sugar, cinnamon, oats, and flour. Add the butter, and using your fingers, a pastry cutter, or a fork cut in the butter until the mixture has the consistency of coarse crumbs. (A food processor may also be used for mixing the streusel.)

7. Sprinkle the tops of the loaves evenly with the streusel. Bake in the center of the preheated oven until the loaves are even golden brown and a cake tester inserted in the center comes out clean, 40 to 45 minutes. Gently remove to racks to cool completely.

Sweet Vanilla Challah

I have transformed my classic challah recipe into a tantalizing sweet bread.
It is customary to serve two challot (the plural of challah) loaves on each Sabbath or festival table.
Challot are made in a variety of sizes and degrees of richness. They are served on white linen to remind the faithful
of the manna "bread from heaven" the Jews received every Friday in the desert. It is traditional
for the baker to burn in the oven a piece of dough known as the challah portion, for which the loaf is named.
Serve wedges with raspberry jam for Valentine's Day morning breakfast.

YIELD: 2 TURBAN LOAVES

1 tablespoon (1 package) active dry yeast
½ cup sugar
1 tablespoon salt
6½ to 7 cups unbleached all-purpose or
　bread flour
1¾ cups hot water (120°)
4 eggs, lightly beaten
½ cup vegetable oil
1½ tablespoons pure vanilla extract

Vanilla Egg Glaze
1 egg yolk
1 teaspoon pure vanilla extract
½ teaspoon sugar

1. *In a large bowl* with a whisk or in the work bowl of a heavy-duty electric mixer fitted with the paddle attachment, combine the yeast, sugar, salt, and 2 cups of the flour. Add the hot water, eggs, oil, and vanilla. Beat hard until smooth, about 3 minutes. Scrape down the sides of the bowl occasionally. Add the remaining flour, ½ cup at a time, switching to a wooden spoon as necessary if making by hand. Continue beating until dough is too stiff to stir.

2. *Turn out the dough* onto a lightly floured work surface and knead until soft and springy and a layer of blisters shows under the skin, about 2 minutes, adding only 1 tablespoon flour at a time as necessary to prevent sticking. The dough needs to be a bit firm for free-form loaves. Place in a greased deep container, turn once to coat the top, and cover with plastic wrap. Let rise at room temperature until doubled in bulk, 1½ to 2 hours.

3. *Gently deflate the dough*, turn out onto a lightly floured surface, and divide into 2 equal portions. Roll each section into a smooth, thick strip about 30 inches long, with one end 2 to 3 inches fatter than the other. Roll to lengthen and taper the thinner end. With the fat end on the work surface, lift the tapered end and wind the rest of the dough around the center section 2 or 3 times, forming a compact coil. Pinch the end and tuck it under. Place the coils, with the swirl pattern facing up, on 1 or 2 greased or parchment-lined baking sheets or 2 9-inch springform pans. Cover loosely with plastic wrap and let rise until almost doubled in bulk, 30 to 40 minutes. Because of the eggs, this loaf does not need to double completely. It will rise a lot in the oven. Twenty minutes before baking, preheat the oven to 350°.

4. *To make the vanilla egg glaze*, in a small bowl, whisk together the egg yolk, vanilla, and sugar. Beat until well blended. Gently brush the dough surfaces with a thick layer of the glaze. Bake the loaves in the center of the preheated oven until a deep golden brown, 40 to 45 minutes. Carefully lift the turbans off the baking sheets with a spatula and place them on racks to cool. If using springform pans, release the sides and then carefully remove the turbans from the pan bases. Let cool completely before slicing.

Mexican Sweet Bread

This basic sweet dough can be used to create a variety of holiday breads
that vary dramatically in shape. Results range from the Twelfth Night rosca de reyes
(king's bread ring) to pan de ferias. Serve a feast of chicken mole, pork-filled tamales, guacamole,
and fresh pinto beans, and finish with slices of your sugar-speckled rosca.

YIELD: 1 RING LOAF

Sponge
¾ cup warm milk (105° to 115°)
½ cup warm water (105° to 115°)
1 tablespoon (1 package) active dry yeast
Pinch of sugar
1 cup unbleached all-purpose flour

Dough
3 to 3¼ cups unbleached all-purpose flour
¼ cup sugar
Grated zest of 2 oranges
1½ teaspoons salt
3 eggs
1 teaspoon pure vanilla extract, or 1 small
 vanilla bean, split lengthwise
3 tablespoons orange brandy
½ cup (1 stick) unsalted butter, at room
 temperature, cut into pieces
½ cup dried currants
½ cup chopped candied orange peel,
 preferably homemade
1 cup mixed chopped Honey-Glazed Dried
 Fruits (following)
1 or 2 china statues of baby Jesus, large pecan
 halves, or whole almond nutmeats

Sugar Crystal Glaze
1 egg yolk, lightly beaten
10 pecan halves or whole almonds
10 pieces crystallized angelica
3 tablespoons unsalted butter, melted
¼ cup granulated or large-crystal
 decorating sugar (available from cake-
 decorating stores)

1. To prepare the sponge: In a large bowl with a whisk or in the work bowl of a heavy-duty electric mixer fitted with the paddle attachment, combine the milk, water, and sugar. Sprinkle with the yeast and stir to dissolve. Let stand until foamy, about 5 minutes. Sprinkle with the flour and beat until smooth. Scrape down the sides of the bowl and cover with plastic wrap. Let stand at room temperature until bubbly, about 2 hours.

2. To prepare the dough: In a large bowl with a whisk or in the work bowl of a heavy-duty electric mixer fitted with the paddle attachment, combine 1½ cups of the flour, the sugar, orange zest, and salt. Add the sponge, eggs, vanilla extract (or scrape out the seeds from the split vanilla bean into the bowl), orange brandy, and butter. Beat until creamy, about 2 minutes. Add the remaining flour, ½ cup at a time, until a soft dough is formed that just clears the sides of the bowl, switching to a wooden spoon as necessary if making by hand.

3. Turn out the dough onto a lightly floured work surface and knead until soft and springy, about 3 minutes, adding only 1 tablespoon flour at a time as necessary to prevent sticking. The dough should not be too dry. Place in a greased deep container, turn once to coat the top, and cover with plastic wrap. Let rise at warm room temperature until doubled in bulk, about 2 hours. Do not rush this dough, as the

full rising time is important to develop the flavor and texture.

4. Turn out the dough onto the work surface and pat into a fat rectangle. Sprinkle with the currants, candied orange peel, and glazed dried fruits and press them in with your palms. Roll up into a cylinder and then smooth into a thick rope 20 to 22 inches long. Push the statue(s) or nuts into the dough and pinch the dough closed to seal. Lay the dough rope on a greased or parchment-lined pizza pan or cake pan 15 inches in diameter and pinch the ends together with water-moistened fingers to form a closed ring. Place a 6-inch cake pan with greased outer sides upside down in the center of the ring to retain the center hole. This pan will help the cake keep its shape. Loosely cover with plastic wrap and let rise at warm room temperature until doubled in bulk, about 1 hour. Twenty minutes before baking, preheat the oven to 375°.

5. To glaze the rosca, brush the entire surface with the egg yolk and gently press the nuts and angelica in a decorative pattern into the top. Bake in the center of the preheated oven until browned and a cake tester inserted into the center comes out clean, 40 to 45 minutes. Remove from the oven and brush with the melted butter and sprinkle with the sugar. Turn off the oven and return the *rosca* to the oven for 5 minutes. Remove immediately and let stand 10 minutes before using a large spatula to carefully transfer from the pan to a rack. Let cool completely before slicing.

HONEY-GLAZED DRIED FRUITS

If extra fruits will be used for decorating the center of the rosca, roll them in sifted powdered sugar for a pretty presentation.

YIELD: ABOUT 1/2 POUND

1¼ cups granulated sugar
¼ cup honey
2 tablespoons light corn syrup
½ cup water
8 ounces whole dried fruit, such as dried apple slices, whole figs, and/or apricot, pear, or peach halves

1. In a deep, medium-heavy saucepan, combine the sugar, honey, corn syrup, and water. Heat over low heat, stirring constantly with a wooden spoon, until the sugar dissolves, about 5 minutes. Using a pair of metal tongs, add the fruit, taking care not to splash. Bring the mixture to a boil without stirring. Immediately reduce the heat to medium so the syrup simmers. Cook the fruit slowly for exactly 15 minutes, stirring gently to avoid burning and basting occasionally. The fruit will plump up.

2. Remove the pan from the heat and immediately place in a pan of warm water to cool the syrup slightly. Using tongs, carefully remove the individual pieces of fruit, letting the extra syrup drip back into the pan. Place on a layer of waxed paper or parchment paper set on a wire rack to cool completely, at least 8 hours. To store, arrange the glazed fruits in layers in an airtight container, separating them with sheets of clean waxed paper or parchment paper that have been brushed with a thin film of corn syrup. Store up to 3 weeks in the refrigerator.

Beyond the beautiful world of liqueur-spiked glazes, silver-coated almonds or other edible treasures such as dragées, bits of candied citrus peel, carved chocolate roses, chocolate coffee beans, and glazed nut halves, one of the most appealing and imaginative ways to decorate breads for celebrations is with fresh flowers and assorted greenery. The rainbow of colors is visually striking against the natural earth hues, and the myriad of shapes softens the basic geometrics of the loaf. Whether your style is innovative or tried-and-true, this style of decorating can become one of your culinary trademarks, as well as a passion.

Consider using traditional flowers associated with a birthday month, such as roses in June and daisies in April, a beautiful and thoughtful gesture. Fill the center of a powdered-sugar-dusted yeast bread baked in a fluted tube mold with a small bouquet of starlike borage, or entwine an egg-rich braid with scarlet runner bean leaves and their delicate tendrils. Tuck a small branch of evergreen citrus shrub, such as kumquat or tangerine, with its fruits attached alongside a loaf. Lay a loaf beside a bunch of fresh cherries with its green leaves intact or some perfectly formed immature persimmons still on the branch.

Flowers have been used for centuries for culinary, chemical, and medicinal purposes, as well as for decoration. They come in an enticing variety of aromas, delicate flavors, and textures. Become familiar with families of edible and inedible blossoms. If you have any doubt, *don't use them.* All flowers of poisonous plants must be completely avoided, even though they can be temptingly beautiful. Without exception, avoid the toxic blossoms and greenery of the crocus (except for the saffron variety), daffodil, oleander, wisteria, poinsettia, foxglove, rhododendron, lily of the valley, avocado leaves, iris, sweet pea, lupine, azalea, and all plants of the nightshade family.

The good news is there is a long list of safe edible flowers from which to choose. They can be found in gardens, in the wild, fresh, from the florist, or dried from the herbalist. Just be certain they have not been sprayed with chemicals. The blossoms from herbs such as lavender, chamomile, anise, hyssop, borage, chives, arugula, sage, thyme, basil, and oregano are charming accents. The flowers of vegetables such as squashes, pumpkins, and fennel are totally edible. Enjoy fragrant fruit-tree blossoms of apple, orange, lemon, plum, and cherry. Edible garden varieties with little flavor but a nice crunchy texture are the tulip, pansy, petunia, sunflower, hollyhock, and gladiolus. Blossoms that are rather bittersweet but beautiful are the iris, nasturtium, johnny-jump-up, honeysuckle, geranium, spicy marigold, calendula, columbine, poppy, chrysanthemum, hibiscus, tiger lily, and primrose.

Old-fashioned flowers that have not been hybridized often have the most intense flavor and fragrance. Roses are a popular choice, either as a whole flower or just a sprinkling of soft petals. I especially love the old-fashioned miniature or wild varieties with only five petals that form large hedges along country lanes. Carnations, rose geraniums, jasmine, gardenias, and lilacs will also decorate a bread with their perfume as well as their color.

Edible wild flowers include red clover, cattails, dandelions, thistle, yuccas, and daisies. If you enjoy foraging for wild flowers, avoid those growing close to busy roads or near orchards, as they may be sprayed with chemicals.

Pick your floral bouquet after the dew is off, but before the heat of the day sets in. Wash the flowers thoroughly in cool water, drain, and then roll them up to dry in paper towels. If not using immediately, refrigerate or place the stems in water to keep them fresh.

Arrange fresh greenery around the cutting board or pedestal plate to create a nest around your loaves on the table for a soft, yet dramatic accent. My favorites include ivy, feathery asparagus fern, shiny leather fern, oval citrus, deeply lobed maple, fig, grape, or round nasturtium leaves.

For a special touch, decorate a celebration or holiday bread with crystallized flowers and herb leaves (page 38). Violets, violas, some small orchids, borage flowers, and pansies are exceptionally easy to work with because of their broad, flat petals that stay intact and their vibrant colors. Crystallized flowers may be made weeks in advance and stored in airtight containers until needed.

Egg decorating became popular during Lent after the Holy Wars, with a rainbow of colors created from boiled flowers, leaves, nut hulls, and vegetable peelings. It has been recorded that the early Christians of Mesopotamia also practiced egg dyeing for spring festivities. As the years went by, decorating with geometric and pastoral themes became a high art, culminating in the intricately detailed folk art of Ukrainian dyed eggs known as *pysanky*. My favorite design is golden heads of wheat, a visual prayer for a bountiful harvest. Loaves reflect the season when colored or decorative eggs are embedded and baked into the loaf or nestled around them as decorations. My Swiss-German friend, Rosmarie, ritually dyes eggs during the spring holiday season here as she did in her native Switzerland, with literally a pound of papery orange-brown onion skins to create boiled eggs with a subtly marbled, ethereal color. To re-create traditional hues, use blue to symbolize the heaven Christ ascended to, orange for the color of the resurrection, green for spiritual rebirth, and red for His blood.

In the fall I like to use small cobs of multicolored corn, still in their papery leaves, and unshelled nuts to mirror some of the ingredients used in baking. Loaves look great in baskets lined with a bed of dried wheat, their tan bearded heads of grain peeking out the sides, or a nest of fresh fig leaves. I have also edged loaves with a long colonial-style swag of dried pomegranates or oranges interspersed with bunches of dried bay leaves and cinnamon sticks, or simply a long garlic braid. Look for swags of fresh or well-made imitation evergreens or holly sprigs during the winter for lining the perimeter or serving baskets. A wreath-shaped loaf may cradle an exquisite beeswax candle and holder in the center or sport a variety of wide ribbons tied around it.

Accompaniments

CHEESE SAUTÉ
Serve as an appetizer with Tuscan Peasant Bread and fresh grapes.
YIELD: 4 SERVINGS

All-purpose flour, for dusting
1 or 2 eggs, well beaten
1 cup fine dried white bread crumbs
8 ounces Monterey Jack, Muenster, or
    mozzarella cheese, chilled and cut into
    ½-inch-thick slices, or one 8-ounce
    round Brie or Camembert
4 to 5 tablespoons unsalted butter
¼ cup chopped fresh chives or green part
    of green onions

1. Preheat the oven to 200°. Place a few tablespoons of flour, the eggs, and the bread crumbs in separate shallow bowls. First, dip the cheese slices in the flour to absorb moisture, then into the beaten egg, and finally in the bread crumbs, coating all surfaces.
2. Melt 2 tablespoons of the butter in a heavy skillet and sauté the cheese slices over medium-high heat until brown and crisp on both sides. Work quickly and carefully, as the cheese will be soft soon after it comes in contact with the heat. Remove with a spatula to a shallow baking dish lined with paper towels and keep warm in the preheated oven.
3. Wipe out the skillet, place over medium heat, and melt another 2 to 3 tablespoons butter. Add the chives or onions and sauté just to warm for 30 seconds.
4. Place the cheese slices on a serving platter and pour the warm chives and melted butter over the top. Serve immediately.

SPICED APPLESAUCE BUTTER
Use a good-quality commercial applesauce for this simple-to-prepare fruit butter.

YIELD: ABOUT 2 1/2 CUPS
One 24-ounce jar unsweetened applesauce
½ cup frozen apple juice concentrate,
    undiluted
2 tablespoons apple brandy, such as Calvados
1½ teaspoons ground cinnamon
½ teaspoon ground allspice
½ teaspoon ground mace
Pinch of ground cloves
2 tablespoons unsalted butter

1. In a heavy saucepan, combine the applesauce, apple juice concentrate, brandy, and spices. Stir with a whisk to combine evenly. Bring to a boil. Immediately reduce the heat to low and add the butter. Simmer uncovered, stirring occasionally, 45 minutes, or until the desired consistency is reached.
2. Remove from the heat and cool to room temperature. Transfer to a covered container and store in the refrigerator for up to 1 month.

CRAWFISH BUTTER
A specialty of my friend, chef Joey Altman.
YIELD: 1 1/2 POUNDS

1 pound crawfish, roughly chopped
1½ pounds unsalted butter, cut into chunks
4 cups water

1. Preheat the oven to 250°. In a deep, 3-quart ovenproof saucepan, combine the crawfish, butter, and water. Cover and bake about 2 hours, until the crawfish is well cooked. Remove from the oven and let cool 30 minutes.
2. Once cool, the red-hued butter will rise to the top and firm up, while the crawfish bodies and butter impurities will sink to the bottom. Scoop out the red butter with a large spoon and divide into desired amounts. Discard the

remaining liquid and solids. Store the butter in the refrigerator up to 3 days or in the freezer up to 1 month.

GRILLED FETA EN PAPILLOTE
This is a great outdoor treat, served with a main course of grilled eggplant and mustard-marinated chicken.
YIELD: 4 SERVINGS

Unsalted butter
8 ounces feta cheese, cut into 4 equal slices
1 tablespoon Hungarian sweet paprika or
    New Mexico chile powder, or to taste
4 thick slices Semolina Sesame Seed Twist
    (page 57) toasted

1. Prepare a charcoal fire.
2. Cut aluminum foil into 4 large squares and butter the center of each square generously. Place a slice of feta atop the butter on each piece of foil and sprinkle with the paprika or chile powder. Wrap tightly closed and place on the grill 4 to 5 inches from the coals. Grill a few minutes, turning once. Remove from the grill and serve each diner a packet. Spread the hot cheese on the toast.

SUMMER CHEESE
Match the herb to your menu.
YIELD: ABOUT 2 CUPS

12 ounces cream cheese, at room temperature
½ cup (1 stick) unsalted butter, at room
    temperature
1 large clove garlic, pressed
1 tablespoon *each* minced fresh marjoram or
    oregano, thyme, basil, and dill
Freshly ground black pepper

1. In a small bowl with a spoon or with an

electric mixer, beat the cheese and butter until fluffy. Add the garlic, herbs, and a few grinds of black pepper and mix well.

2. *Scrape into a container* and top with a few more grinds of black pepper. Cover tightly. Refrigerate overnight to meld the flavors. Serve at room temperature.

California Tomato Ketchup

This tangy puréed condiment can be made with anything from plums to mushrooms. I make enough from meaty Roma (plum) tomatoes all summer long for short-term refrigerator storage, in a glass spring-top jar, without the fuss of preserving.
Yield: About 4 cups

6 pounds ripe Roma tomatoes, cored and coarsely chopped
1 large white onion, cut up
½ large red bell pepper, seeded, deveined, and cut up
1 large shallot, chopped
1 clove garlic, pressed
1¼ cups unfiltered apple cider vinegar
1 cup light brown sugar or honey
¼ cup sherry vinegar
1 teaspoon whole allspice
1 teaspoon whole cloves
1 teaspoon black peppercorns
1 cinnamon stick, 2 inches long
1 large bay leaf
1 teaspoon ground nutmeg or mace
Pinch of dry mustard

1. *In a food processor* fitted with the metal blade, combine the tomatoes, onion, bell pepper, shallot, and garlic. Process until just smooth. Place in a large, deep nonreactive saucepan. Add the vinegar and sugar or honey. Place the whole spices in a cheesecloth bag and add to the pan along with the ground nutmeg or mace and dry mustard. Bring to a boil, uncovered, over medium heat. Reduce to a brisk simmer and cook, stirring often, until the mixture is reduced by half, about 2 hours, or until desired consistency.

2. *Remove and discard* the spice bag and add salt to taste. Serve warm, at room temperature, or chilled. Store in a covered container in the refrigerator up to 1 month.

Orange–Passion Fruit Curd

Looking like a shriveled pink or purple egg, passion fruit has intensely fragrant pulp that easily mixes with other fruits such as guava, pineapple, berries, lime, orange, and apricot. A ripe passion fruit sounds sloshy inside when it is shaken. Whole fruits may be frozen in freezer bags for months, waiting for the right occasion to be juiced (see note). Passion fruits are grown in California and imported to the United States from New Zealand. In case of a serious addiction, use the convenient frozen fruit purées, imported from France and widely used by professional bakers, available in Latin markets and specialty-food stores. This is a wonderful fruit curd for spreading on homemade breads.
Yield: About 2 cups

½ cup (1 stick) unsalted butter
⅔ cup passion fruit juice (see introduction)
¼ cup orange juice
Grated zest of 2 oranges
¾ cup sugar
4 whole eggs plus 2 egg yolks

1. *In the top pan* of a double boiler set over simmering water, melt the butter. Meanwhile, in a bowl with a whisk, in a blender, or a food processor fitted with the metal blade, beat together the passion fruit juice, orange juice, orange zest, sugar, whole eggs, and egg yolks.

2. *With the water at a simmer,* slowly add the egg mixture to the butter, stirring constantly with a whisk. Cook over medium heat, stirring constantly, until thickened, a full 10 minutes. Pour into a jar and let cool, then cover and store in the refrigerator up to 3 weeks.

NOTE: To juice a passion fruit, halve the fruits over a strainer set over a bowl. Scoop out the yellow pulp and seeds into the strainer. Press on the seeds with a fork to extract as much juice as possible, usually about 2 tablespoons per fruit. The seeds are also edible, and the pulp and seeds can also be puréed together in a blender. Refrigerate until needed.

Olive Pesto

This is also wonderful spread on slices cut from nearly any crusty loaf.
Yield: About 1 cup

One 6-ounce can California pitted black olives, drained
¼ cup freshly grated Parmesan or Asiago cheese
¼ bunch fresh Italian (flat-leaf) parsley, stemmed
1 tablespoon capers, rinsed and drained
3 tablespoons fruity olive oil
1 tablespoon fresh lemon juice
1 teaspoon crumbled fresh thyme leaves or a large pinch of dried thyme leaves
Freshly ground black pepper to taste

1. *In a blender* or in a food processor fitted with the metal blade, combine all the ingredients and, using on-off pulses, process to form a rough-textured purée. Alternatively, grind the ingredients together in a mortar using a pestle.

2. *Store in a covered container* in the refrigerator up to 5 days.

GRILLED CHEESE IN FRAGRANT LEAVES

As these packets cook over a charcoal fire, the fragrance of the grape leaves is infused into the cheese. Fresh fig leaves may be substituted for the grape leaves.

YIELD: 8 SERVINGS

8 to 12 ounces hard cheese, such as Gruyère or smoked Cheddar, or 1 pound fresh goat cheese

16 to 24 fresh grape leaves, washed and patted dry

1 loaf Italian Whole-Wheat Walnut-Raisin Bread, thinly sliced (page 95)

1. Prepare a charcoal fire in a grill. Cut or slice the cheese into 16 thick slices that can easily be wrapped in the grape leaves. Turn each leaf so that the heavily veined side is face up. Place a piece of the cheese in the center of a leaf. Fold the base of the leaf over the cheese and then wrap completely in the leaf. Use a second leaf, if necessary, to cover the entire surface of the cheese. Carefully secure with a toothpick. Repeat with the remaining cheese slices and leaves.

2. Place the wrapped bundles on the grill rack 4 to 5 inches above the coals. Grill, turning once, just until the cheese melts, about 5 minutes' total cooking time. To serve, present each guest with 2 bundles of cheese to unwrap and spread while still warm on the bread slices.

GRAPE JELLY

Small batches of lovely homemade jelly can be made from good varietal grape juices (bottled or reconstituted frozen) or crushed fresh fruit. I have many memories of long hours spent juicing my own Concord grapes by steam extraction, but simply crushing and pressing them is much easier. Grape jellies made at home tend to be a bit softer set than commercial brands. It is important to follow the directions exactly for the best results.

YIELD: ABOUT 2 1/2 CUPS

1¾ to 2 pounds white or red table or varietal grapes, or 1½ cups commercial grape juice

1¾ cups sugar

3 tablespoons (half of a 1¾-ounce package) powdered fruit pectin

⅓ cup water

1. Crush the fresh grapes in a blender or a food processor fitted with the metal blade. Pour the crushed grapes through a colander lined with a double layer of cheesecloth set over a bowl and squeeze to separate the juice from the seeds and skin. You should have 1⅓ to 1⅔ cups juice. Discard the solids. Place the juice in a saucepan and bring to a boil. Reduce the heat to low, cover, and simmer 10 minutes. Let cool to lukewarm before using or cover and refrigerate.

2. In a medium bowl, combine 1 cup of the grape juice and 1½ cups of the sugar. Stir to moisten evenly. Gently warm the juice, if necessary, to dissolve the sugar. Set aside. In a medium, heavy saucepan, combine the pectin and the water. Heat until warm, stirring with a whisk to dissolve the pectin. Do not boil or use a microwave oven. Add the remaining ¼ cup sugar and ½ cup grape juice to the pectin mixture, stirring constantly. Immediately remove from the heat and let stand 15 minutes, stirring twice.

3. Slowly add the juice-sugar mixture to the pectin mixture, stirring constantly until the sugar is dissolved. Pour into jars and let stand, uncovered, at room temperature until set, 12 to 18 hours. Cover with lids and store in the refrigerator up to 2 months.

MAPLE PUMPKIN BUTTER

This butter is made in the oven, an easy alternative to cooking it for long hours in an old-fashioned kettle over an open fire or on a stove-top.

YIELD: ABOUT 2 CUPS

3 cups pumpkin purée (homemade, page 105, or canned)

½ cup light brown sugar

½ cup pure maple syrup

⅓ cup unfiltered apple or pear juice

2 teaspoons ground cinnamon

½ teaspoon ground ginger

½ teaspoon ground cloves

1. Preheat the oven to 300°. In a medium saucepan, stir together all the ingredients and bring the mixture to a simmer. Transfer the hot mixture to a 9-by-13-inch baking dish and spread it in an even layer. Bake, uncovered, in the center of the preheated oven, stirring every 20 minutes (3 times total), until thick, about 1¼ hours, or until desired consistency.

2. Remove from the oven and cool slightly, then scrape into a spring-top jar. Cool to room temperature, then store up to 1 month in the refrigerator.

CHERRY CHÈVRE

The Indians of the Great Lakes region traditionally dried wild cherries as a snack. Today, Michigan is known for producing fabulous dried sour cherries and the Northwest provides the market with dried sweet Bings. The concentrated cherry flavor is positively addicting. Look for them in the produce section of specialty-food markets.

YIELD: ABOUT 1 1/2 CUPS

¾ cup pitted dried cherries
¼ cup water
¼ cup cherry liqueur, cherry juice, or
    white grape juice
8 ounces fresh soft goat cheese, such as
    domestic *fromage blanc* or imported
    Montrachet, at room temperature
2 tablespoons unsalted butter, at
    room temperature

1. *Combine the cherries*, water, and liqueur or juice in a small saucepan. Bring to a boil and reduce until most of the liquid is evaporated, about 5 minutes. Set aside to cool.
2. *Purée the cherries* in a food processor fitted with the metal blade or in a food mill. In a small bowl with a wooden spoon or an electric mixer, cream together the goat cheese and butter until smooth. Add the cherry paste and stir just until mixed. Transfer to a covered container and refrigerate until serving.

APRICOT-PIÑA MARMALADE

Apricots and pineapple have lots of natural sweetness, yet both flavors boldly stand out on their own. This spread is good on cream cheese sandwiches.

YIELD: ABOUT 1 1/2 CUPS

One 8-ounce can crushed pineapple in
    heavy syrup
6 ounces dried apricot halves, chopped
¼ cup frozen unsweetened orange or
    tangerine juice concentrate, undiluted
Grated zest of 1 orange or 2 tangerines
¼ cup mild honey, or more to taste

1. *Drain the pineapple*, capturing the syrup in a small saucepan. Set the pineapple aside. Add the apricots and juice concentrate to the syrup and bring to a boil. Remove from the heat and let stand 20 minutes to plump the apricots.
2. *Add the pineapple*, citrus zest, and honey to the apricot mixture. Place the pan over medium heat and bring to a simmer. Cook uncovered, stirring occasionally, until thickened, 10 to 15 minutes. Remove from the heat and scrape into a clean container. Let cool to room temperature; the marmalade will thicken more as it cools. Cover and refrigerate up to 2 months.

Table of Equivalents

The exact equivalents in the following tables have been rounded for convenience.

METRIC

g = gram
kg = kilogram
mm = millimeter
cm = centimeter
ml = milliliter
l = liter

US/UK

oz = ounce
lb = pound
in = inch
ft = foot
tbl = tablespoon
fl oz = fluid ounce
qt = quart

WEIGHTS

US/UK	Metric
1 oz	28 g
2 oz	56 g
3 oz	84 g
4 oz (¼ lb)	112 g
5 oz (⅓ lb)	140 g
6 oz	168 g
7 oz	196 g
8 oz (½ lb)	224 g
10 oz	280 g
12 oz (¾ lb)	296 g
14 oz	392 g
16 oz (1 lb)	450 g
1½ lb	675 g
2 lb	900 g
3 lb	1350 g

LENGTH MEASURES

⅛ in	3 mm
¼ in	6 mm
½ in	12 mm
1 in	2.5 cm
2 in	5 cm
3 in	7.5 cm
4 in	10 cm
5 in	13 cm
6 in	15 cm
7 in	18 cm
8 in	20 cm
9 in	23 cm
10 in	25 cm
11 in	28 cm
12 in/1 ft	30 cm

OVEN TEMPERATURES

Fahrenheit	Celsius	Gas
250	120	½
275	140	1
300	150	2
325	160	3
350	180	4
375	190	5
400	200	6
425	220	7
450	230	8
475	240	9
500	260	10

LIQUIDS

US	Metric	UK
2 tbl	30 ml	1 fl oz
¼ cup	60 ml	2 fl oz
⅓ cup	80 ml	3 fl oz
½ cup	125 ml	4 fl oz
⅔ cup	160 ml	5 fl oz
¾ cup	180 ml	6 fl oz
1 cup	250 ml	8 fl oz
1½ cups	375 ml	12 fl oz
2 cups	500 ml	16 fl oz
4 cups/1 qt	1 l	32 fl oz

Acknowledgments

Many people helped me compile the information and recipes for this collection and although the majority are acknowledged in the text, I also wish to thank: Judy Adam, Peggy Fallon, Margaret 'Aunt Marge' Hensperger, Nick and Judy Larsen, Christy Salo, and especially Mary Jo Turek, Donna Germano, and Jesse Cool for their ever enthusiastic support.

And as always, 'thank yous' to editors Bill LeBlond and Leslie Jonath for their careful supervision; Gretchen 'miz dezign' Scoble for her thoughtful design collaboration; and my part-time fairy godmother and literary agent, Martha Casselman, for her enthusiasm, hard work, ever-helpful recommendations, and general hand-holding.

Deep appreciation goes to my team of conscientious recipe testers: Judy Adam, Lisa Carlson, Martha Casselman, Sallie Doeg, Cynthia Dominguez, Pamela Farrell, Teresa Gubbins, Maureen Lucas, Judy Matkin, Jacqueline Higuera McMahan, Marie Meseroll, Berit Meyer, Lou Seibert Pappas, Fran Pershing, Roberta 'Bobbe' Torgerson, and Diane Wellck.